Christoph Weber
Uncast

Spector Books

→ p. 203–213
not yet titled (pinhole camera stop-motion setup), 2015
Baryta prints
36 × 22 cm

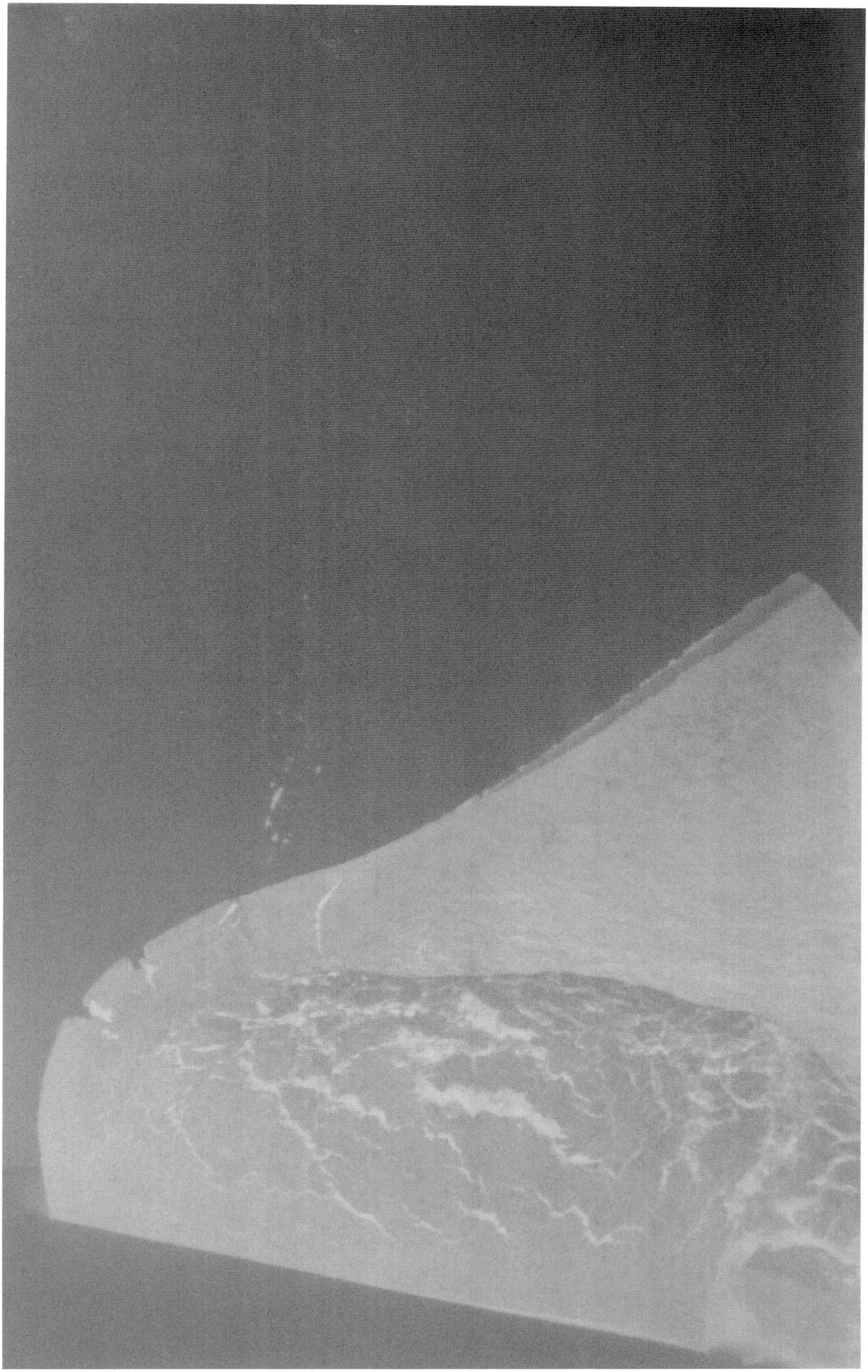

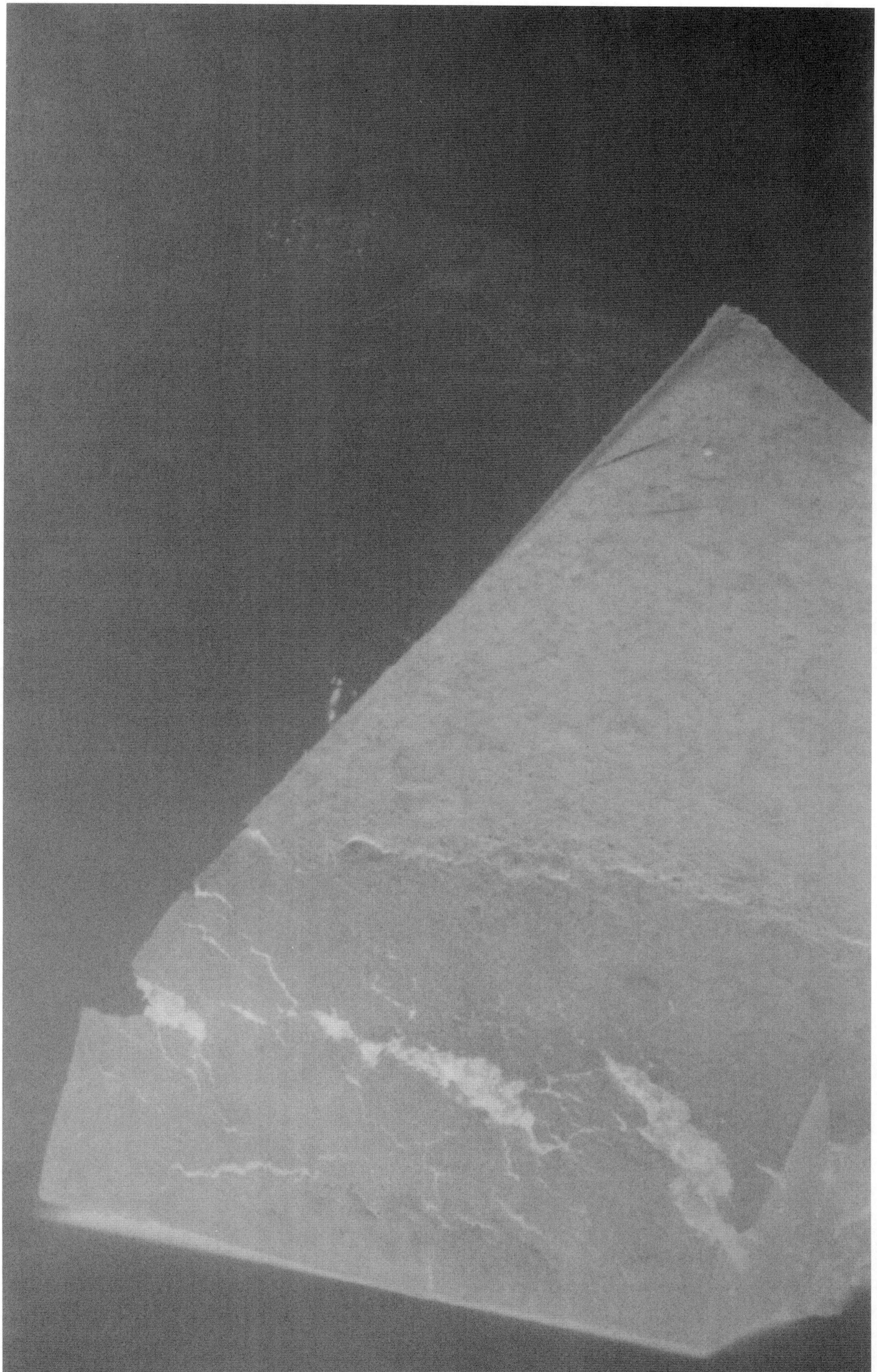

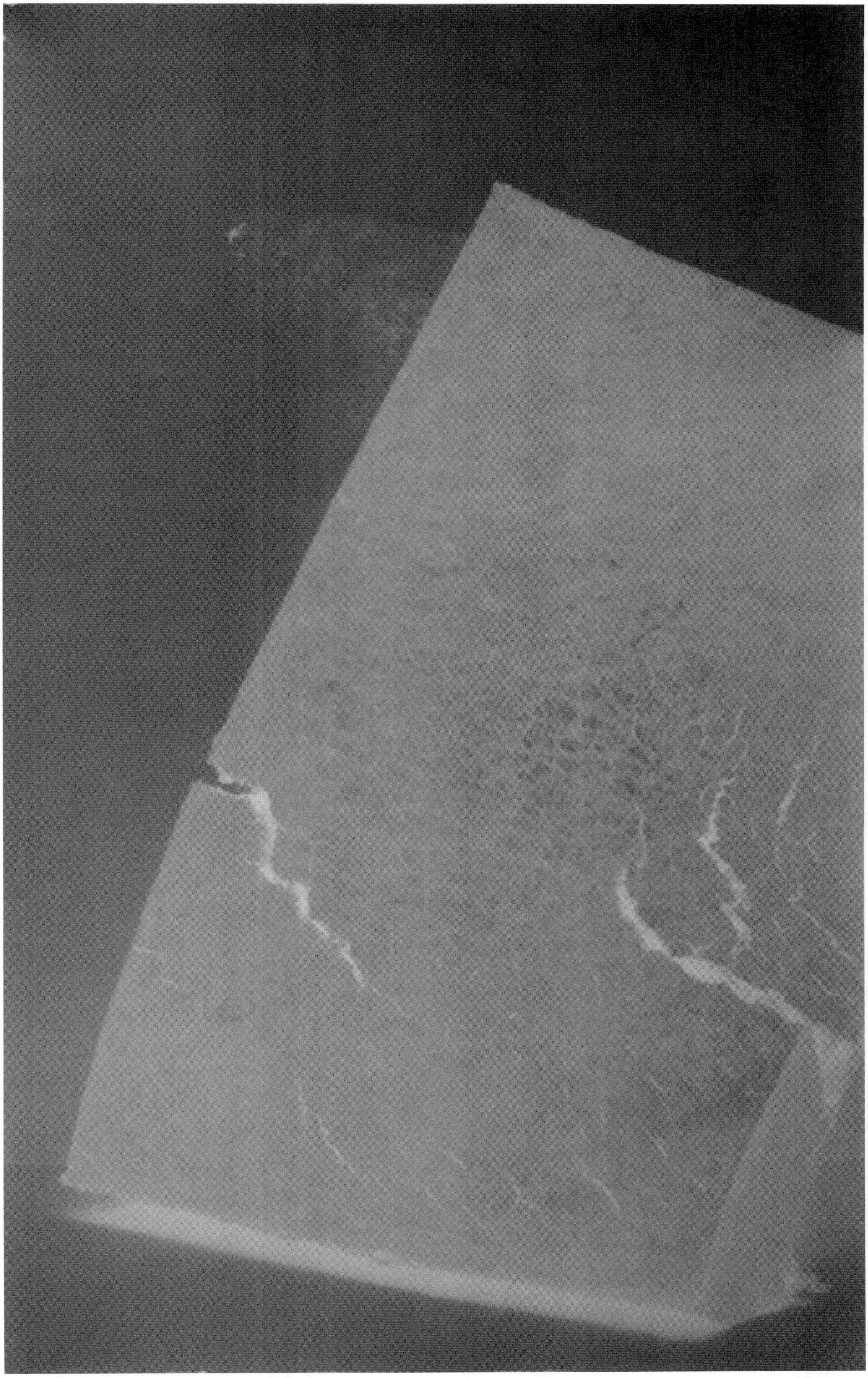

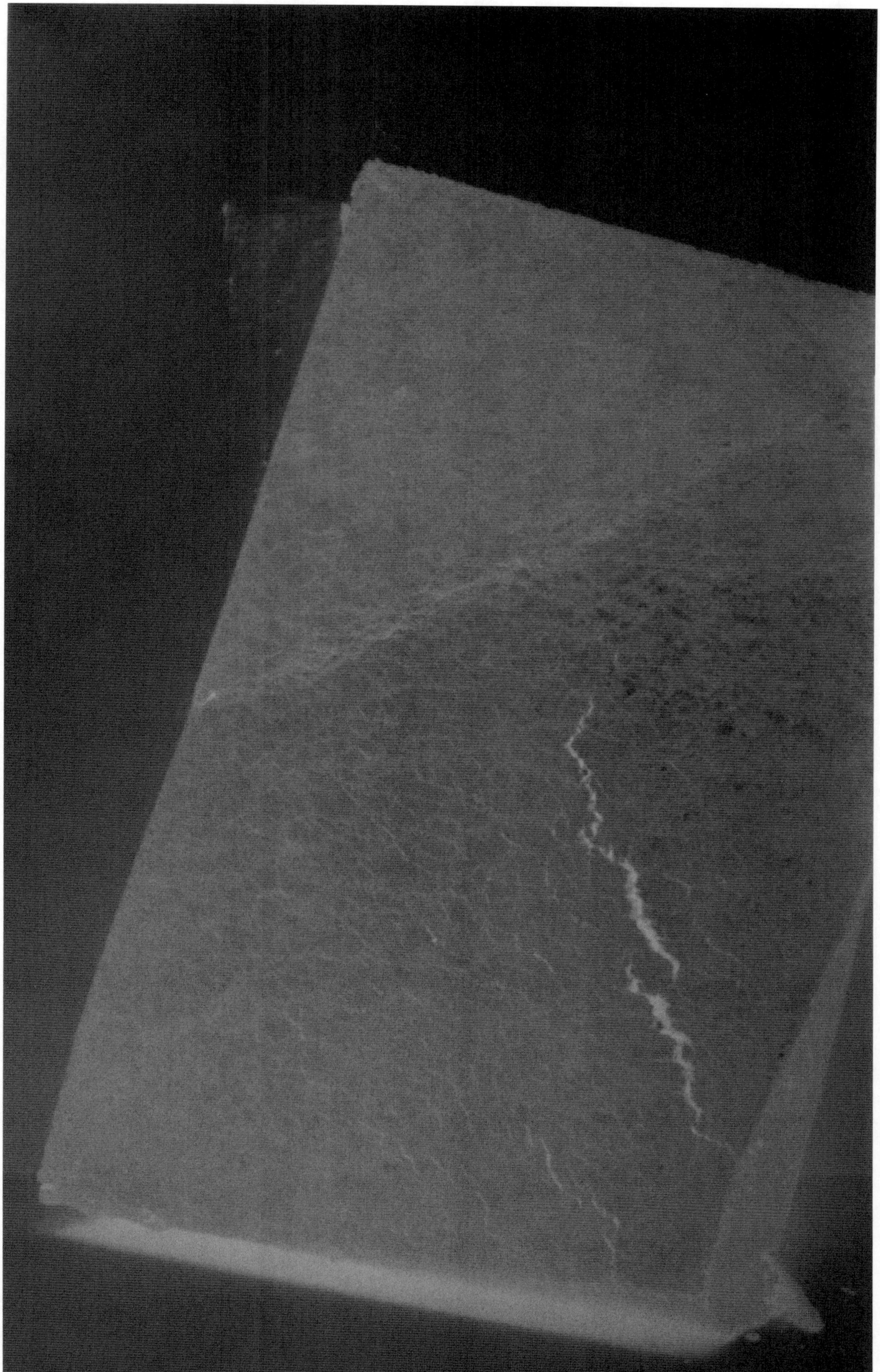

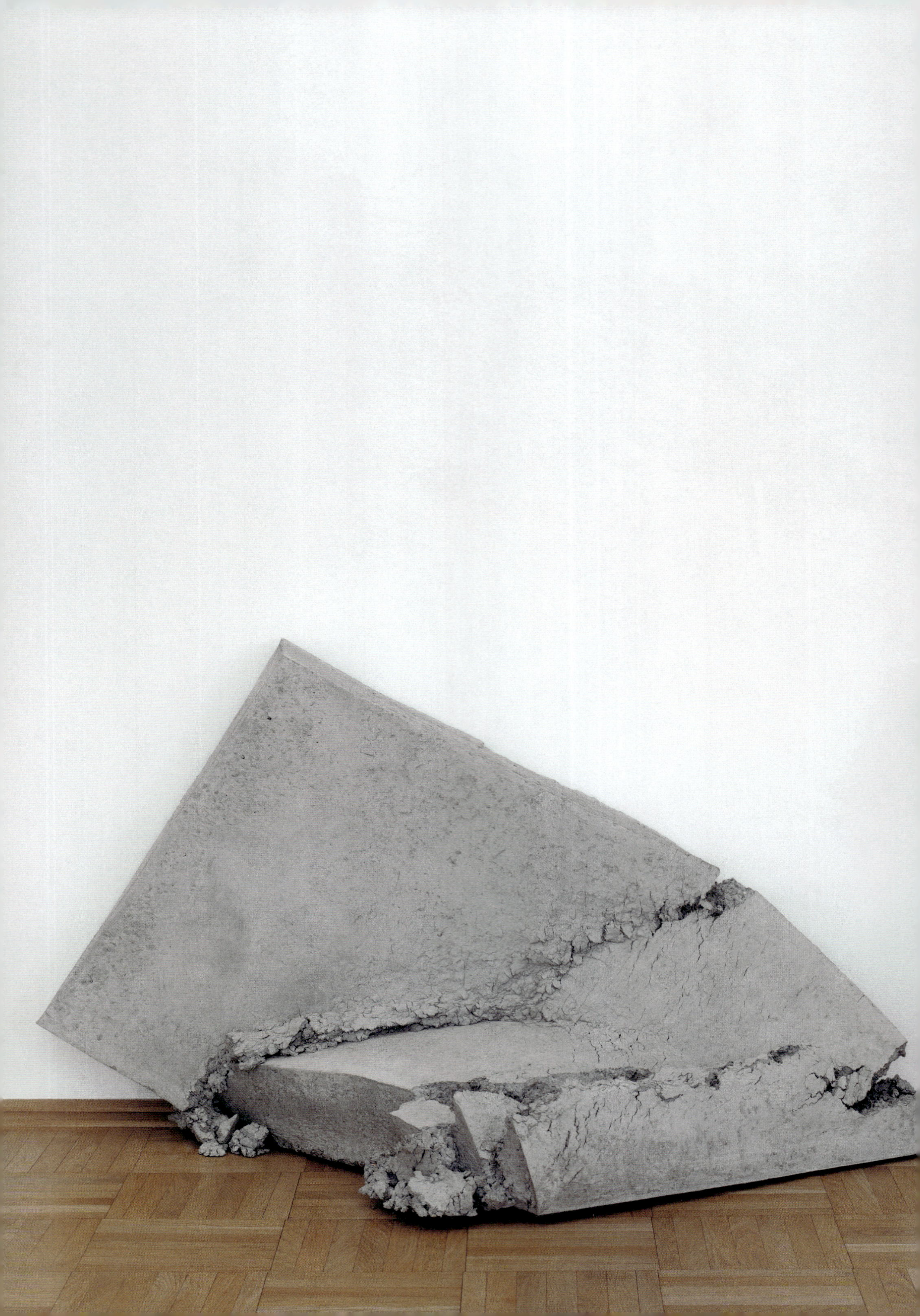

Not yet titled, never will be

Sadie Plant

Concrete cures; it doesn't dry. The process does end, but it takes a long time: concrete is still curing long after it has become hard enough to use. Concrete is a kind of runny rock, a liquid limestone that can be poured into a mould or even sprayed onto a surface to attain the strength and appearance of quarried stone. It is a mixture of water, aggregate, and cement, which is a powder cooked from stone that was once at the bottom of the sea. Its production transforms the raw material of rock into a remarkably versatile and malleable substance. Since the invention of modern cement in the mid-nineteenth century, the excavation of stone and its redistribution in concrete form all around the world has been conducted on such an enormous scale that it is perhaps the clearest marker of human intervention on and below the surface of the earth. Bridges, tunnels, dams, canals, walls, pipes, railways, runways, and roads: concrete is the crucial substance of the entire structure and infrastructure of the modern world.

Christoph Weber's concrete was just about to turn into a standard slab when the process was arrested, stopped in its tracks. Like a cake taken out of the oven too soon, or a photographic plate prematurely brought to light, each of these not quite ready-mades stands, or rather doesn't quite stand, paused on its way to assuming its proper industry standard form, not quite up to the shape it was supposed to take. These pieces were going to be slabs, but they didn't quite make it, they never arrived. Not yet titled, not yet finished, never will be.

The result is incongruous. The slabs look soft and pliable, more like textiles than blocks of stone, but they are in fact as fixed and solid as any uniform concrete slab. They appear to have lost, or never quite attained, their shape, but of course they have lost nothing; they are simply as they are. One series is arranged as a sequence of five slabs, which appear to be slowly sliding down the wall, slumping to the floor, each less stable than the last: the first almost holding itself upright; the last folded in on itself, buckling under its own wet weight. The series is in fact supposed to run from left to right: the slab that has almost completely collapsed was the first to have its shuttering removed, after just 90 minutes, when the concrete was too fresh, and each subsequent slab was given a little longer to solidify before it was released. The last is almost standing, but hasn't quite managed to maintain its shape.

→ p. 40
not yet titled, 2015
1/5 parts
140 × 766 × 77 cm

They could be stills from a stop-motion sequence, frames of a narrative which would conclude with a stable concrete block: the story would end with the finished work. But Weber does not frame the series with an unformed heap or a final piece: the world has no need for yet another perfect block. Instead we are shown the story in between; captured are the moments on the way, the stages of development implicit in every finished block, but normally not let out of the box.

It's not that the slabs have not dried properly: cement sets and hardens, but drying is peripheral to the process of curing, the final stage in concrete's long passage to itself. Water makes it plastic and malleable: it needs to be wet in order to be workable. Some of this water evaporates, but this is not what makes the concrete hard. It is in fact a process of hydration, rather than dehydration, which makes concrete stiffen, solidify, and gain its strength. A series of exothermic chemical reactions begins when water is added to cement and ends long after a concrete form can be considered strong enough to fulfill the purpose for which it has been cast. It seems so solid, dead and dry, but it is water that makes concrete hard. So crucial is water to its chemistry, that concrete can almost be said to be a means of trapping liquid, making water set.

Concrete is cooked in a series of processes that employ a culinary vocabulary of ingredients, recipes, ovens, and mixers, not to mention all the crushing, baking, cooling, grinding, stirring, pouring, spreading, and setting. These terms are just as likely to be found in a kitchen as they are at a cement works. It is in myths about the cooking of food that Levi-Strauss divines the difference between nature and culture, the unelaborated and the elaborated: food in the raw is life in the raw, and cooking marks the shift into the cultural. Some kinds of cooking involve only the most minimal processing of food: roasting over a fire is a matter of cooking with air, an immediate and direct use of heat that can lead to food that is well cooked on the surface but raw inside. Others are more thorough and elaborate: boiling requires the mediation of pots and pans and water too, and uses fire to heat the pot and the water to cook food. But all kinds of cooking mediate between the natural and the cultural world. Cooking is a moment of transition, a shift between dimensions, a step between two worlds.

This distinction can of course be played in many ways, as Levi-Strauss does in relation to food: it might be said that the most elaborated processes of cooking have an affinity to the most elaborated forms of cultural life. But food that is barely touched, the least mediated food, also belongs to the most refined cultural plane: sushi is far more sophisticated than boiled fish; the bourgeoisie favours salad over fast, processed food.

→ p. 40
not yet titled, 2015
2/5 parts
140 × 766 × 77 cm

The work of stonemasons might also be considered far more sophisticated than that of construction workers mixing and pouring their concrete on site, and buildings cast in concrete might be seen as impoverished and crude when compared to buildings sculpted out of stone. But in terms of the complex nature of its production, its unique material qualities, the sheer extent of its use, and the scale of its impact on the world, concrete is exemplary cultural stuff. The making of rock by grinding, baking, and steeping stone, distributing it on a global scale, and pouring it into negative spaces formed by moulds or shuttering on site: these are infinitely more elaborate processes than cutting and using stone fresh, as it were, from the ground. As a construction material, concrete has a plasticity that constitutes a break with the necessities of stone and makes entirely new forms and structures possible: it is the stuff of contingency. The scale of its use, its ubiquity, and its crucial role in the erection of the entire military and industrial edifice, make concrete one of the most present and dominant expressions of anthropogenic impact on the world.

But concrete does as much to scramble distinctions between nature and culture, origin and artifice, as it does to solidify them. The production of concrete continues the long journey made by limestone, itself a sedimentary rock, which forms in warm and shallow seas alive with corals, algae, and the skeletons and shells of underwater organisms rich in calcium carbonate. This fossilised marine environment is the limestone that is later quarried, crushed, and baked into cement. When water is added to the mix, it is this ancient underwater world that assumes a new and massively redistributed role on the surface of the earth.

Modern concrete — made from Portland cement — was developed in the nineteenth century, but the use of stone did of course survive: some cities celebrate the purity of such raw material, defining themselves by the natural simplicity and local nature of the stone with which they are built. Jerusalem owes its identity not only to the stone backdrop of the Knesset and the stones of the Western wall, but to its whole built environment, which must, by law, be constructed using local limestone, "Jerusalem stone". Or at least, its buildings have to appear to be built from this stone, even when they are in fact concrete clad in a just few millimeters of stone. Tel Aviv, on the other hand, to the west, is a city of concrete, not of stone. This is the city of experimentation: just as stone stands for tradition, religion, and stability in Jerusalem, the city set in stone, the concrete curves and contours of Tel Aviv's Bauhaus buildings were designed to represent the modern, the secular, the adventurous side of a city facing the future and sea.

→ p. 40
not yet titled, 2015
3/5 parts
140 × 766 × 77 cm

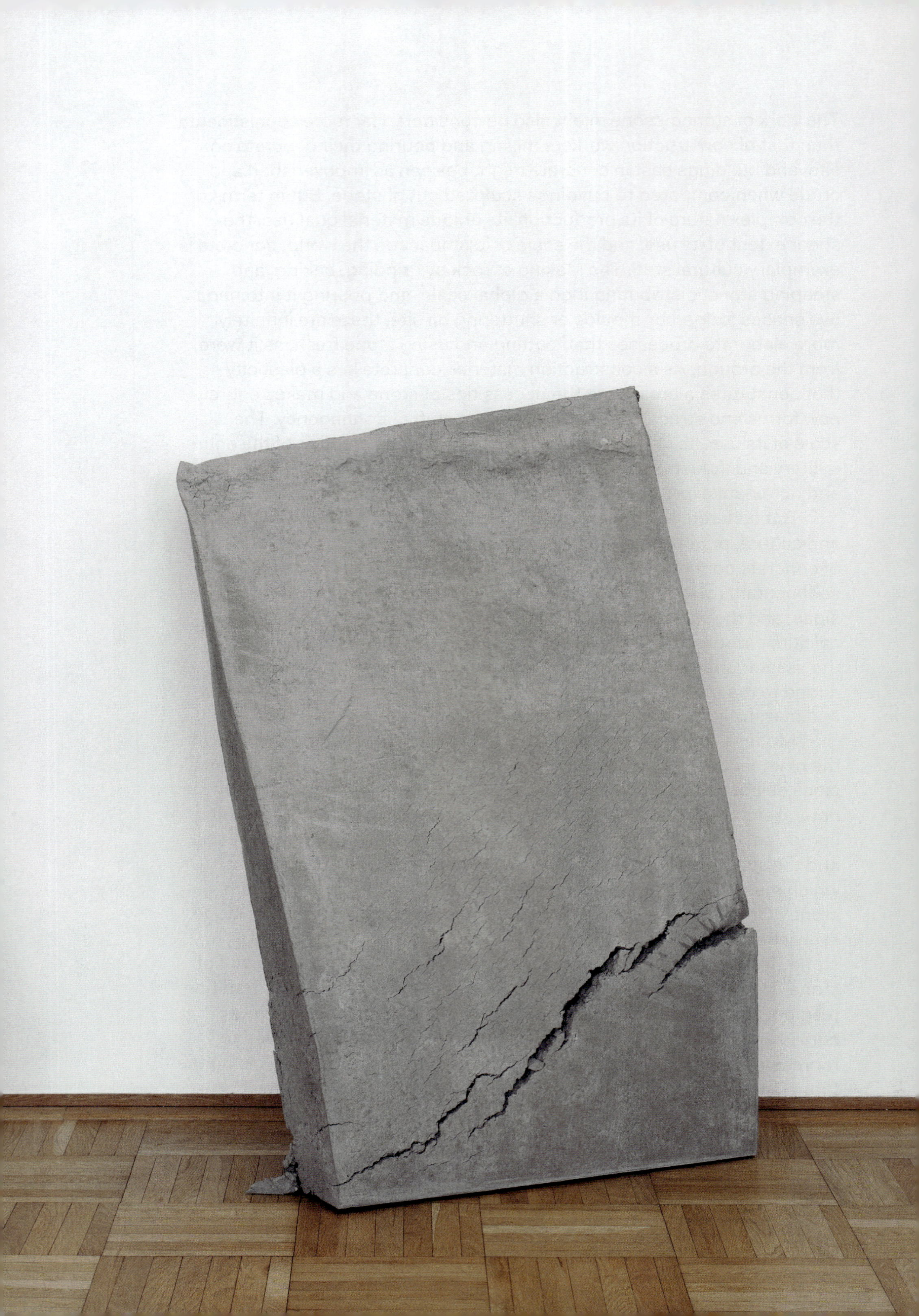

Tel Aviv's architects explored the qualities proper to concrete, what it could do that stone could not. But rather than providing a basis for experimental design, concrete's plastic properties are more often channelled into the production of blocks of easy, cheap, and convenient artificial stone. This is concrete at its most conventional, dull and drab; a standard and monotonous expression of the standard building blocks of modern culture. And if Tel Aviv took its special shape from concrete's very malleability, the landscape to the east of Jerusalem is marked by concrete at its orthodox extreme: a brute show of strength and uniformity in the form of a tall and implacable wall. This concrete has been cooked to perfection and properly cured, its liquidity locked into the rigidity of a standardised form. Tel Aviv's architects took careful account and great advantage of concrete's unique qualities, but the wall's engineers are using it simply as a substitute for stone, stuff to be set in an established mould.

It is in this standard use of concrete, the production of blocks, the building of barriers, that Weber intervenes. His concrete exceeds the standard form, refuses to be held and slotted into place. It breaks the mould, evades its proper destiny, interrupts the standard story that would make it fit for purpose in the construction industry or military machine. In Levi-Strauss's terms, it would be rotten, not too raw or under cooked; in a concrete plant it would be thrown away.

Weber's blocks are neither standing stones nor standard concrete slabs, nor are they rotten scraps or half-baked goods. They may seem immature and insecure, but this belies their solidity; they are as fixed and finalised as concrete blocks can be. They have the appearance of unfinished, uncooked goods, but they are locked into strange forms of their own, one of which is the mould of modern art. Weber's concrete journey is not broken, but diverted to the gallery, where concrete meets culture once again and curing converges with curation.

→ p. 40
not yet titled, 2015
4/5 parts
140 × 766 × 77 cm

→ p. 40
not yet titled, 2015
5/5 parts
140 × 766 × 77 cm

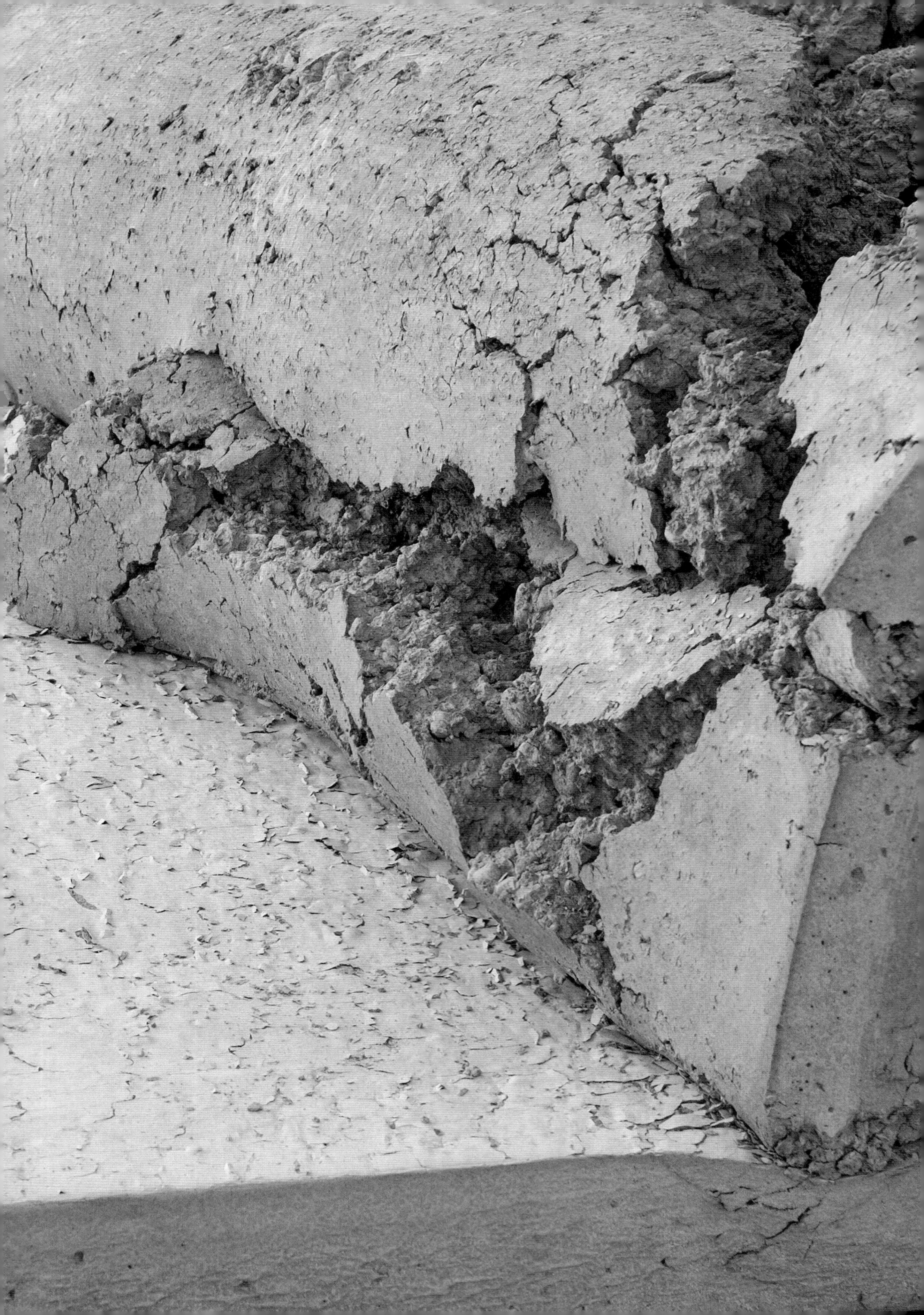

Sculptural Bodies: Lying, Hanging, Unfurling... Situating Christoph Weber's Sculptural Works

Konrad Bitterli

Concrete, concrete, concrete
concrete, concrete, concrete, concrete
concrete washed,
concrete ready-mixed,
concrete finely reinforced,
We're building a world to last
more than fifty thousand years.

[...]

Clean and low-maintenance, beautiful, germ-free
you can never have enough of it,
mixed, reinforced,
fine-washed, fair-faced,
concrete, concrete, concrete,
concrete, a coloured concrete paradise.

Gerhard Polt, *Concrete*

The contrast between the neo-classical interior of St. Gallen's grand museum and Christoph Weber's raw concrete sculpture could not be any greater. Massive, immutable, and yet fragile, the sculpture lies on the fine parquet floor and "occupies" the light exhibition space, its supine form giving the impression that it has suddenly collapsed and broken apart in a great movement of unfolding and unfurling. Striking fissures streak across its surface, branching into countless finer lines. Seemingly granular extrusions protruding between the bulges on one side are perceived as elegant folds on the other. Even with these delicate differentiations of form, the sculpture has a terse sense of self-evidence, as though a vigorous motion has been solidified, the traces of a massive gesture caught in the act.

→ p. 60
not yet titled, 2014
58 × 149 × 103 cm

The work is basically an angular, industrial, grey concrete slab, several centimetres thick, which the artist has raised on one side during the hardening process as though to gently fold the tough material. Weber has provoked and captured a precise moment of transformation, a point of enormous material stress at which control of the substance was lost and one form tipped into another. On the back, the process has produced a regularly shaped curve, while from the front the material seems to have collapsed under its own weight, connecting the distortions to the structure as a whole. The movement that is trapped within the concrete is transformed into elegant curves and abrupt breaks, unfoldings and fault lines. It is a creative process that can be traced intellectually through the gesture of lifting, the beginning of the "folding," the precarious moment of tipping into material overload, and the force of the collapse. All of this speaks in a figurative sense to the equal importance of construction and destruction as elements of the creative process.

Not yet titled, 2014 is so named with a wink and a nod to the fact that the act of naming a work is as crucial as giving it form. This is abundantly clear when one reconstructs the thinking behind the work. With its slabs, folds and faults, Weber's sculpture could be (mis)understood as an accelerated experiment or an artistic model of tectonic processes over an immeasurable period of time, possibly a simulation of geological phenomena. But the material refuses such a partial natural historical reading: as the functional stuff of construction, the language of concrete makes unambiguous reference to industrial scale manufacturing in architecture and city planning, perfectly exemplifying the promise of modernity. Dreams of utopian societies and visionary urbanism did not, however, last very long. Even when it finds its way into a song by someone like the German cabaret artist Gerhard Polt, concrete is now associated with the non-places of the inner city: inhospitable residential buildings in congested areas, the forgotten spaces between roads and railways, and a general sense of blight on the landscape. The word is sometimes used as a metaphor for the apocalyptic sentiments echoed in the "No Future" attitude of late 1970s punk where "concrete" refers to the rigidity of traditional class structure and bourgeois power, not least because concrete is the stuff of bunkers and fortifications.[1]

1 Cf. Thomas Trummer, "Precariously Balanced Roughness," in *RES* (June 2013) p. 50–54. The author refers to the symbolic power of concrete, making explicit reference to the punk movement of the 1970s, squatters, and the anti-nuclear movement.

→ p. 60
not yet titled, 2014
58 × 149 × 103 cm

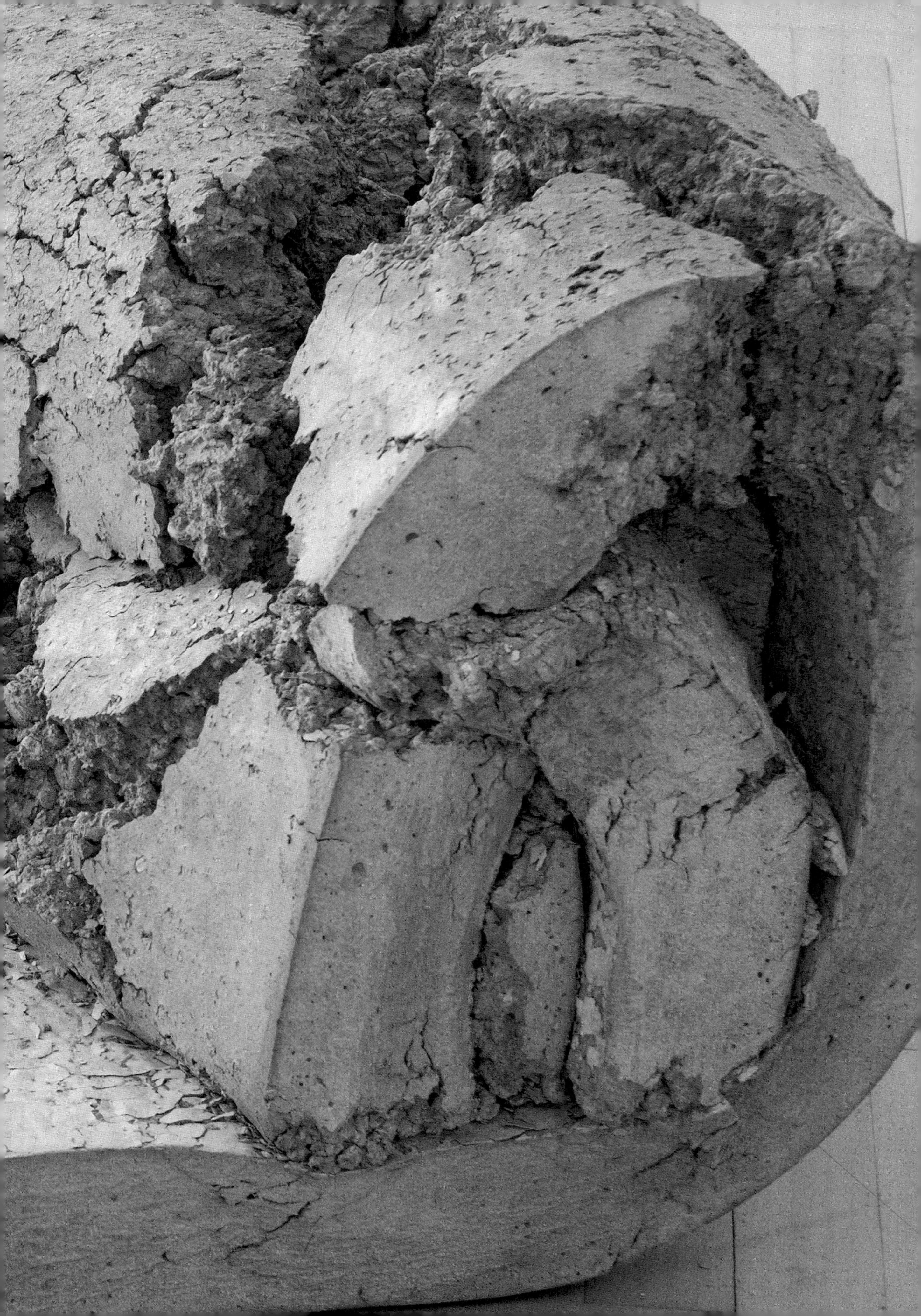

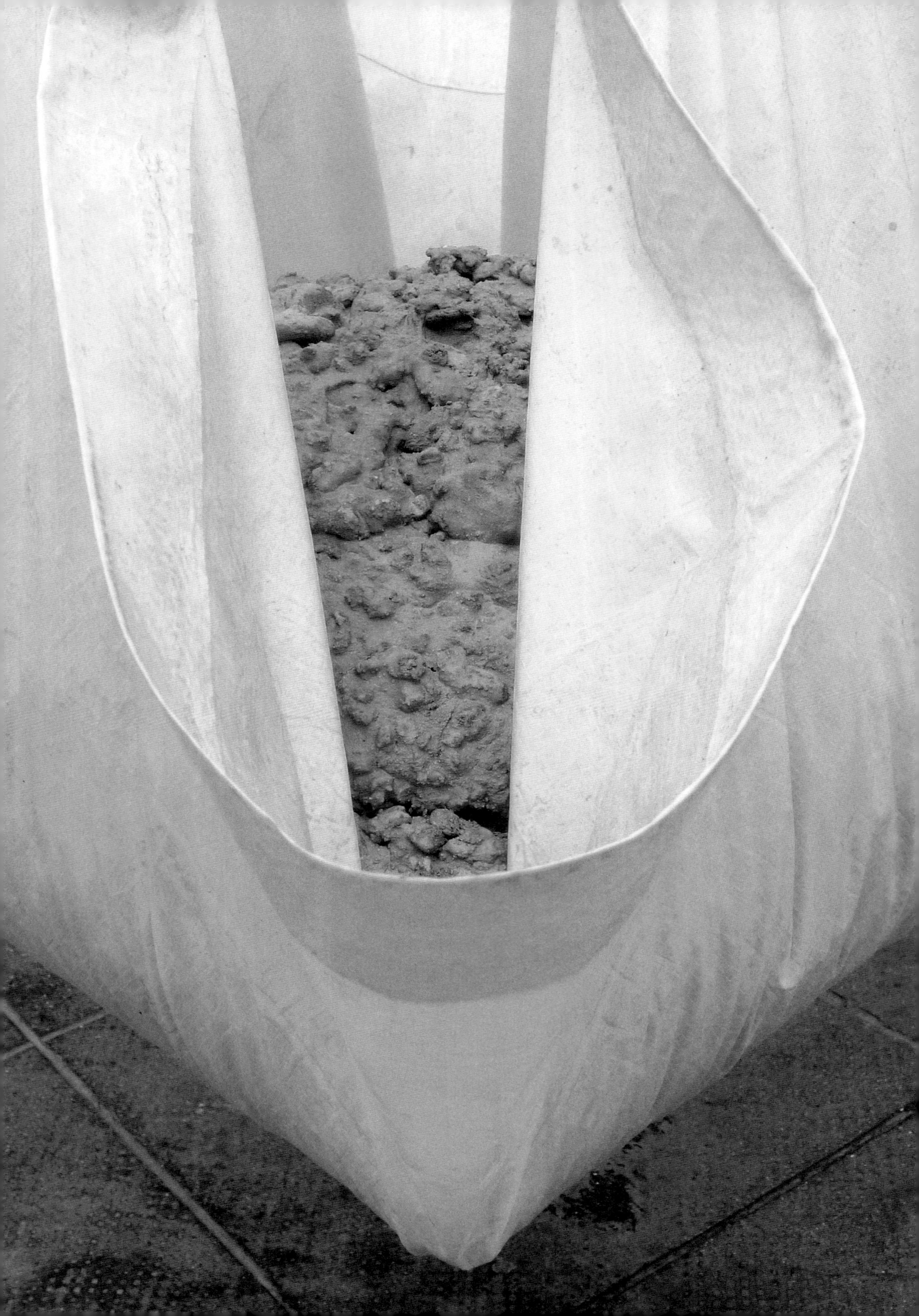

Material: traditions and qualities

Artistic materials are never, therefore, simply neutral, but have imagery of their own. That imagery, along with the history of their use and the traditions of art history on which they draw, remains inscribed in the things they form and "resonates" in each new work. Concrete has often been used in fine arts in relation to architecture, as with the modernist "Kunst am Bau," while the apparently limitless possibilities of "béton brut" have brought a certain sculptural quality to construction. It is amazing that contemporary concrete sculpture so rarely refers to these traditions. Distant reference is made in the towering concrete steles of Isa Genzken (* 1948), and in the sculptural interventions of Manfred Pernice (* 1963), whose "concrete castings" take up the formal language of actual architecture and transform isolated elements into unique hybrid objects whose purpose remain unclear. Other artists use classical applications of the material to produce surprising forms: Lutz / Guggisberg (* 1968 / 66) make small and medium sized concrete sculptures, which have a surreal playfulness of their own. Kilian Rüthemann (* 1979), for his part, sprays liquid concrete onto walls to produce monumental drawings in space, which challenge the crude building material's capacity to adhere to the walls of the white cube.

It is the quality of the material and the design opportunities thrown up by the peculiarities of its plasticity and production that fascinate Christoph Weber. His ability to turn the process of curing to his own advantage, intervening at exactly the right moment to subject his material to the most diverse forces, lifting it, turning it , letting it fall apart, gives his work its unique character. These are the movements, which remain apparent in the finished sculpture: the work is process frozen or hardened. It may make a powerful first impression, but there is nothing monumental about **not yet titled**. Still, it does evoke the metaphors of violence and power, which are inherent in the material. Simply in the acts of folding and collapsing his material, Weber is able to stretch conventional conceptions of vulnerability and fragility and pack his sculptures with complex metaphors of power and powerlessness, creation and destruction....

A look back: processes in art

Op Losse Schroeven. Situaties en Cryptostructuren and Live in Your Head. When Attitudes Become Form were two epochal exhibitions held in 1969, one at the Stedelijk Museum in Amsterdam, the other at the Kunsthalle Bern. Together with *Eccentric Abstraction*, held three years earlier at the

→ p. 90
Beton (gehoben), 2012
359 × 62 × 59 cm

Fischbach Gallery in New York, these exhibitions made an enormous contribution to the emergence of an expanded field of sculpture, which moved beyond the neutrality and rigid severity of minimalism. So-called post-minimalist art marked a conscious departure from the position represented by Donald Judd, breaking with the traditional understanding of art as artefact in favour of more process-based approaches. Artists such as Eva Hesse, Richard Serra, and Keith Sonnier expanded the canon of materials to include neon, latex, and polyester, and other hitherto untried substances in an effort to render their materiality visible. This "anti-illusionistic" art made careful use of the qualities of materials and material traces of the creative process, rather than denying their importance. And with works protruding from the walls, hanging from ceilings, spanning the walls, occupying the corridors, post-minimalist art was also characterized by fresh approaches to the use of space. Forty years later, Christoph Weber's sculptures make these moves as well: they dangle from the ceiling, lean against the wall, hang around, lie on the floor and, as with **not yet titled**, simply occupy the space. This is a work in which the artist transforms the strictly minimalist form of a concrete slab into a shape that is ultimately uncontrollable and so exceeds the austere aesthetics of minimalist art.

In the space of contemporary sculpture

The *Post / Post Minimal* exhibition at the Kunstmuseum St. Gallen in 2014 pitched some outstanding post-minimalist works—from Bill Bollinger, Gary Kuehn, Richard Serra, and Keith Sonnier—against sculptures by contemporary artists, from Katinka Bock to Christoph Weber, whose work pursues the sculptural possibilities opened up in the late 1960s and early 1970s. In contrast to this period, the art of today is less concerned with moving beyond the conventional artistic canon as it is in broadening its contents and materials. Artistic approaches no longer define themselves in terms of bold gestures or radical breaks with tradition, but instead build naturally and smoothly on the formal research of previous generations, linking it to other artistic experiences and creating works informed by unique sensibilities of their own. The four sculptures Weber exhibited here—**Beton (gehoben)** (concrete [raised]), **Beton (gerollt)** (concrete [rolled]), **Beton (gewickelt)** (concrete [coiled]), and **not yet titled**—are emblematic of this shift. In a text accompanying the exhibition, Céline Gaillard outlines the significant moments of Weber's artistic approach: "For him [the artist], the properties of the material and its symbolic power give it an

Beton (gehoben) → p. 90
Beton (gerollt) → p. 92
Beton (gewickelt) → p. 58
not yet titled → p. 60

→ p. 92
Beton (gerollt), 2012
82 × 58 × 11 cm

inherent meaning. He uses the process of curing to allow the act of manipulation to become visible as a performative moment. As if conducting a series of experiments, Weber explores the material's potential by searching for the ideal moment of hardening. Whether by lifting or rolling, the conditions he wrests from this archetypal twentieth-century building material are fundamentally at odds with its standard industrial usages. Weber...is basically playing with both the properties of the material and the conventions of its use."[2] Thomas Trummer describes this concrete sculpture as a kind of a "stress-test for thing-ness,"[3] which opens metaphorically onto the two crucial aspects of contemporary art: its material properties and formal content. It is their close entanglement, highly developed in both material and intellectual terms, that testifies to the eminently contemporary nature of Christoph Weber's works. They are distinguished not only by their sense of their own materiality and the artistic processes to which it gives rise, but also by their ability to realise the metaphors latent in objects, as only the work of art can do. Weber's sculptures are substantial, but they also exemplify the precarious nature of the "human condition" in Gerhard Polt's lyrical "paradise of coloured concrete."

2 Céline Gaillard, "Exhibition text" for *Post / Postminimal. The Rolf Ricke Collection in Dialogue with Contemporary Artists*, Kunstmuseum St. Gallen 2014, unpublished.

3 Thomas Trummer, op. cit.

In the background (p. 39):
Bill Bollinger, Untitled, 1970
Richard Serra, Duplicate (Cut Piece), 1970
Gary Kuehn, Straw Piece, 1963
Gary Kuehn, Untitled, 1968
Richard Serra, Coils [Lead Piece], 1968
Richard Artschwager, Untitled, 1967

→ p. 58
Beton (gewickelt), 2014
14 × 33 × 130 cm

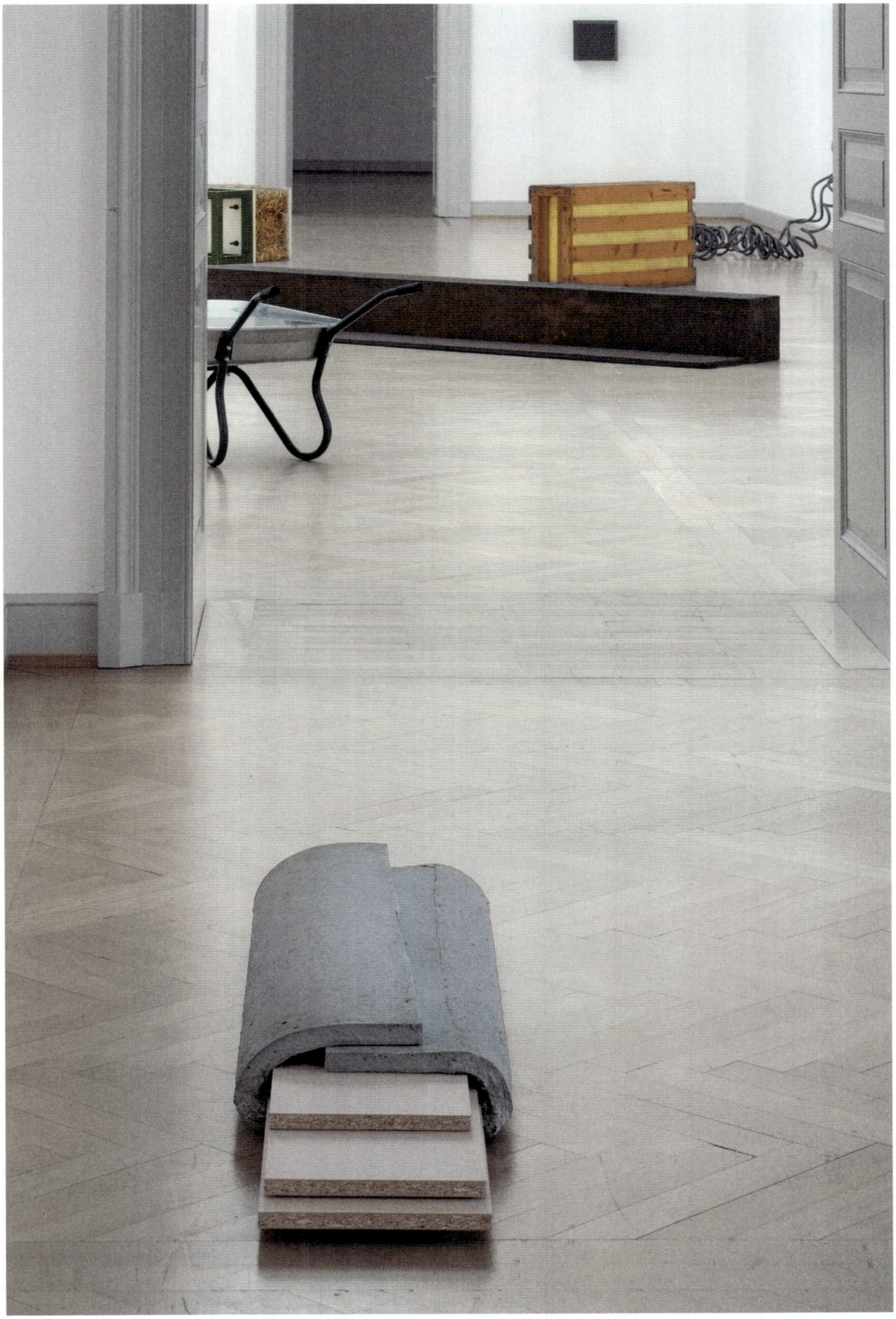

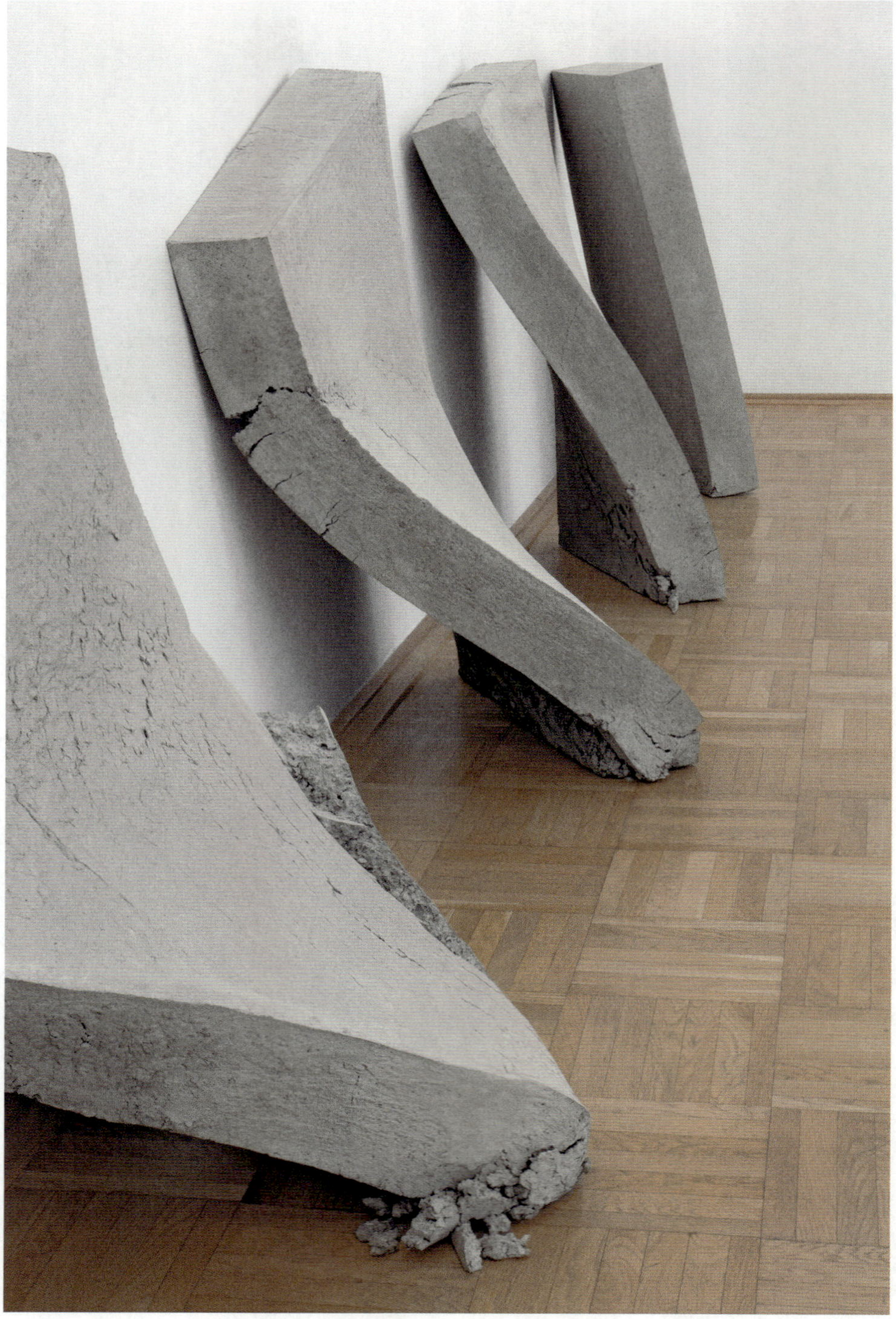

not yet titled, 2015
Concrete
5 parts
140 × 766 × 77 cm

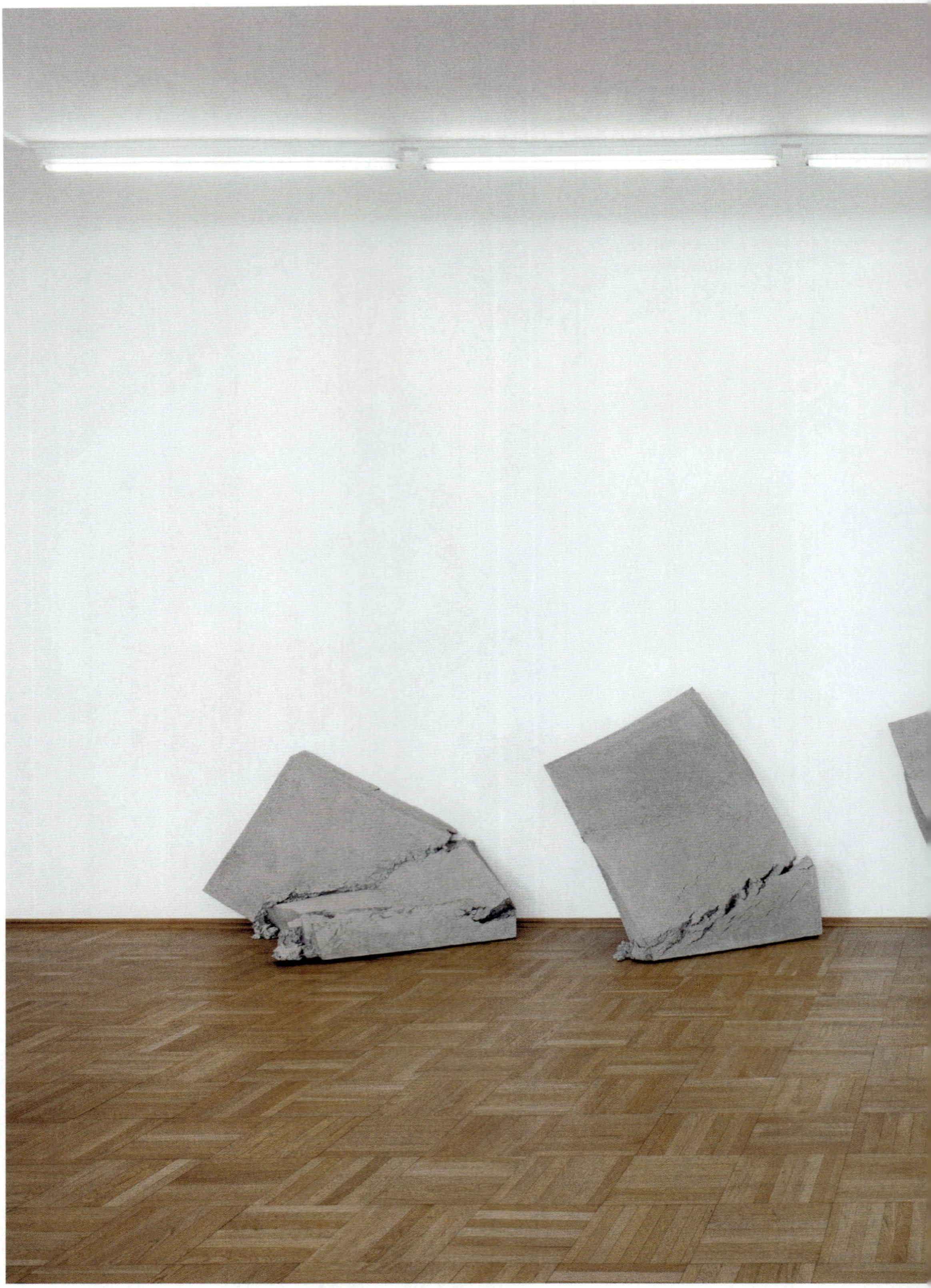

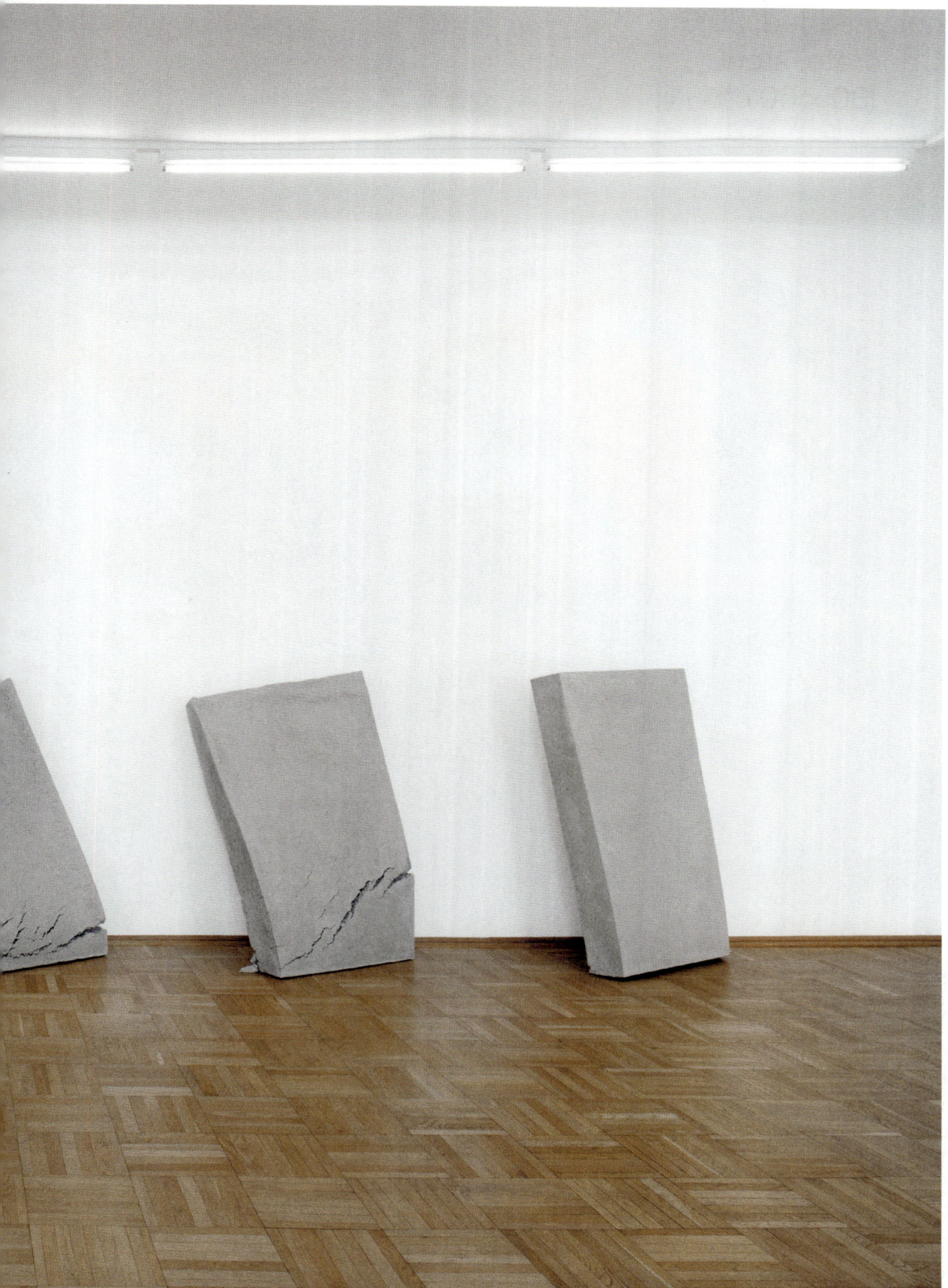

not yet titled, 2015
Concrete, steel
18 × 130 × 60 cm

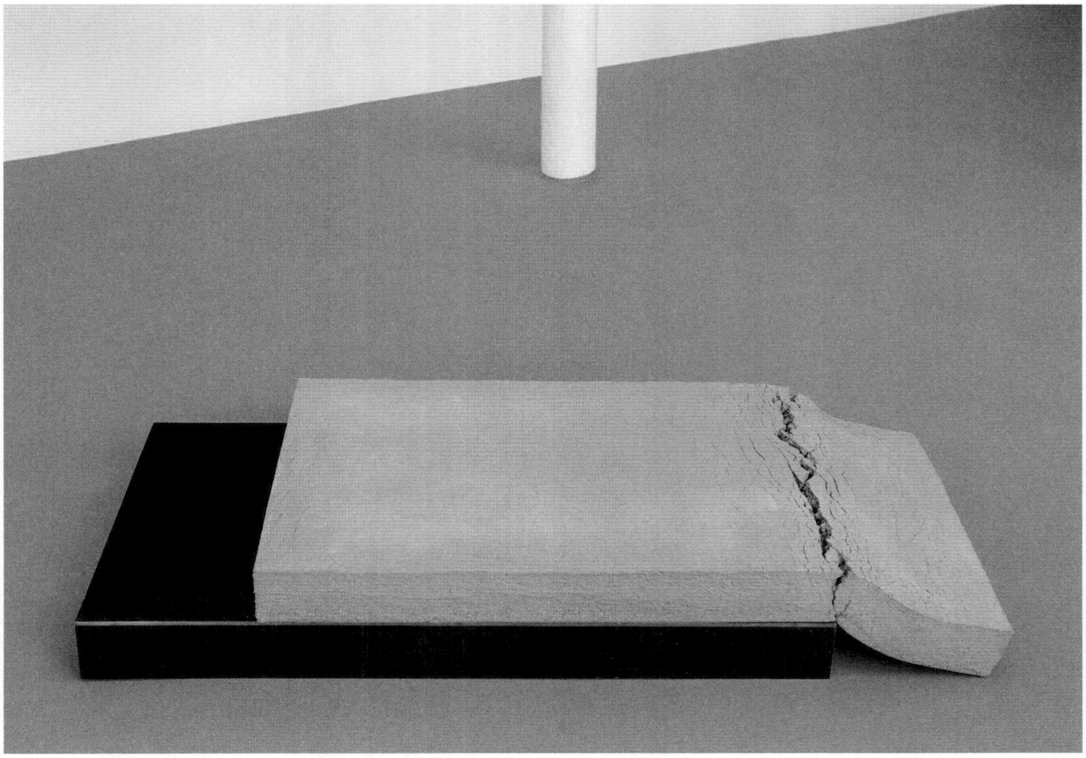

not yet titled, 2015
Concrete
120,5 × 44 × 22,5 cm

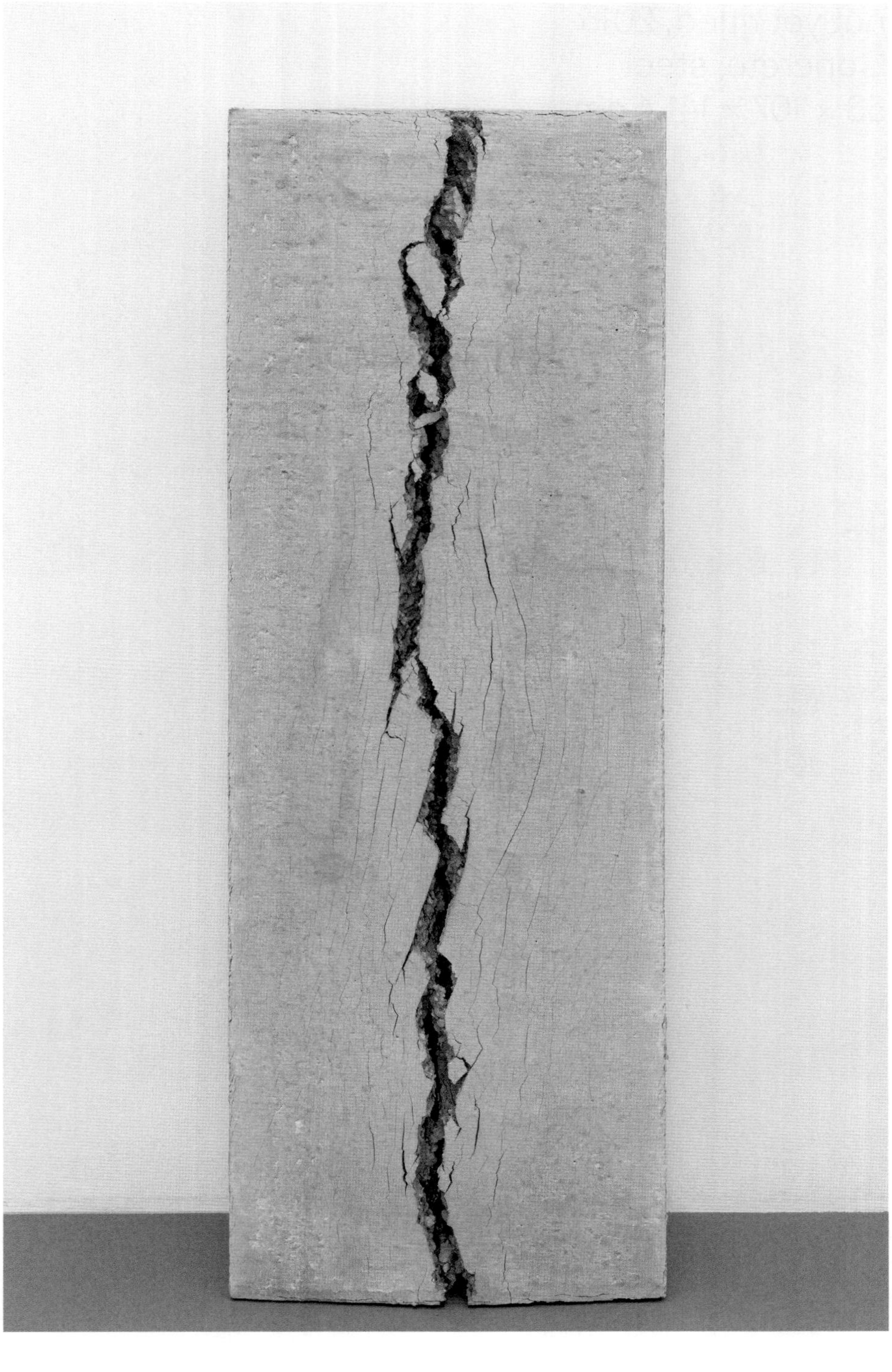

not yet titled, 2015
Concrete, steel
53 × 107 × 141,4 cm

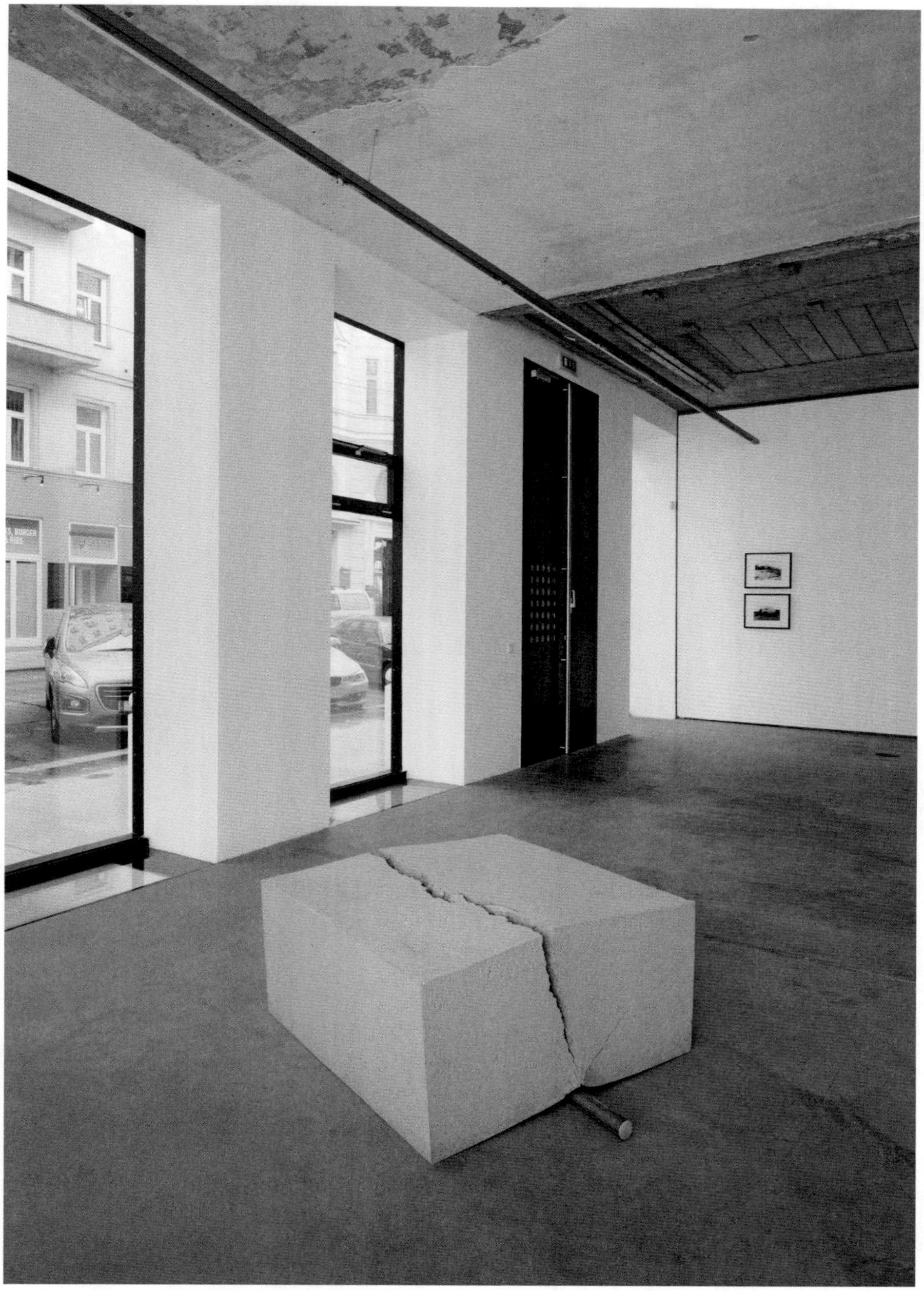

not yet titled, 2014
Concrete, steel
17 × 111 × 150 cm

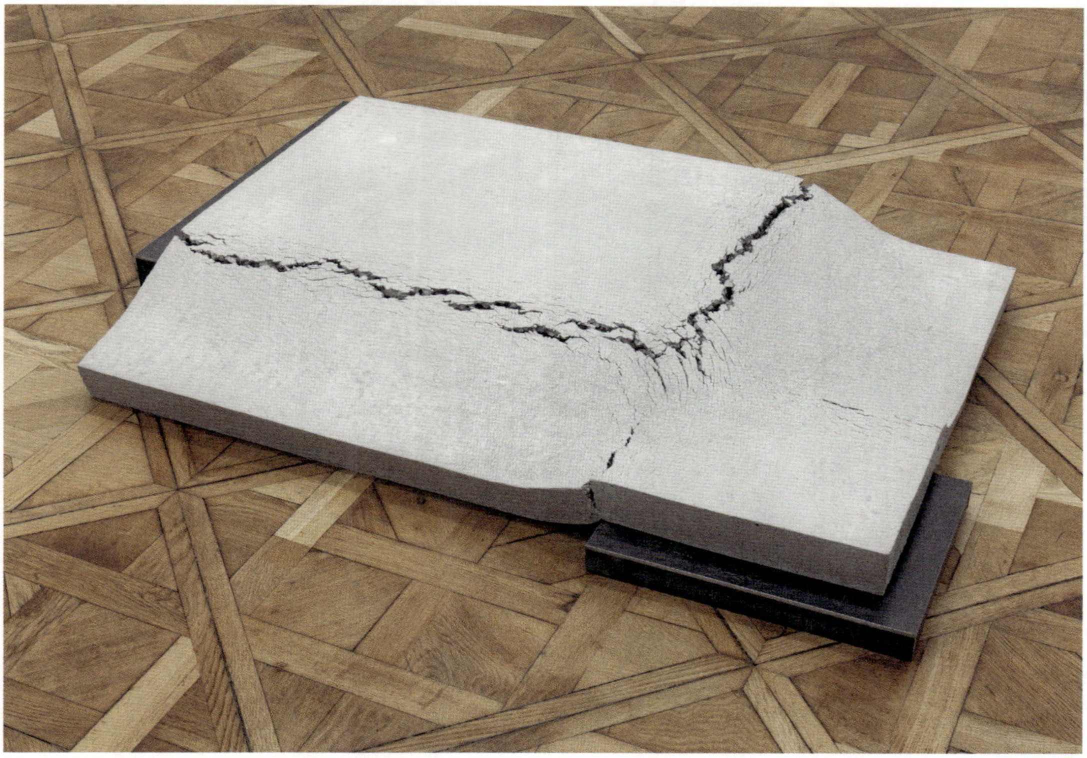

not yet titled, 2014
Concrete
128 × 103 × 55 cm

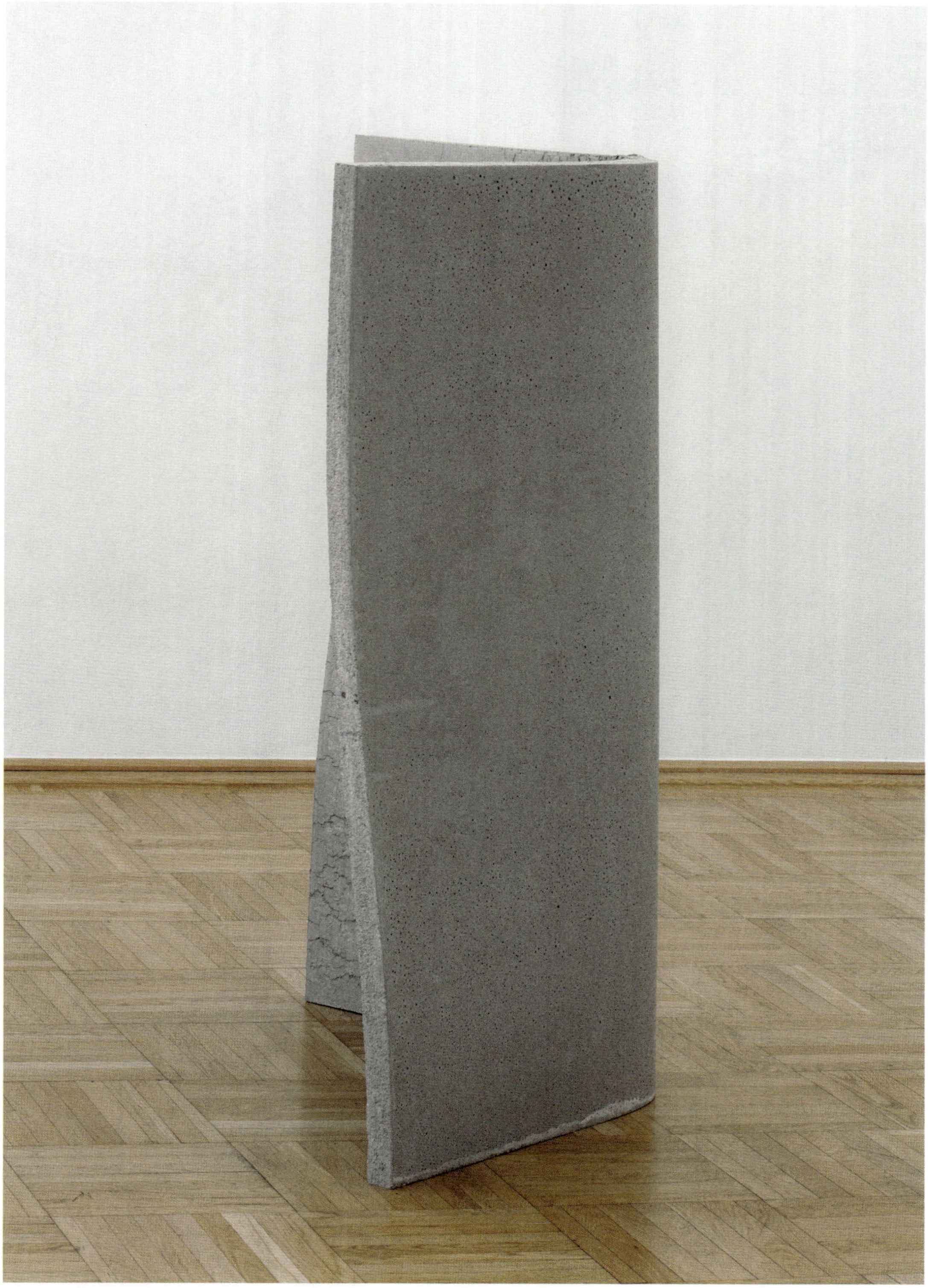

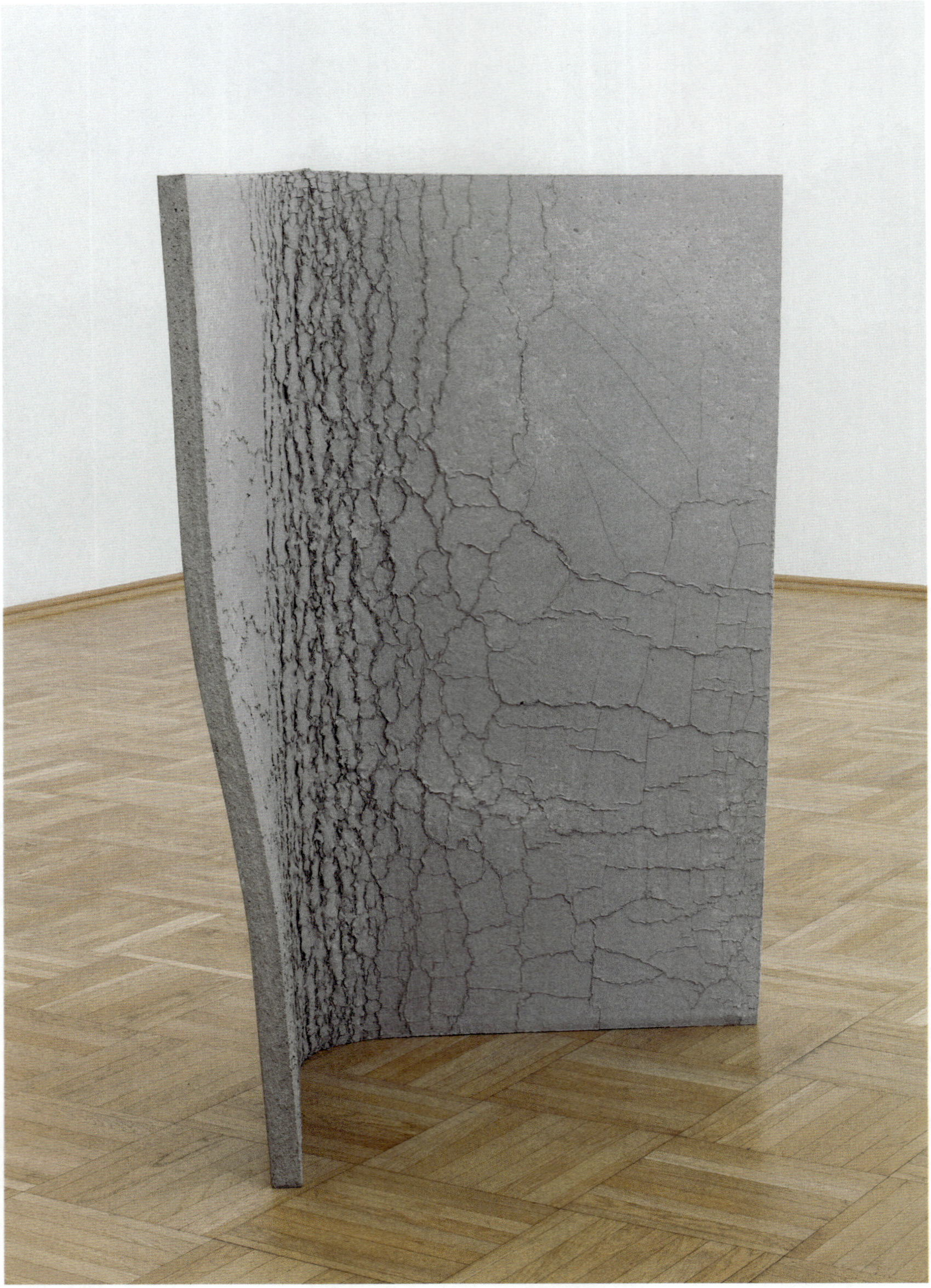

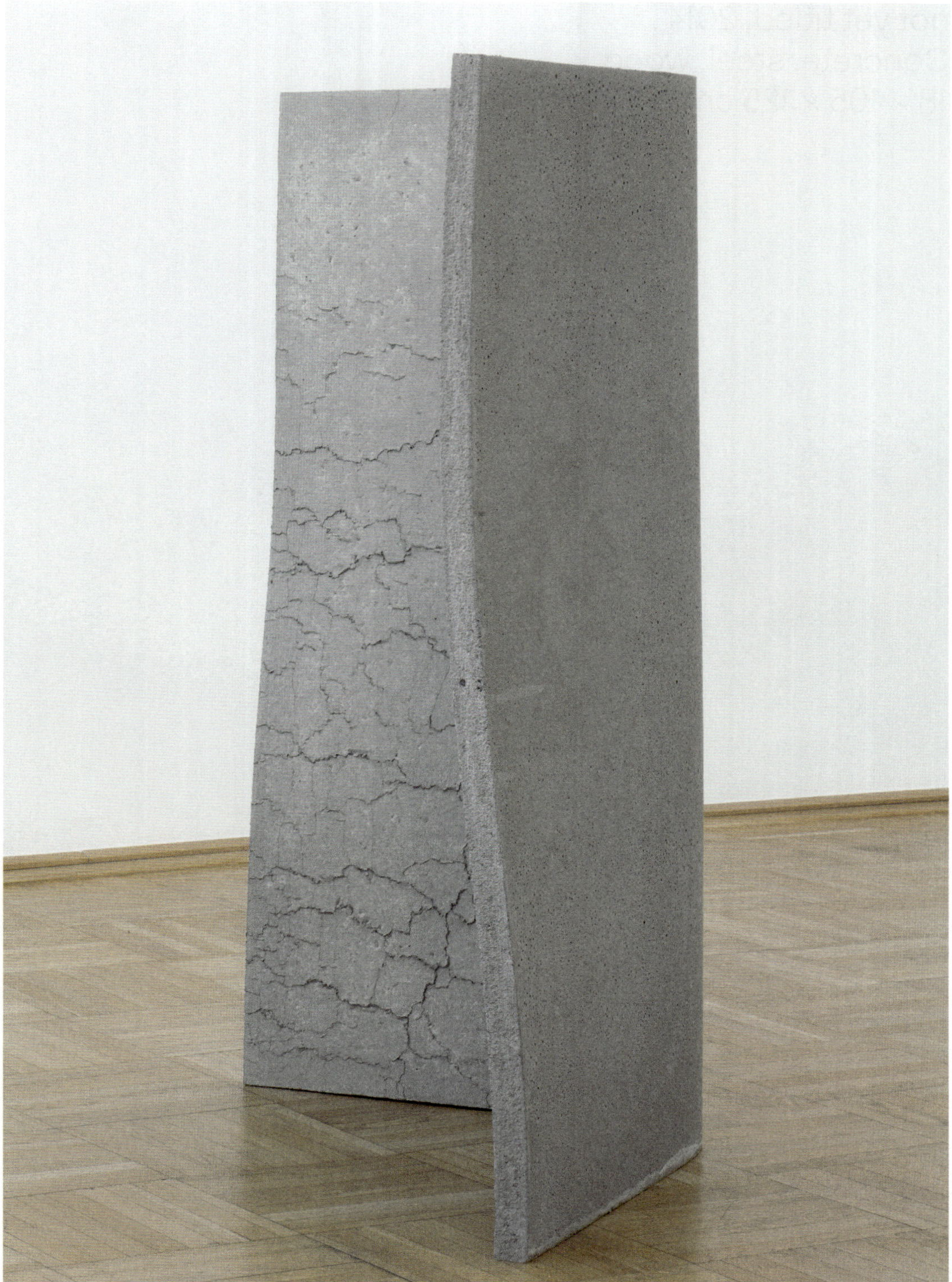

not yet titled, 2014
Concrete, steel, wood
18 × 105 × 125 cm

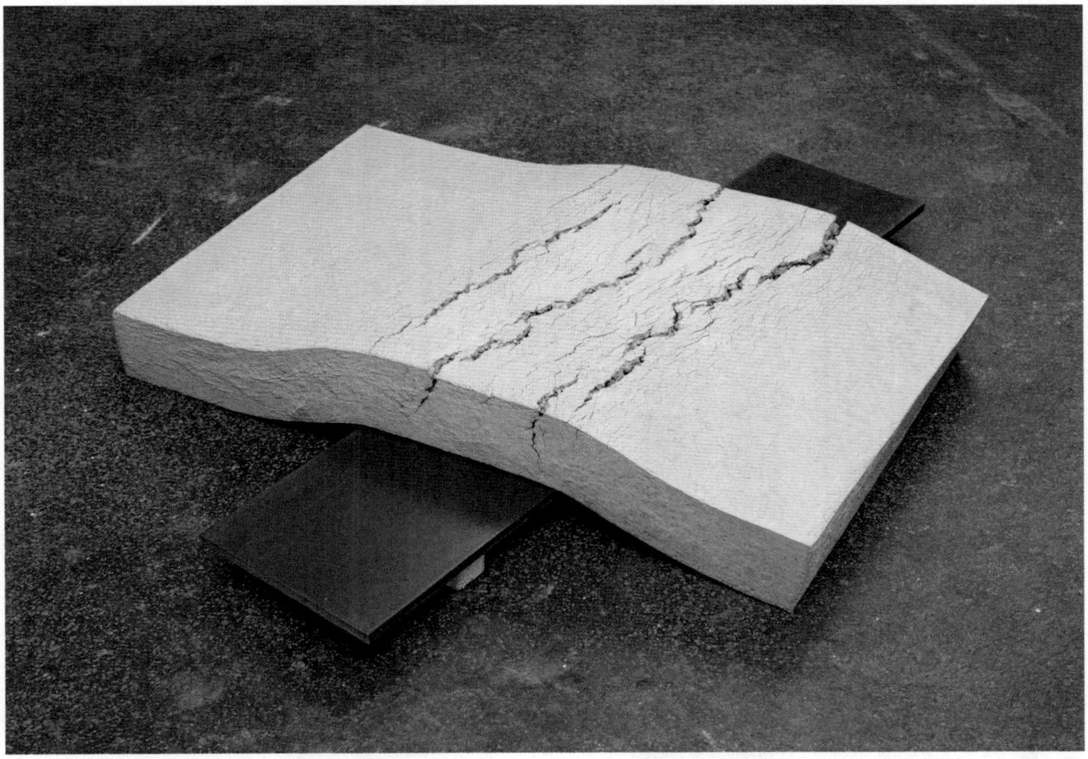

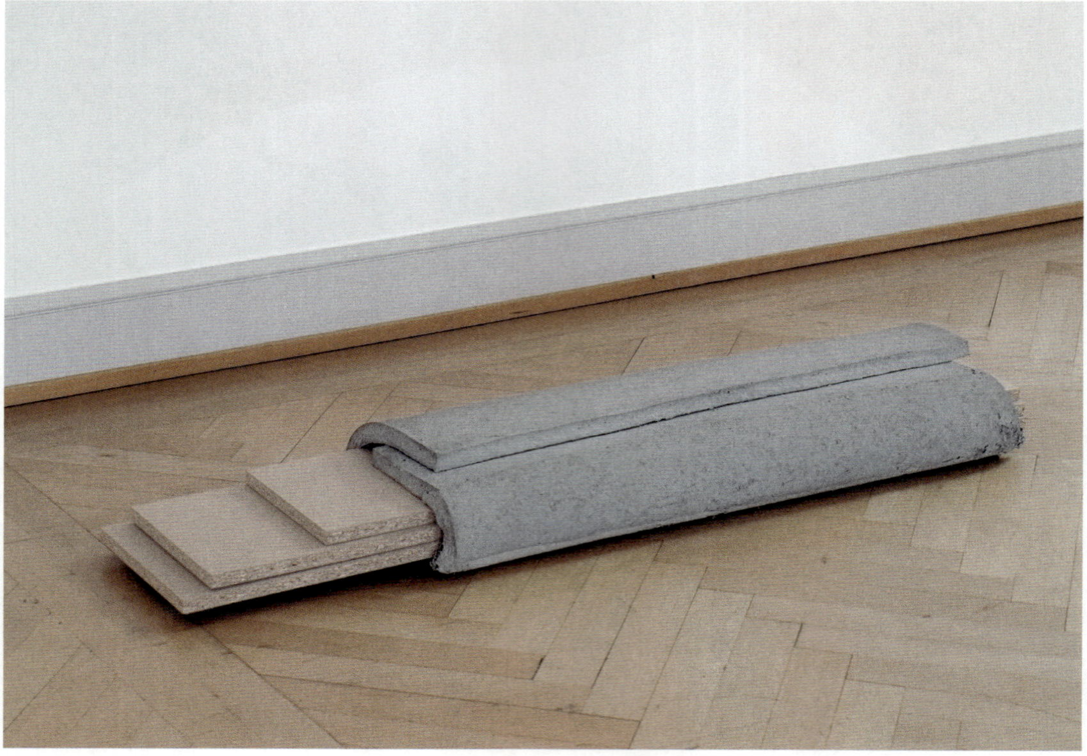

Beton (gewickelt), 2014
Concrete, particleboard
14 × 33 × 130 cm

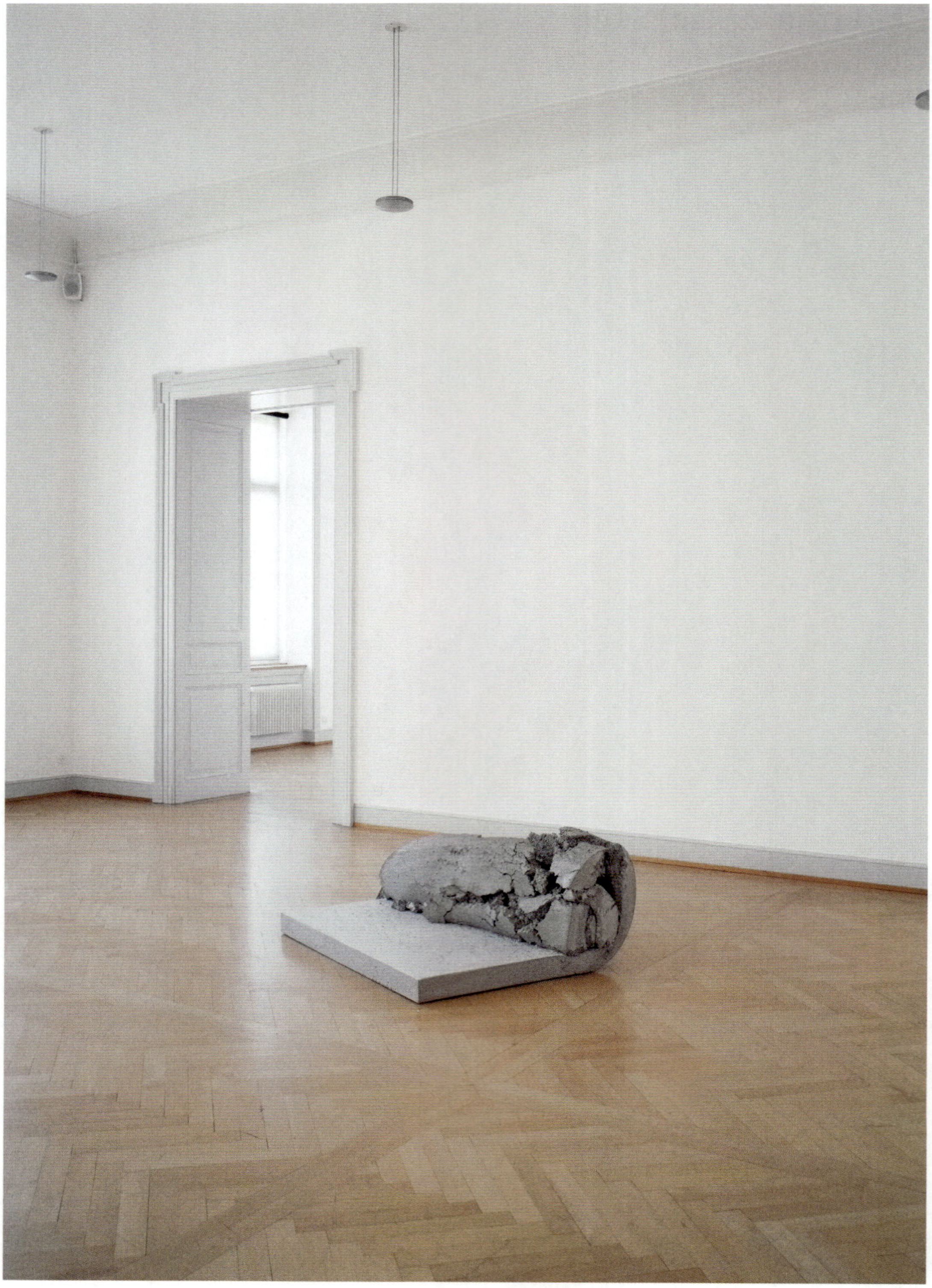

not yet titled, 2014
Concrete
58 × 149 × 103 cm

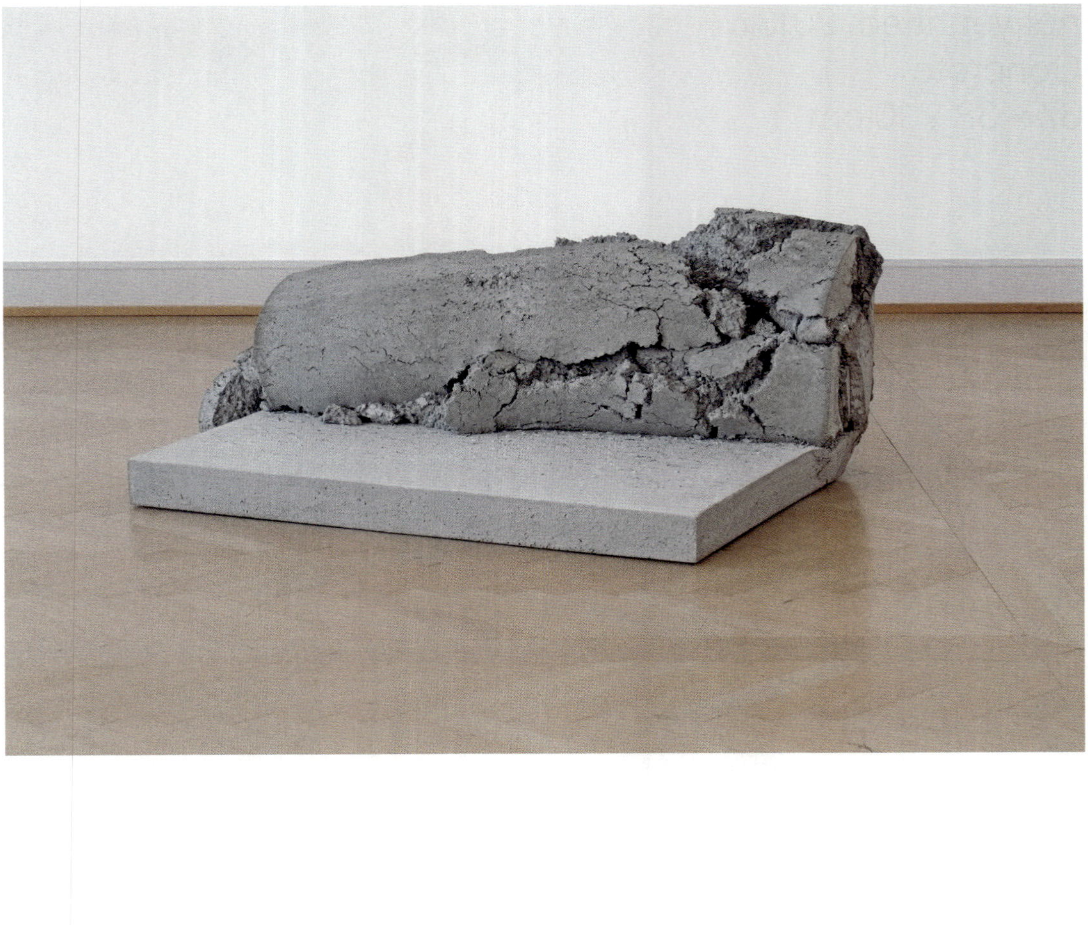

not yet titled, 2013
Concrete
37 × 38 × 10 cm

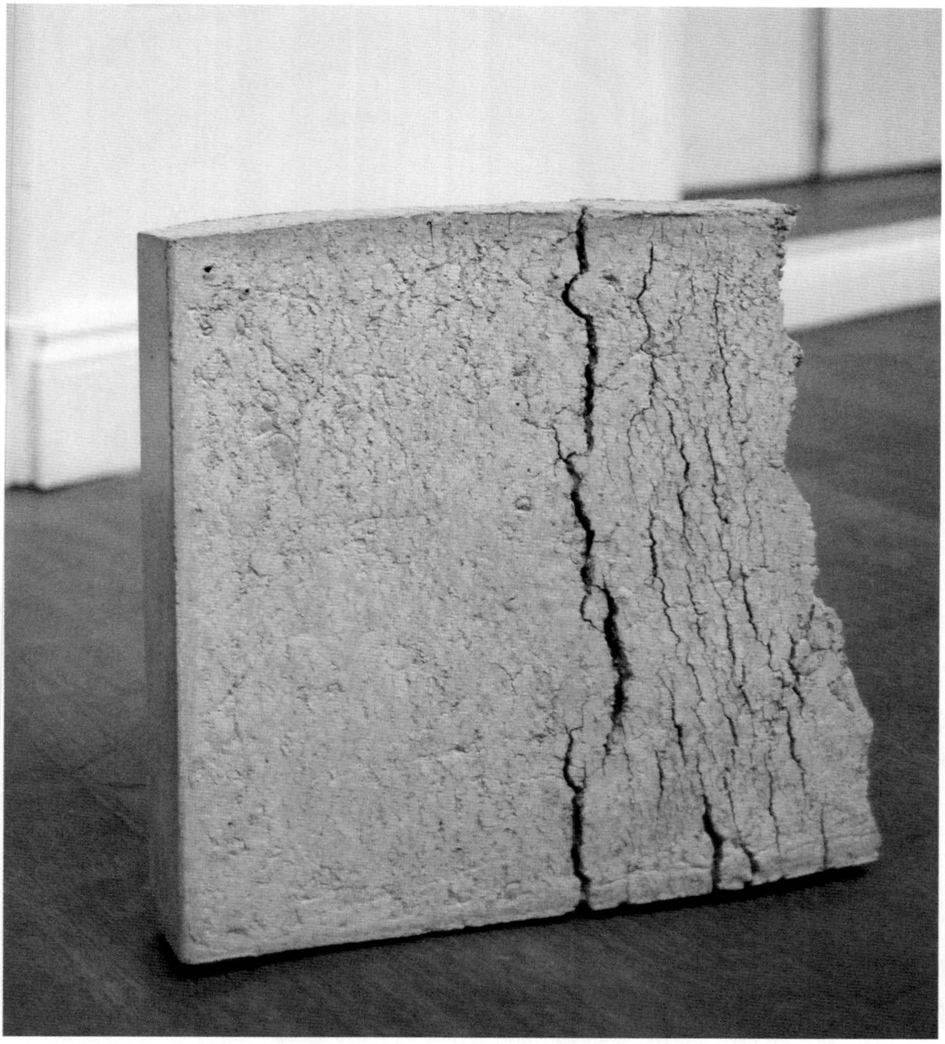

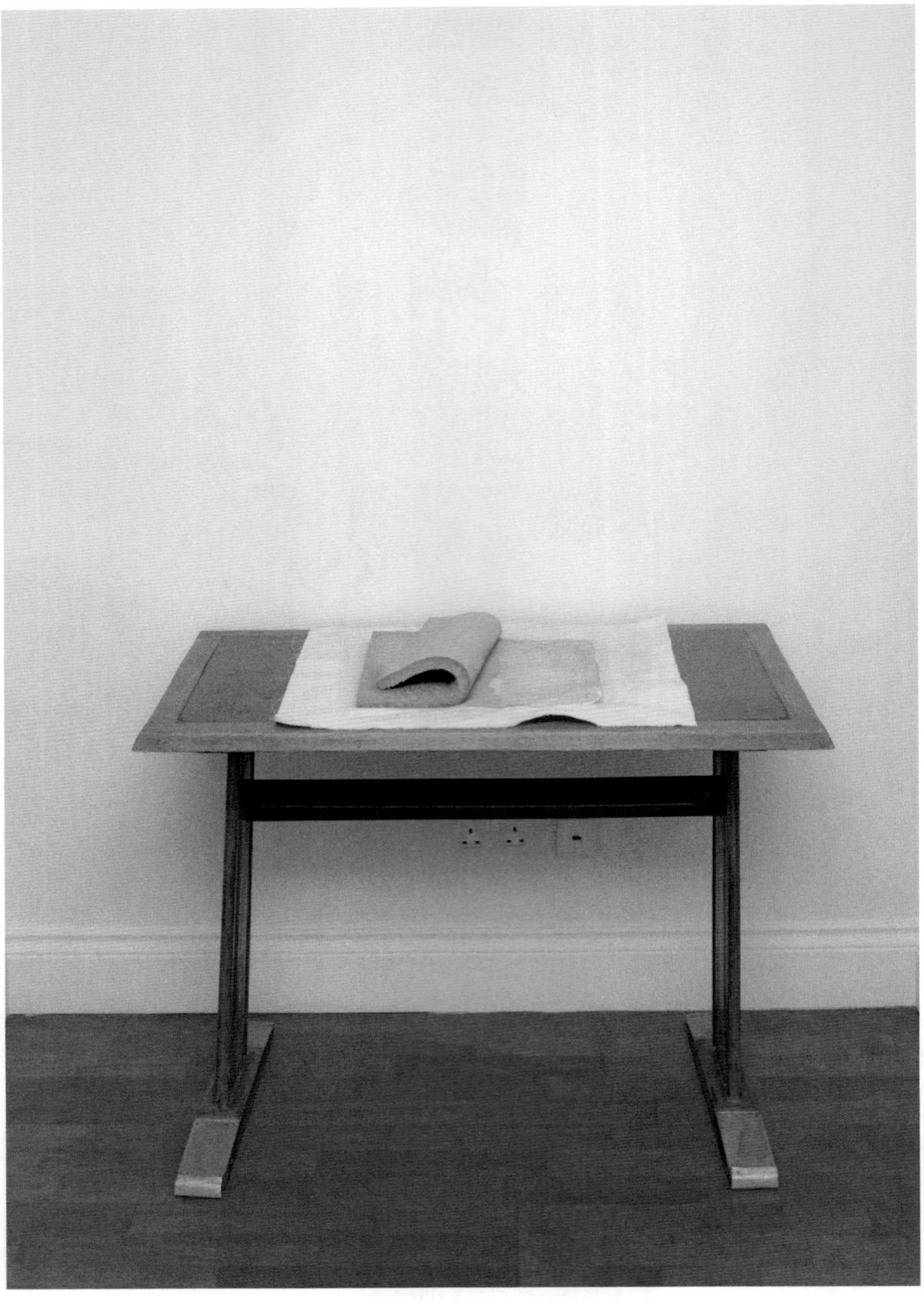

Beton (gefaltet), 2013
Concrete, cotton
7,5 × 58 × 62 cm

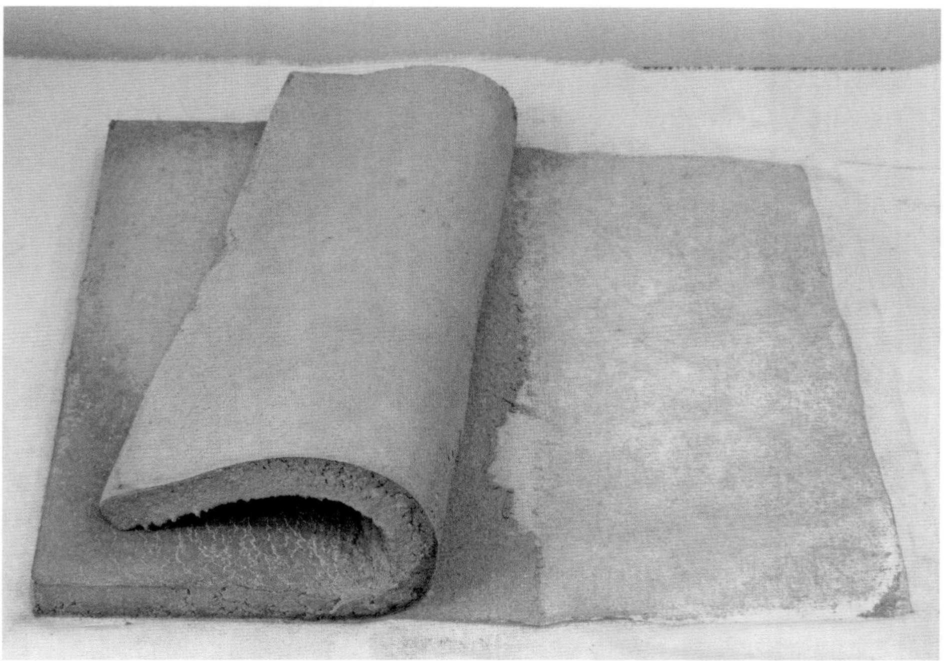

not yet titled, 2012
Concrete
29 × 98 × 75 cm

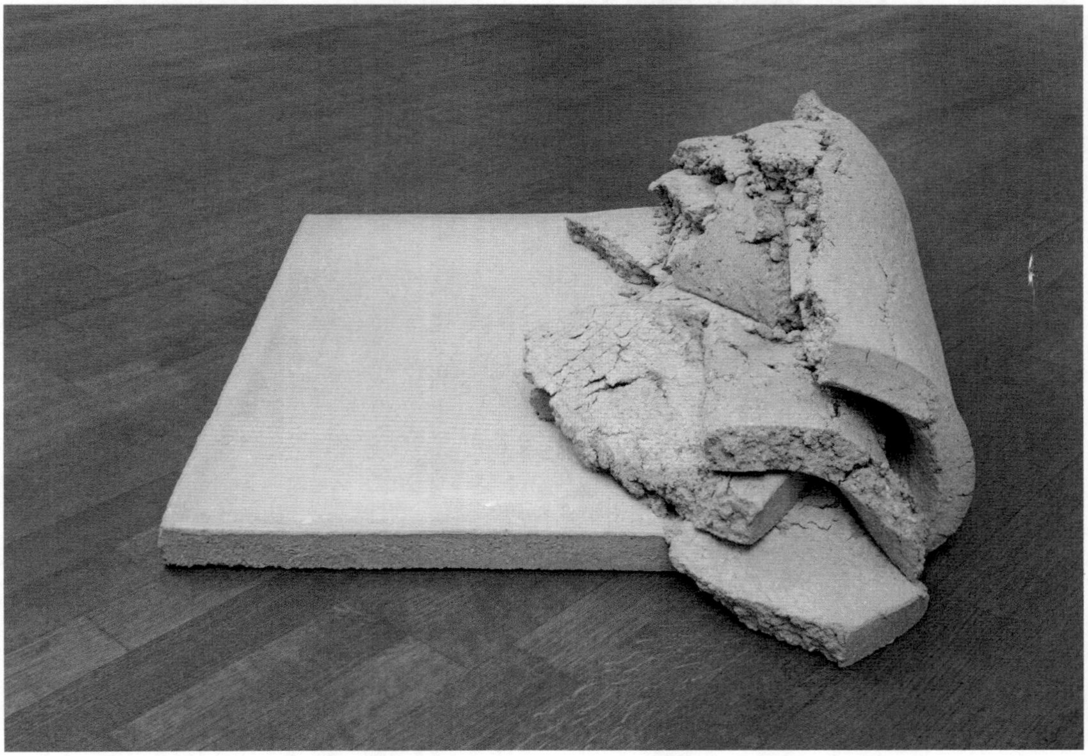

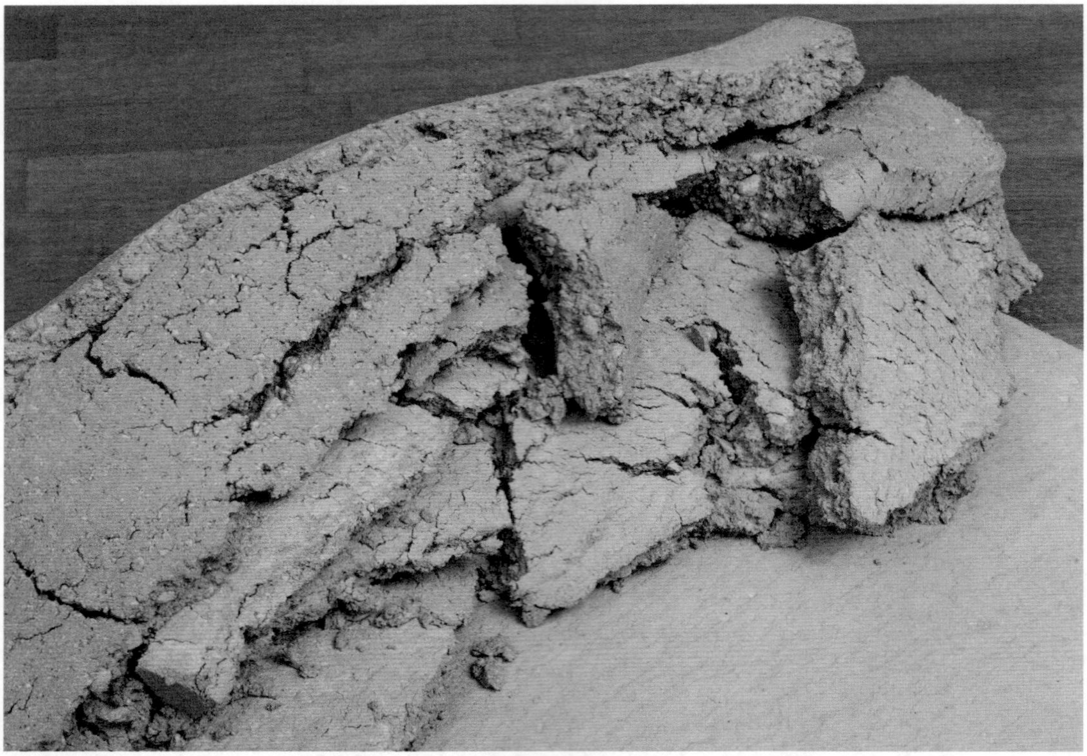

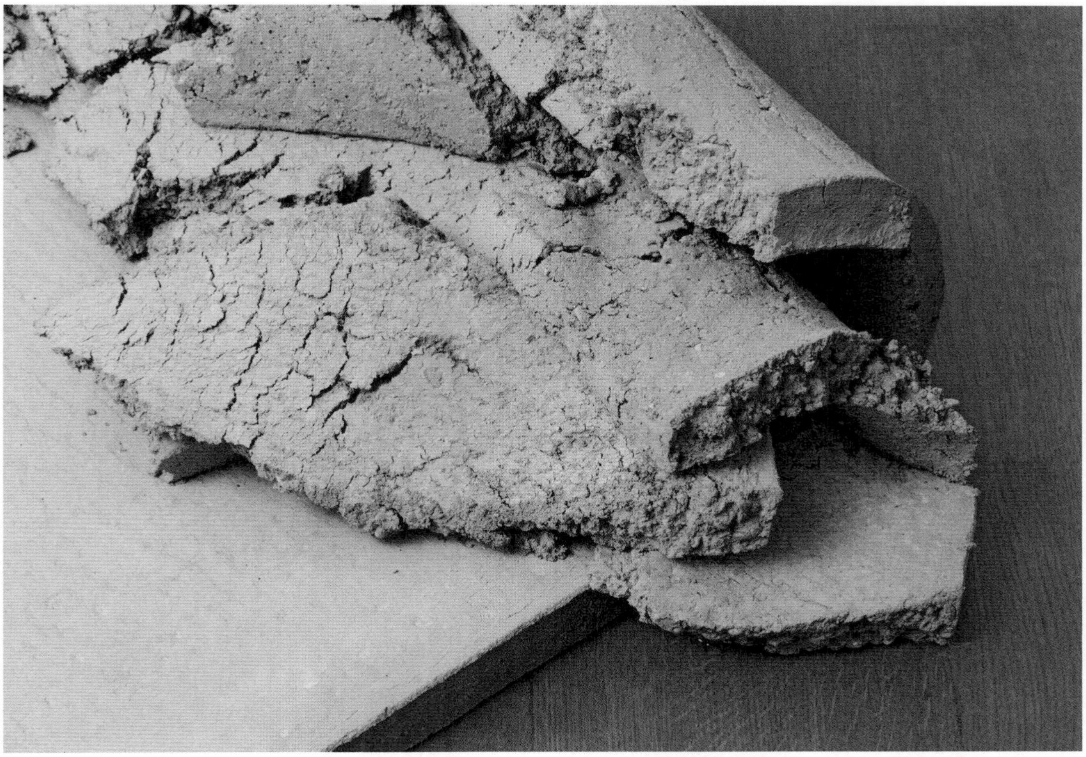

Schade, dass Beton nicht brennt, 2012
Concrete
40 × 60 × 20 cm

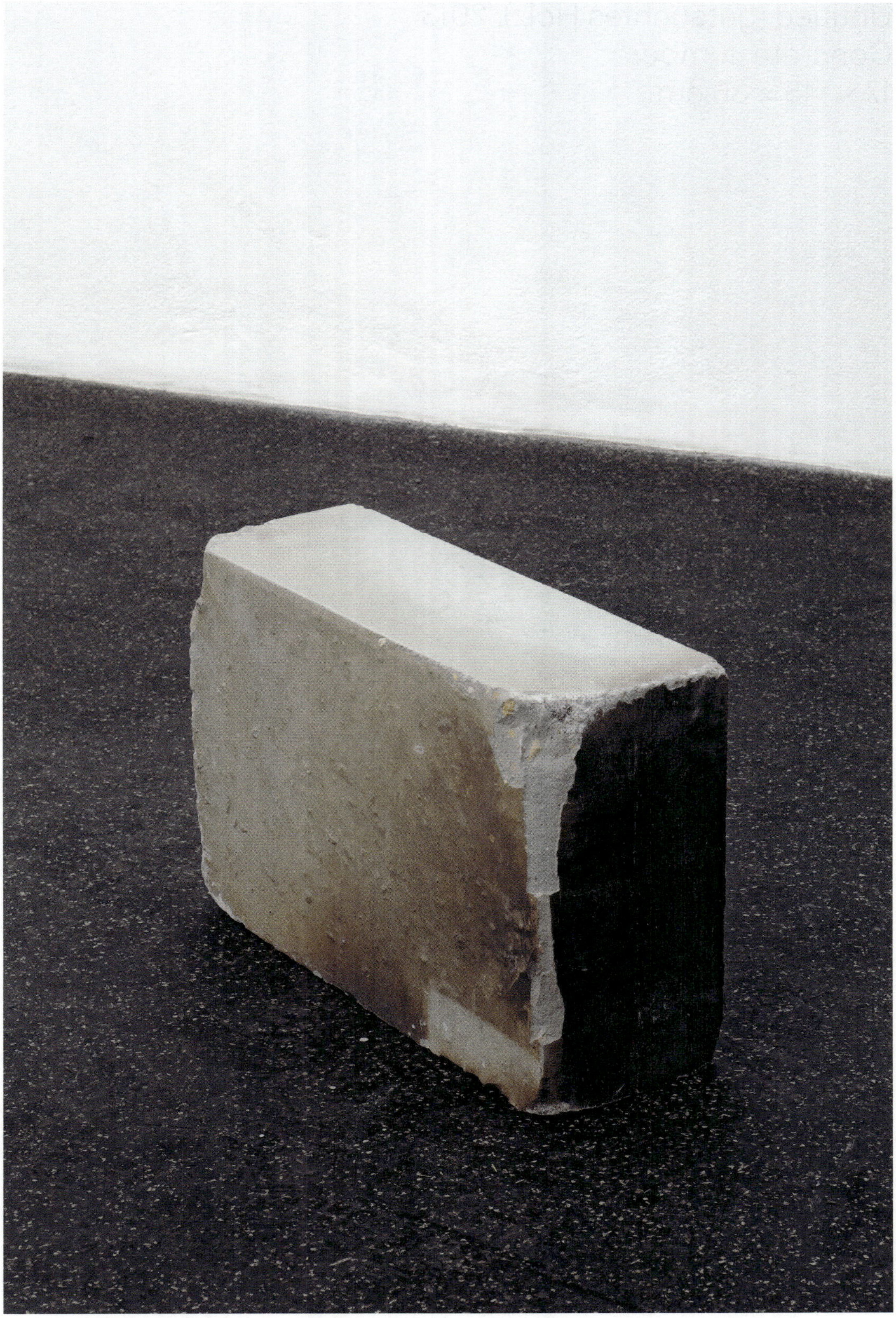

Untitled (getauchtes Holz), 2013
Concrete, lumber
17 × 145 × 36 cm

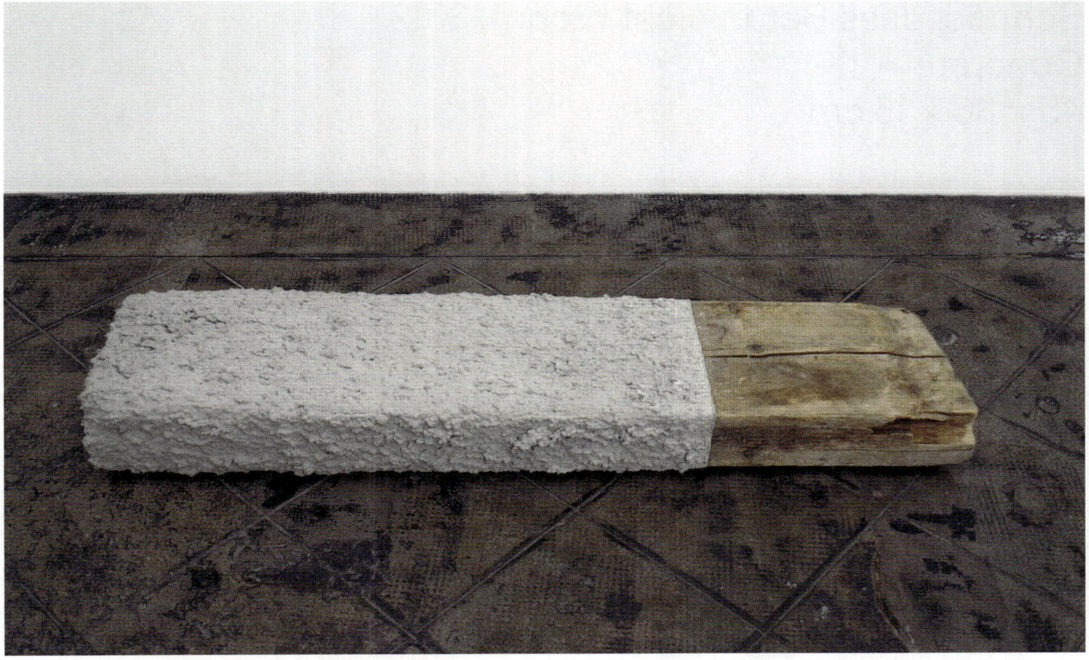

Schade, dass Beton nicht brennt, 2012
Concrete
45 × 30 × 15 cm

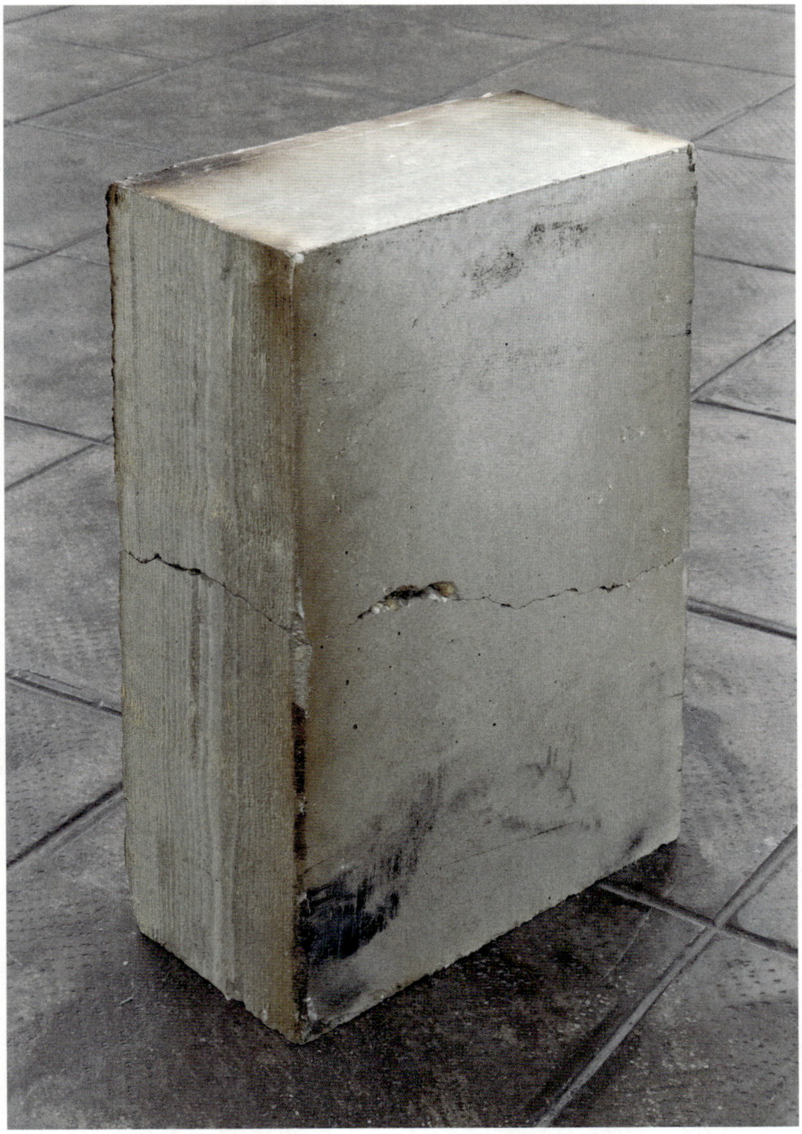

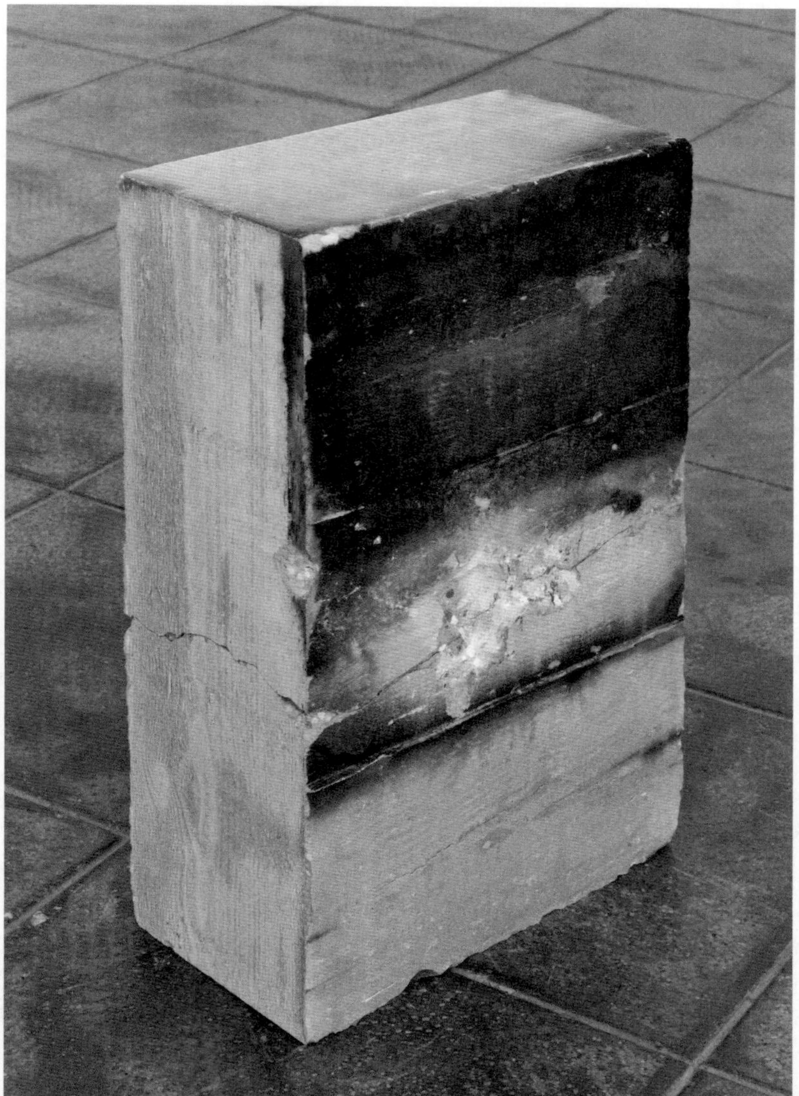

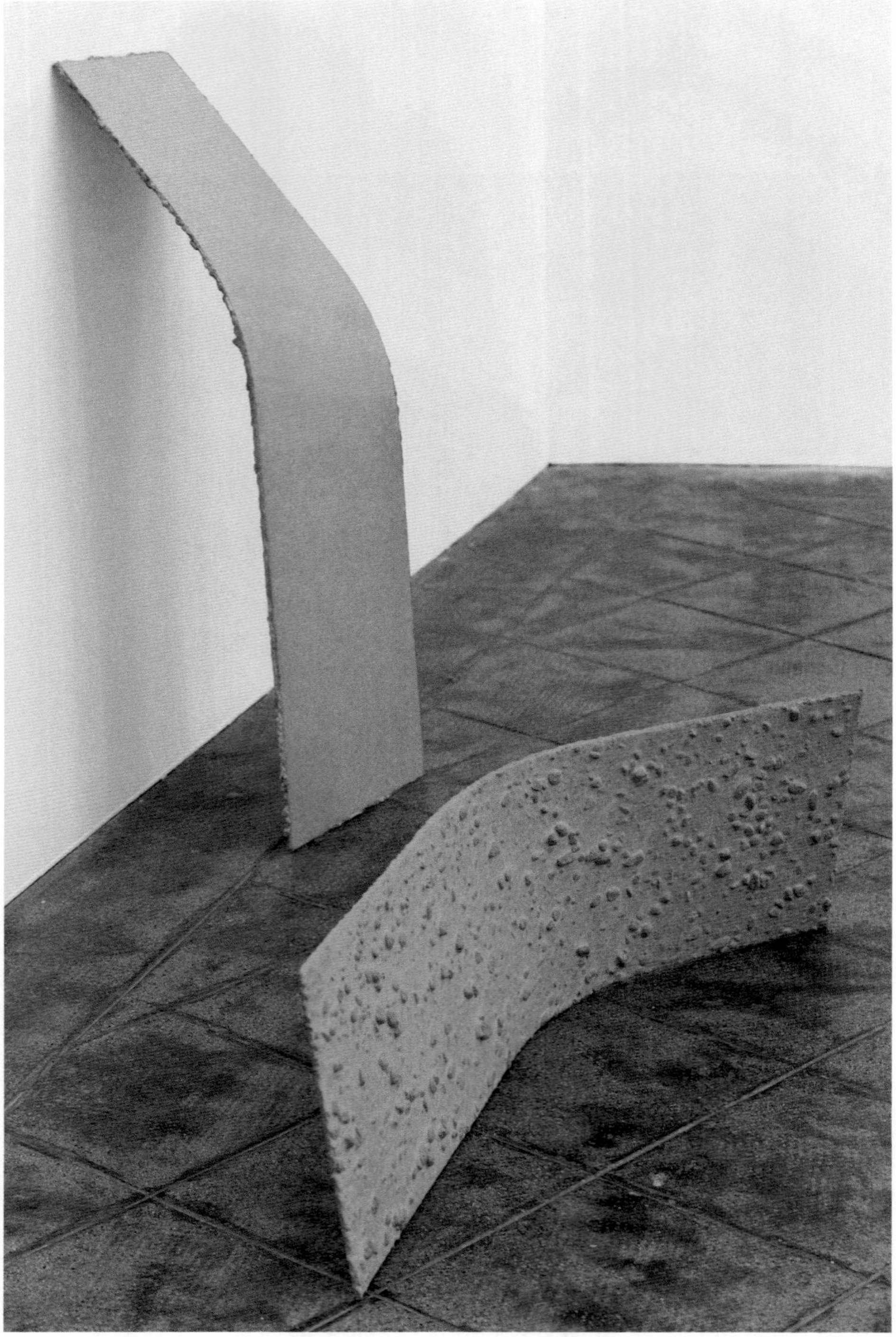

bent inversion
(lehnend), 2012
Concrete
109 × 37 × 0,7 cm

bent inversion
(seitlich stehend), 2012
Concrete
36,6 × 115 × 0,7 cm

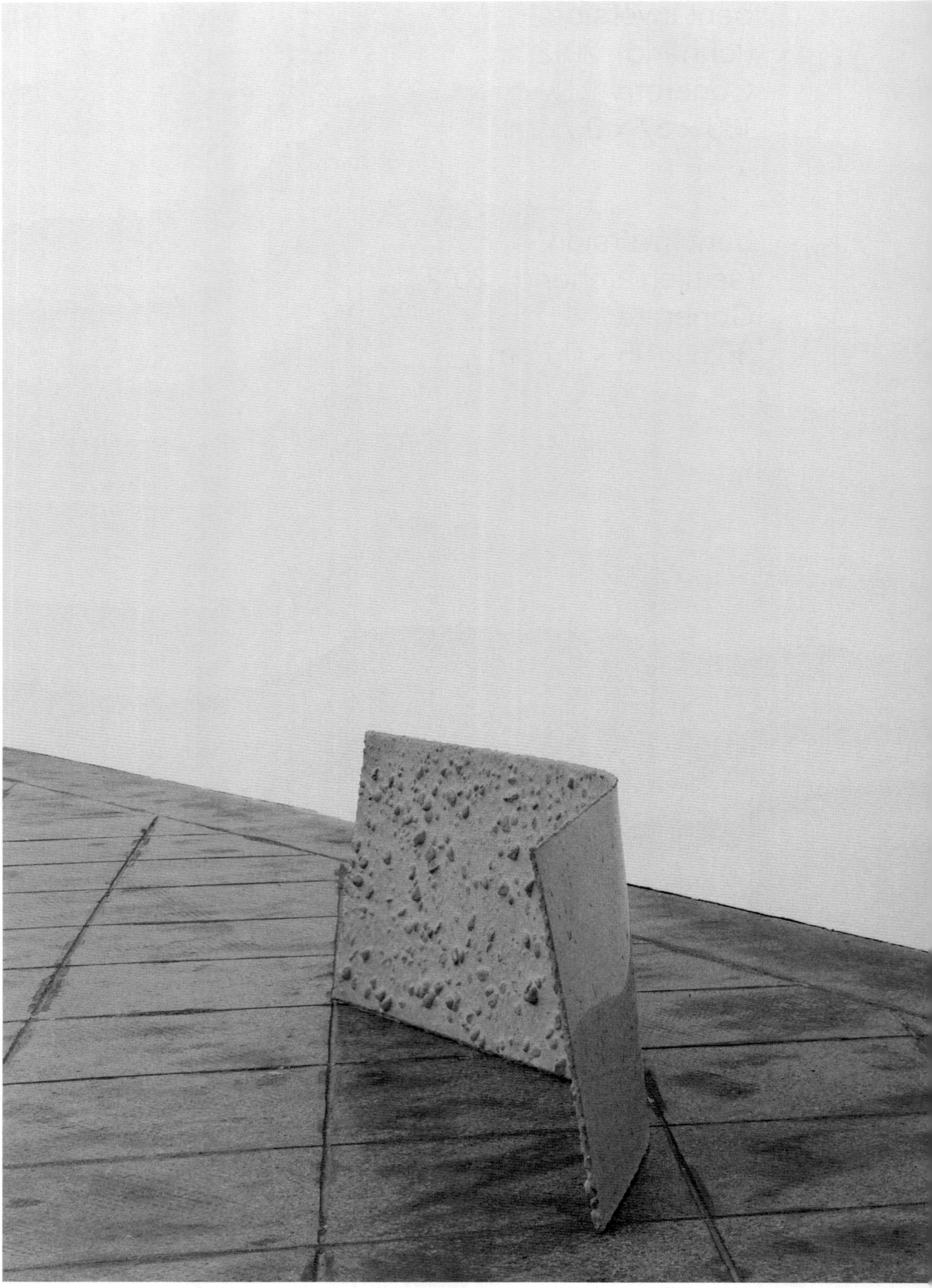

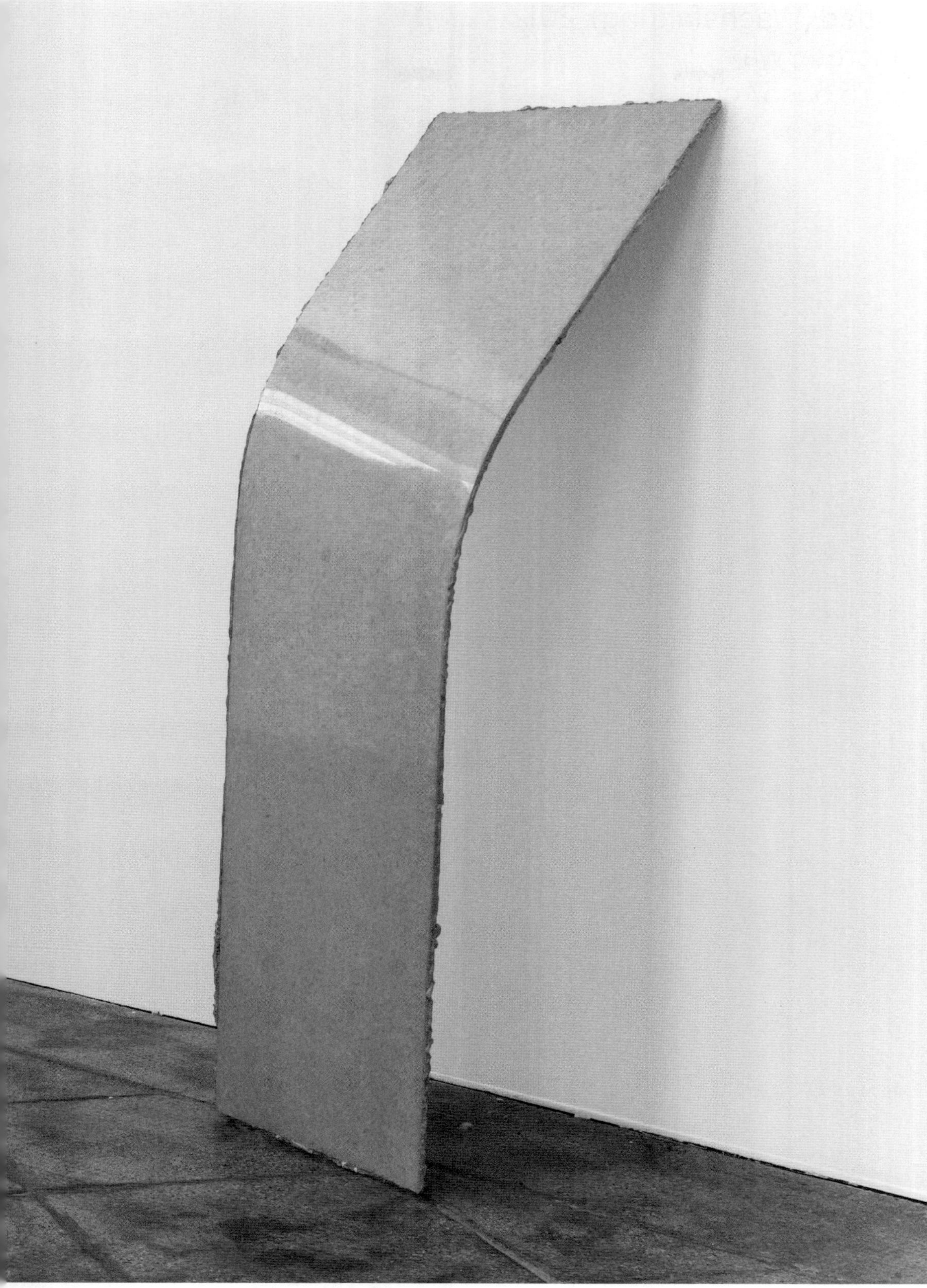

Untitled (Wachsfaltung), 2012
Concrete, wax
13 × 75,5 × 57 cm

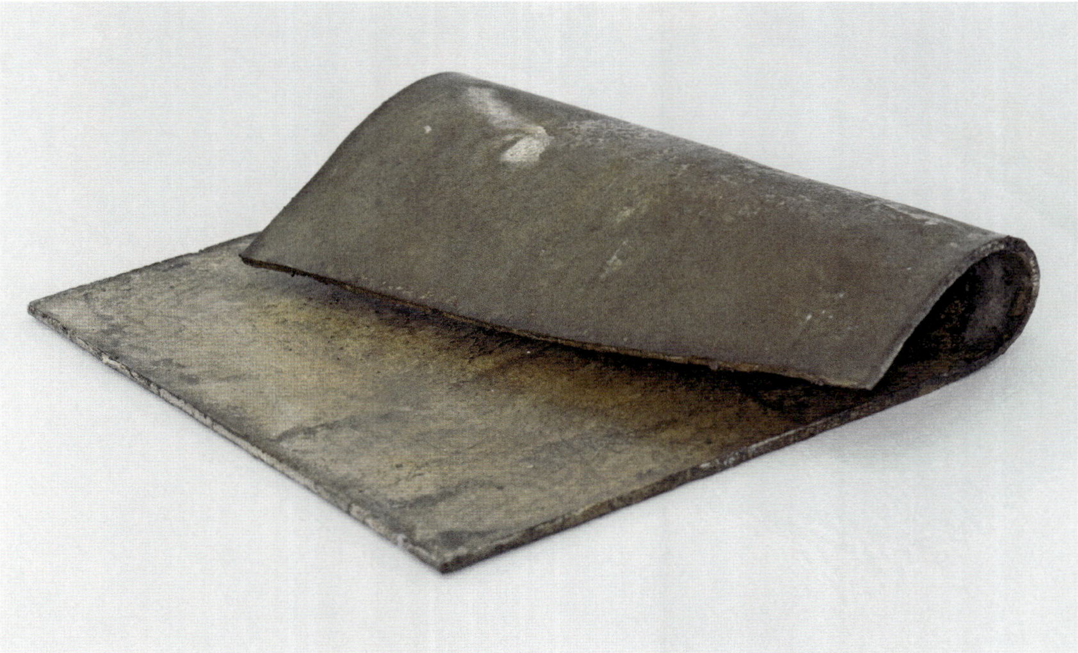

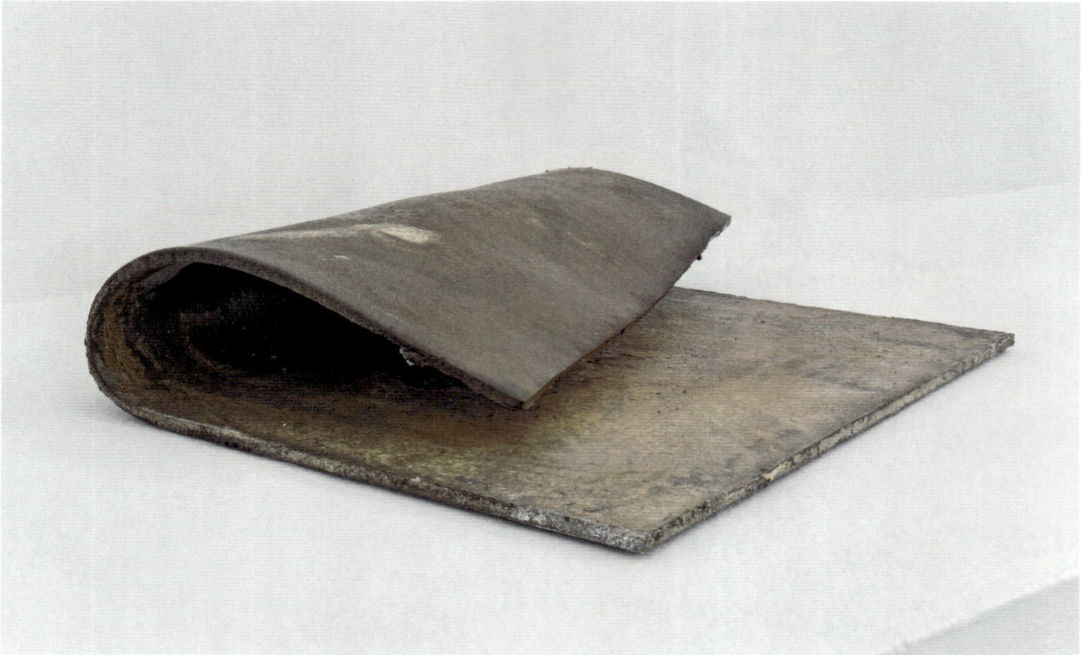

Beton (gehoben), 2012
Tarp, concrete, wirerope
359 × 62 × 59 cm

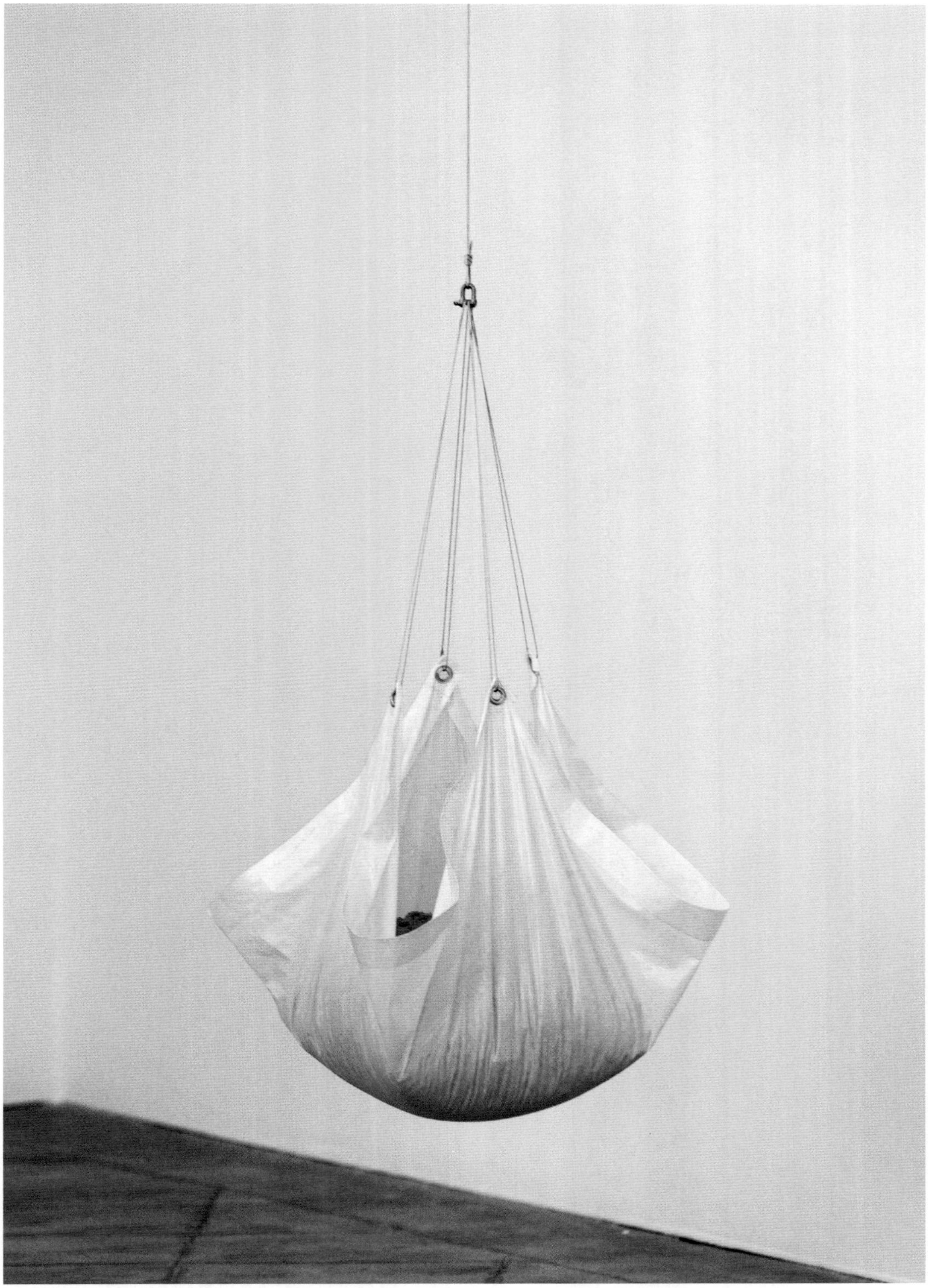

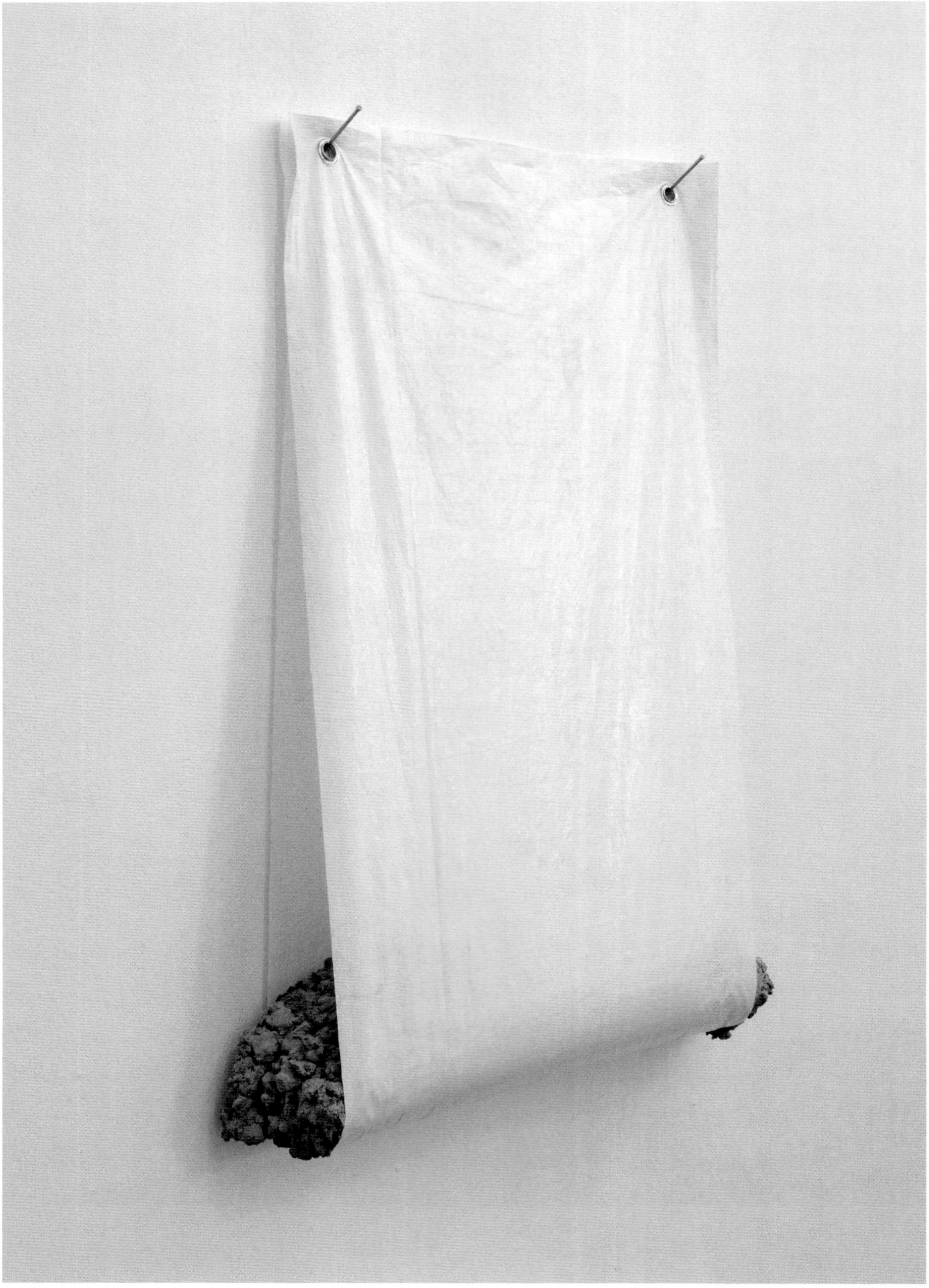

Beton (gerollt), 2012
Tarp, concrete, nails
82 × 58 × 11 cm

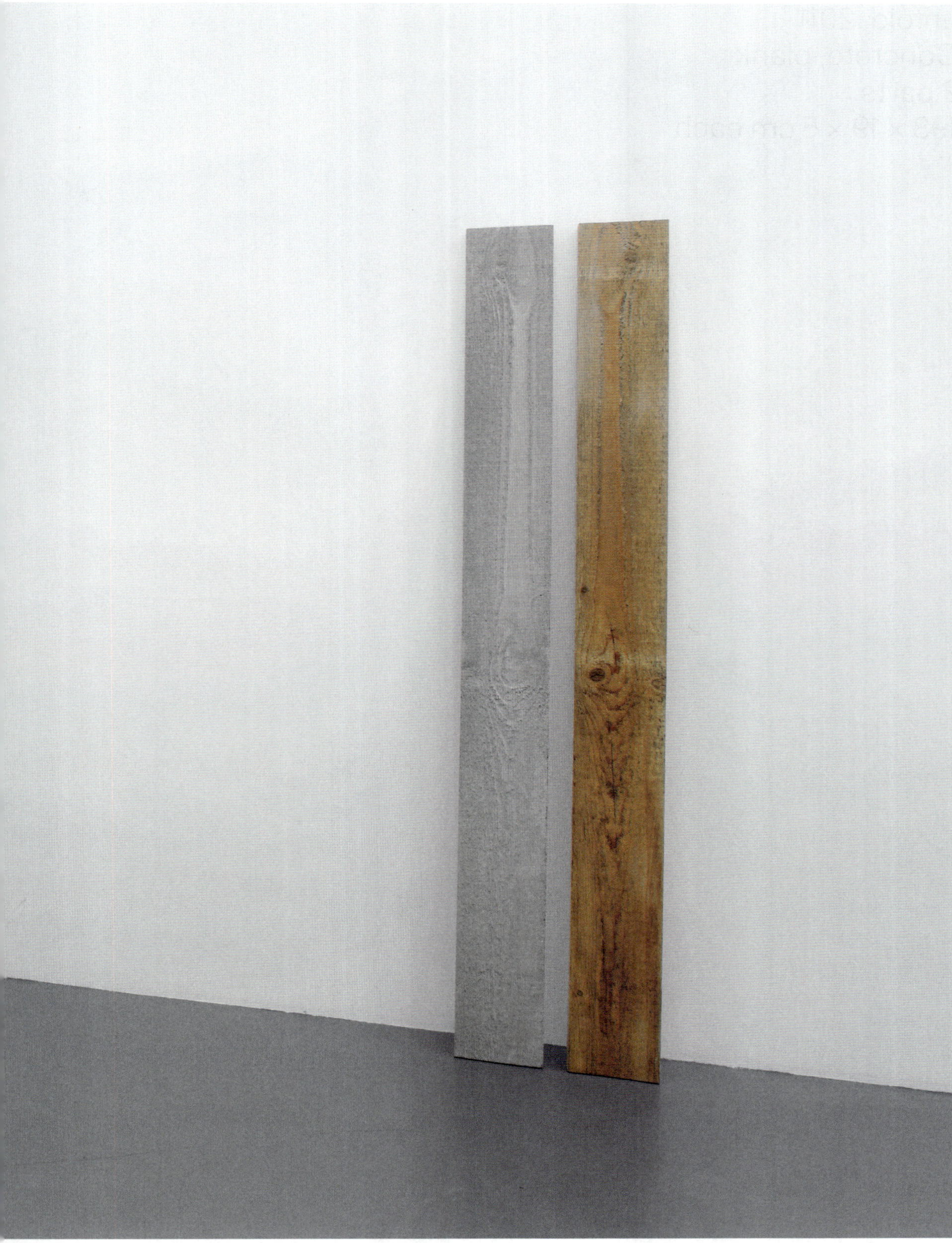

unfold, 2011
Concrete, plank
2 parts
198 × 19 × 5 cm each

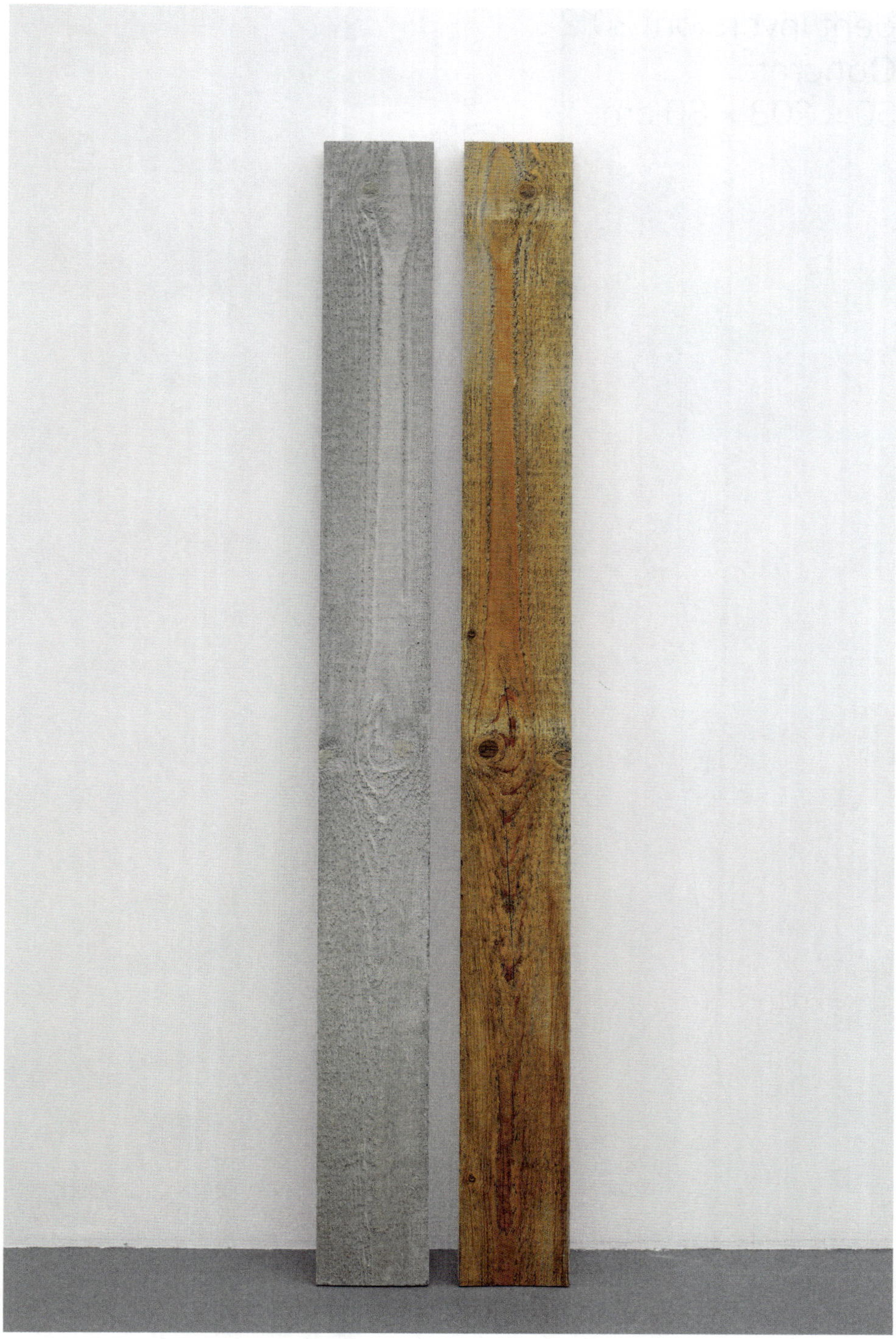

bent inversion, 2012
Concrete
50 × 208 × 80 cm

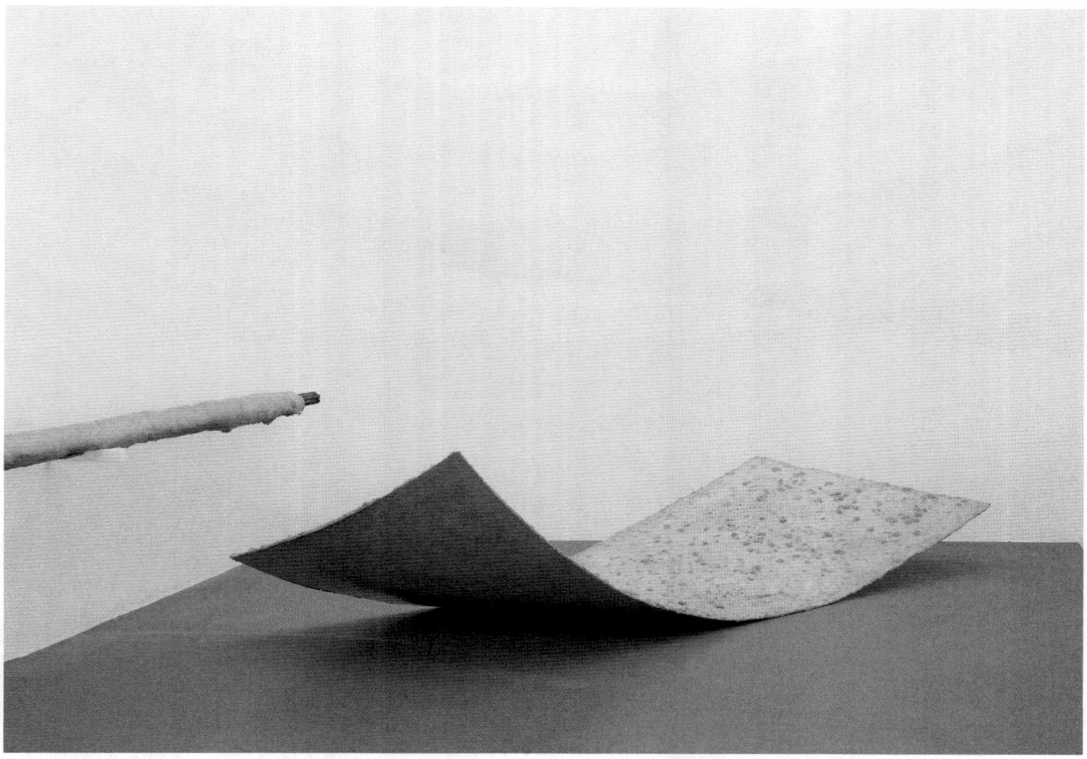

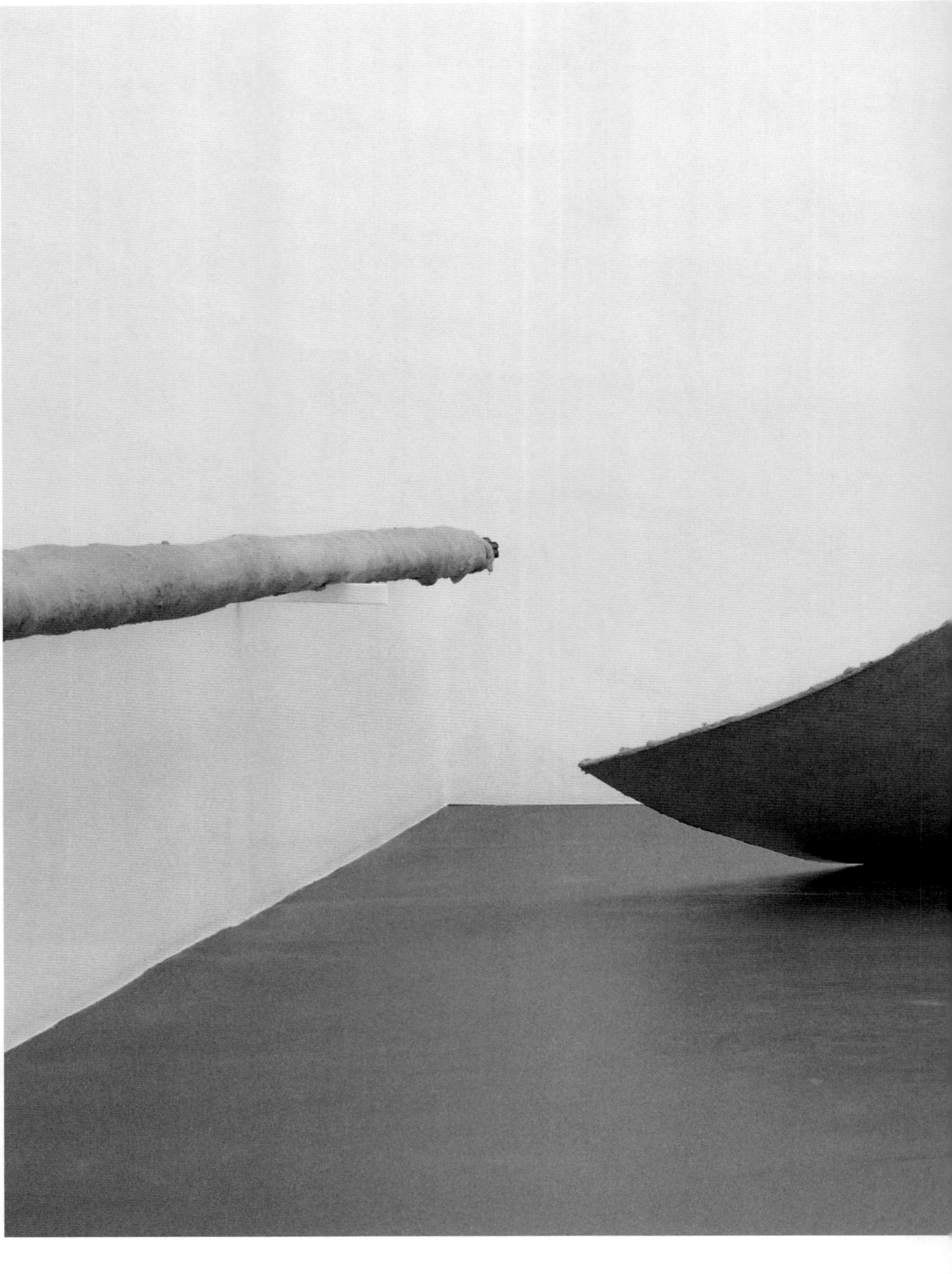

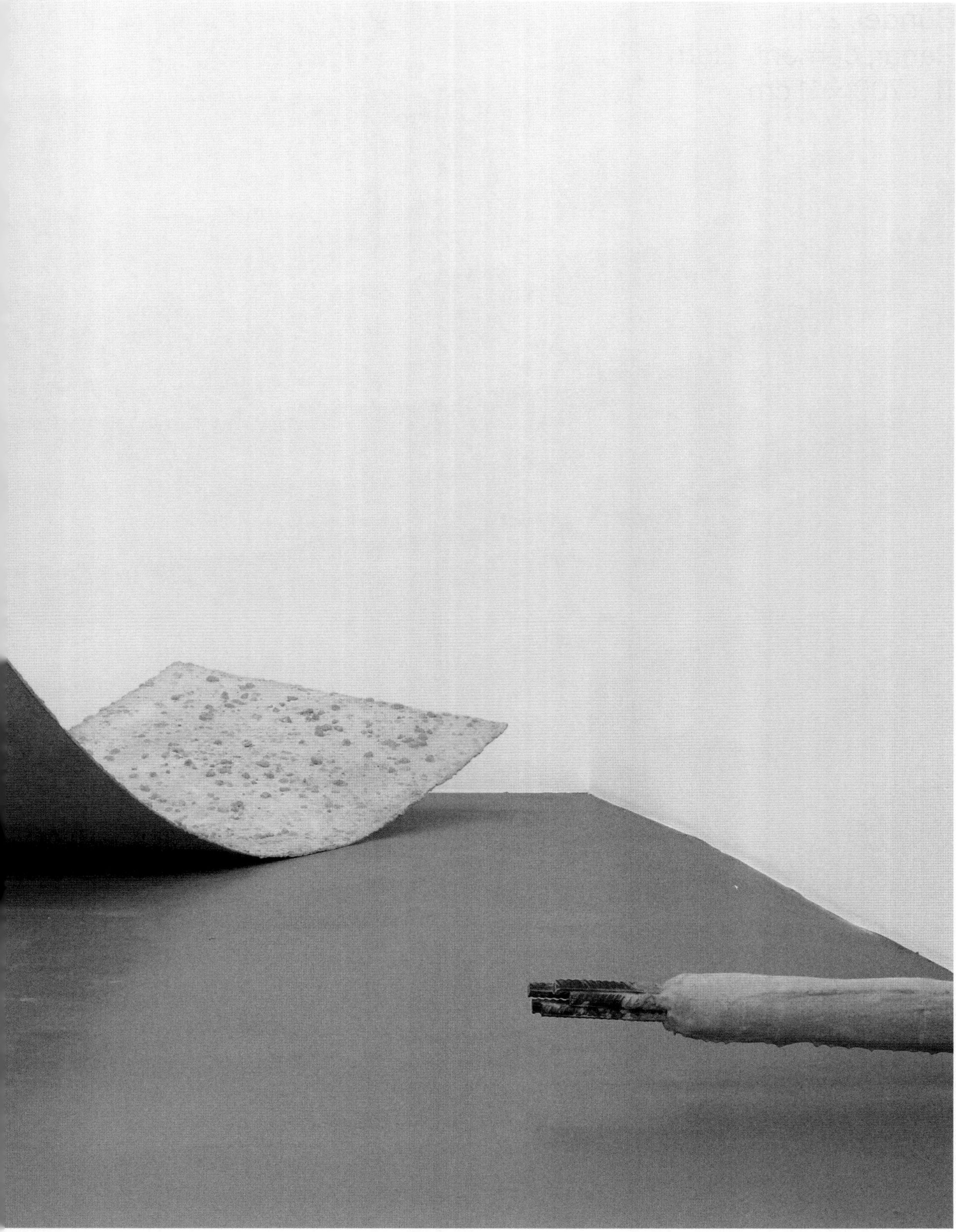

Bündel, 2012
Rebar, cement, cloth
11 × 700 × 11 cm

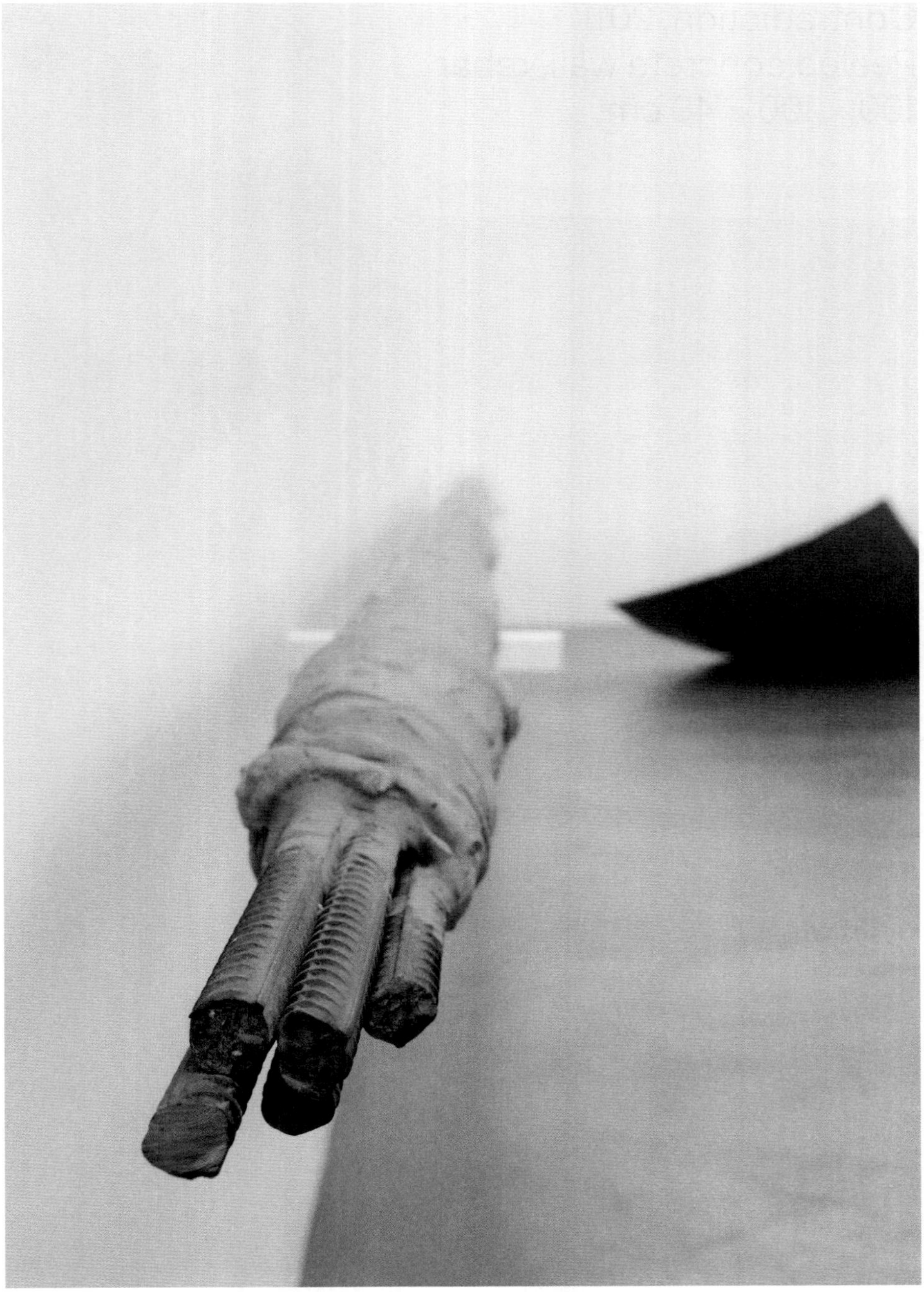

Contradiction, 2011
Peeled concrete wall, rebar
100 × 100 × 40 cm

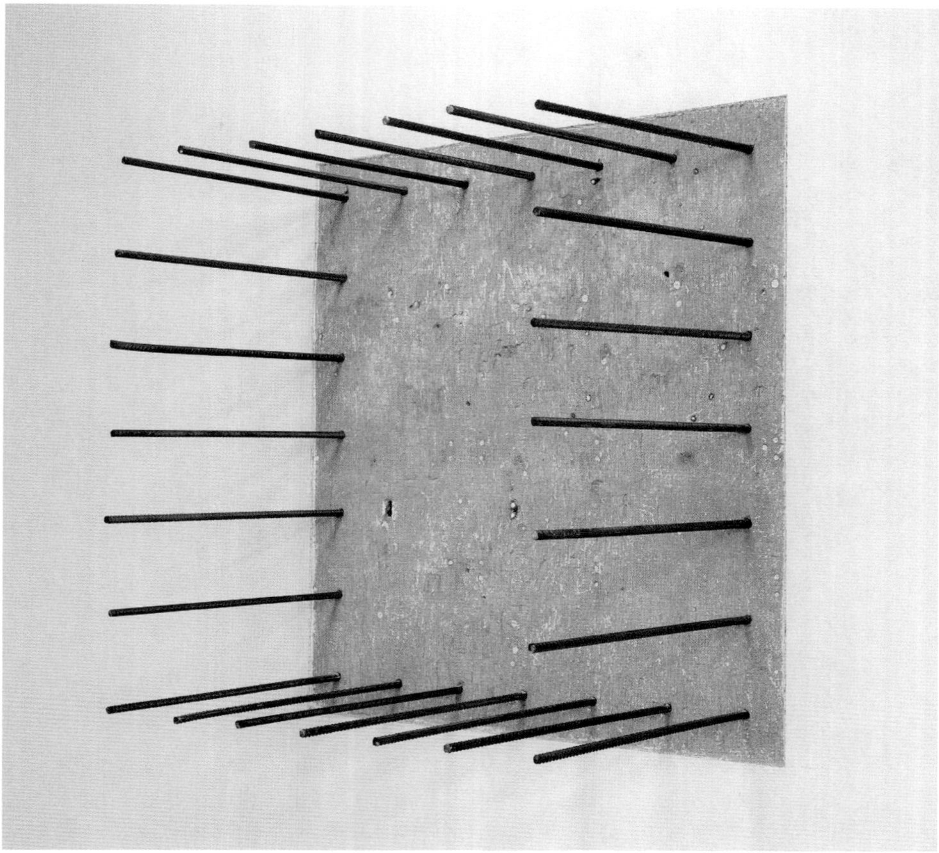

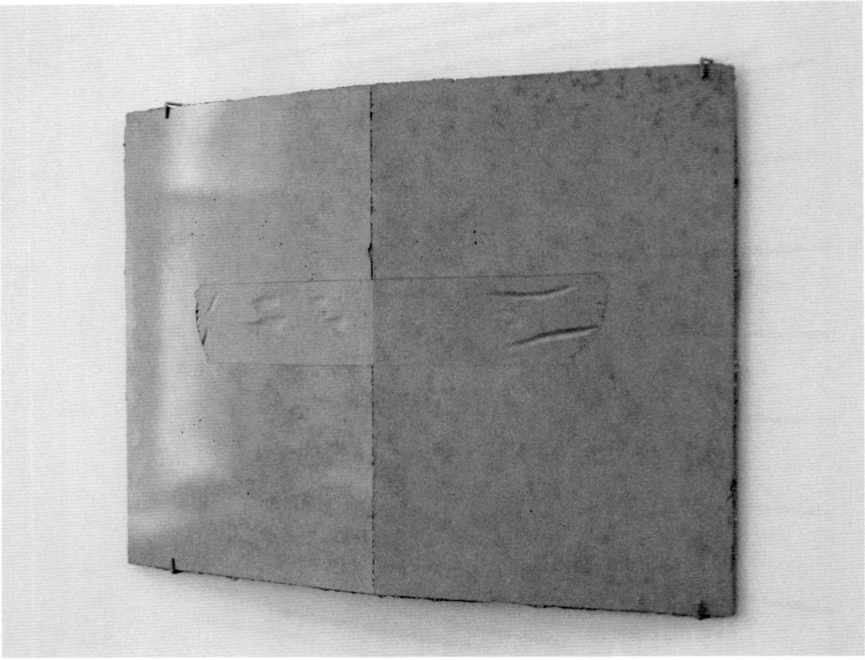

inversions, 2011
Concrete, nails
29,7 × 42 × 3 cm

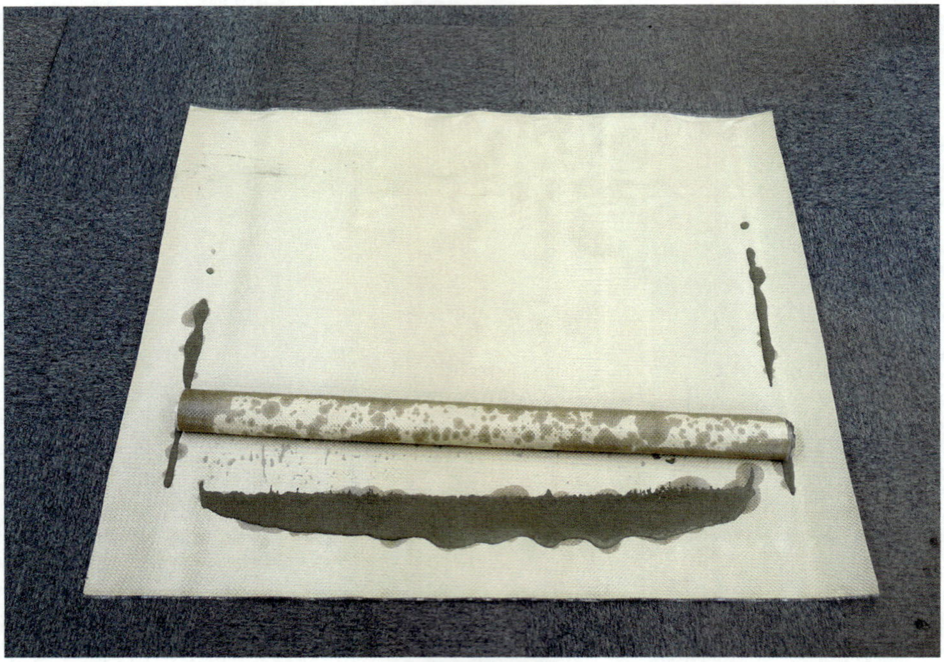

not yet titled, 2011
Concrete, paper
6 × 100 × 88 cm

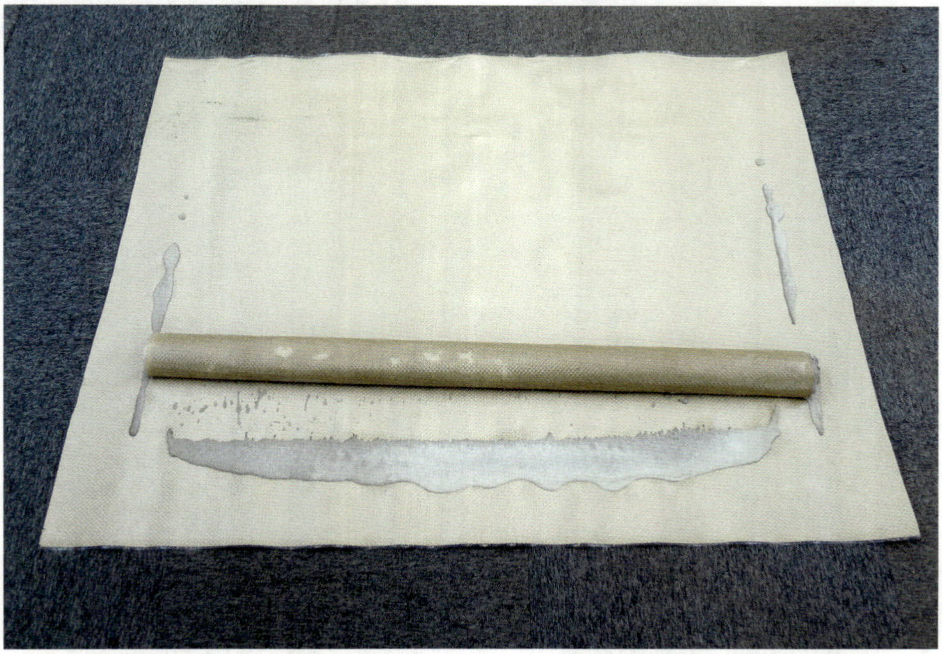

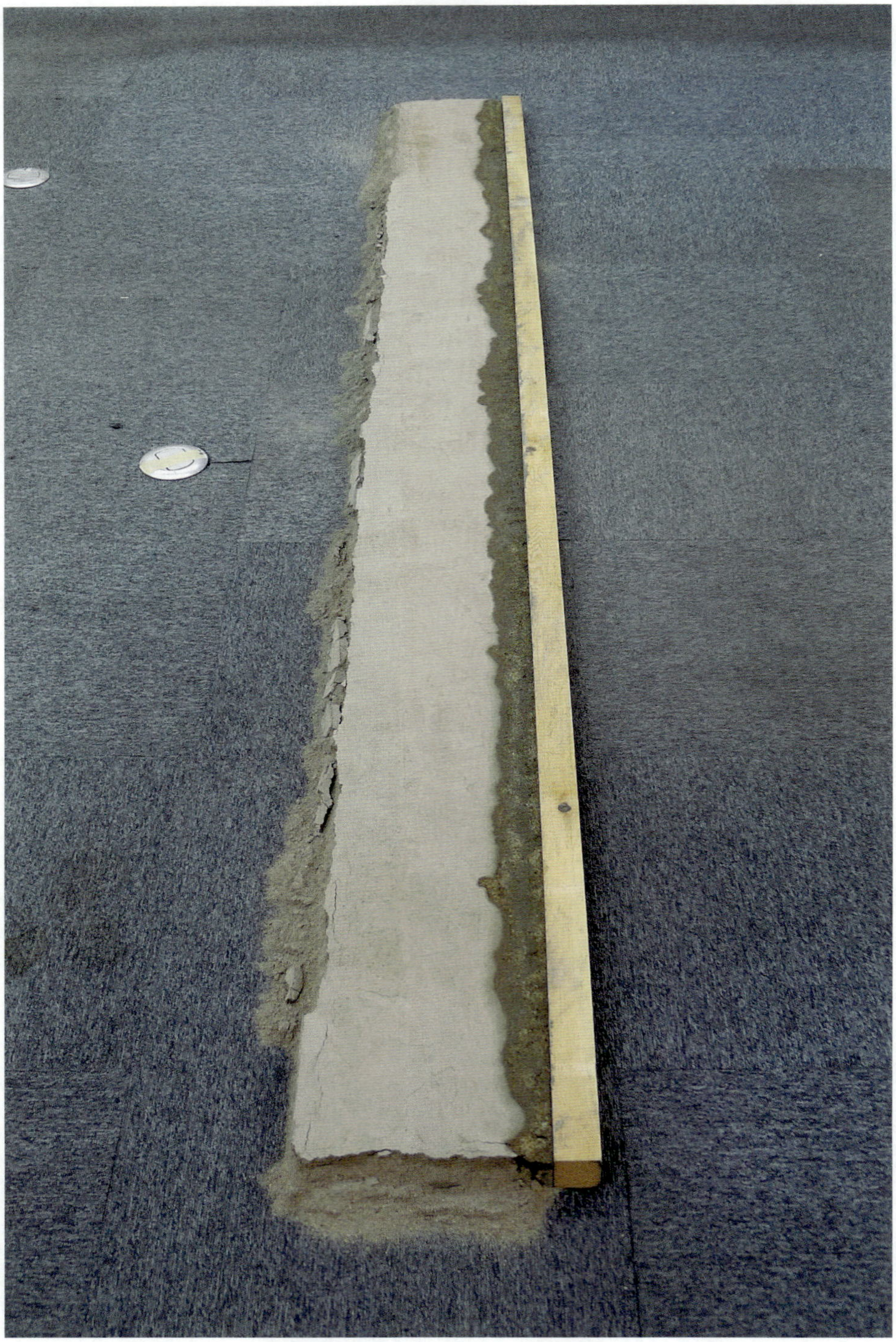

Untitled (Baseline), 2009
Sand, cement, water, lumber
Dimensions variable
Here: 5 × 35 × 350 cm

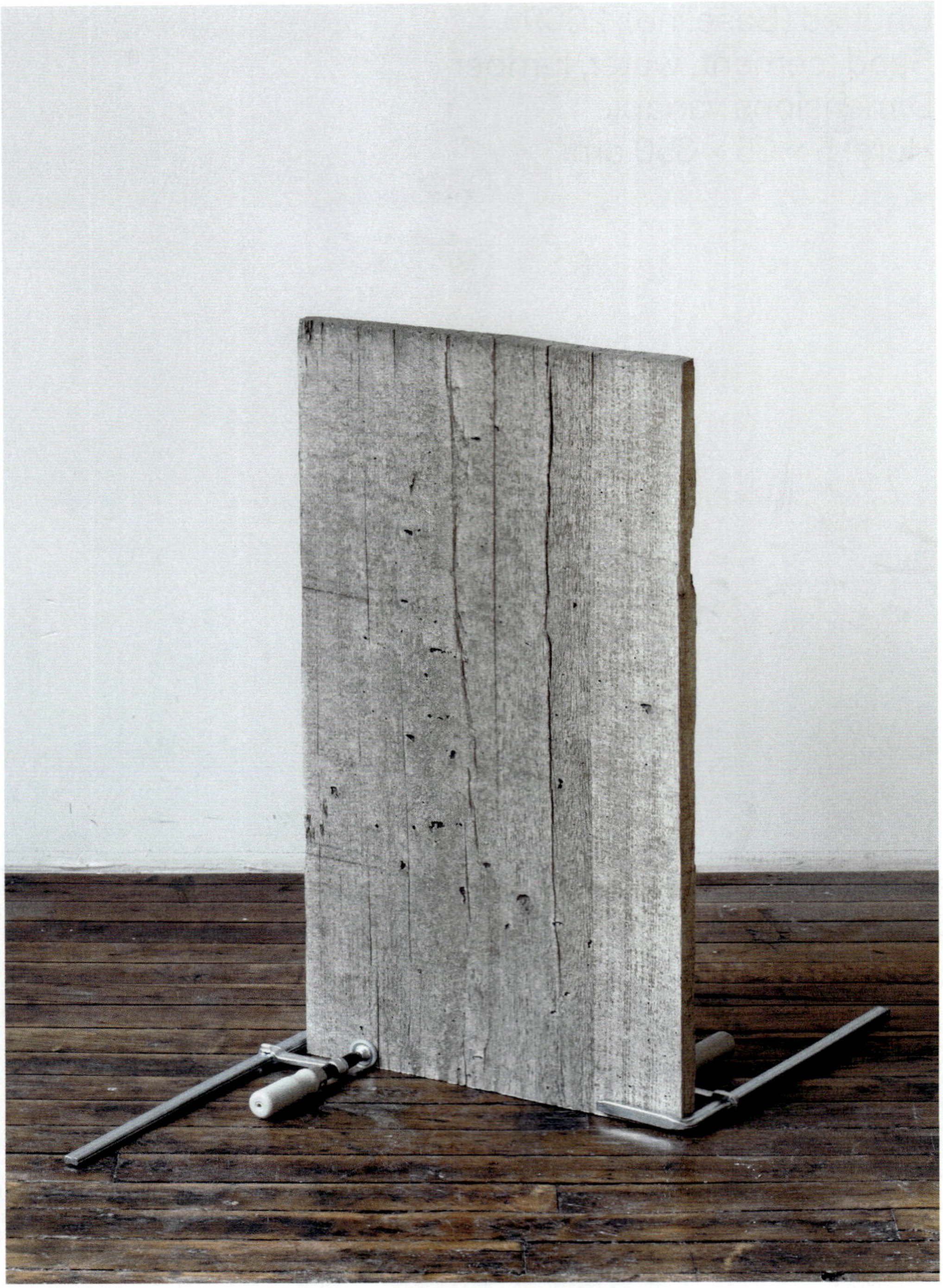

not yet titled, 2010
Concrete, clamps
63 × 37 × 60 cm

Untitled (bewehrtes Wachs), 2014
Wax, aluminum mesh
65 x 34 x 35 cm
Pedestal
9 x 68 x 68 cm

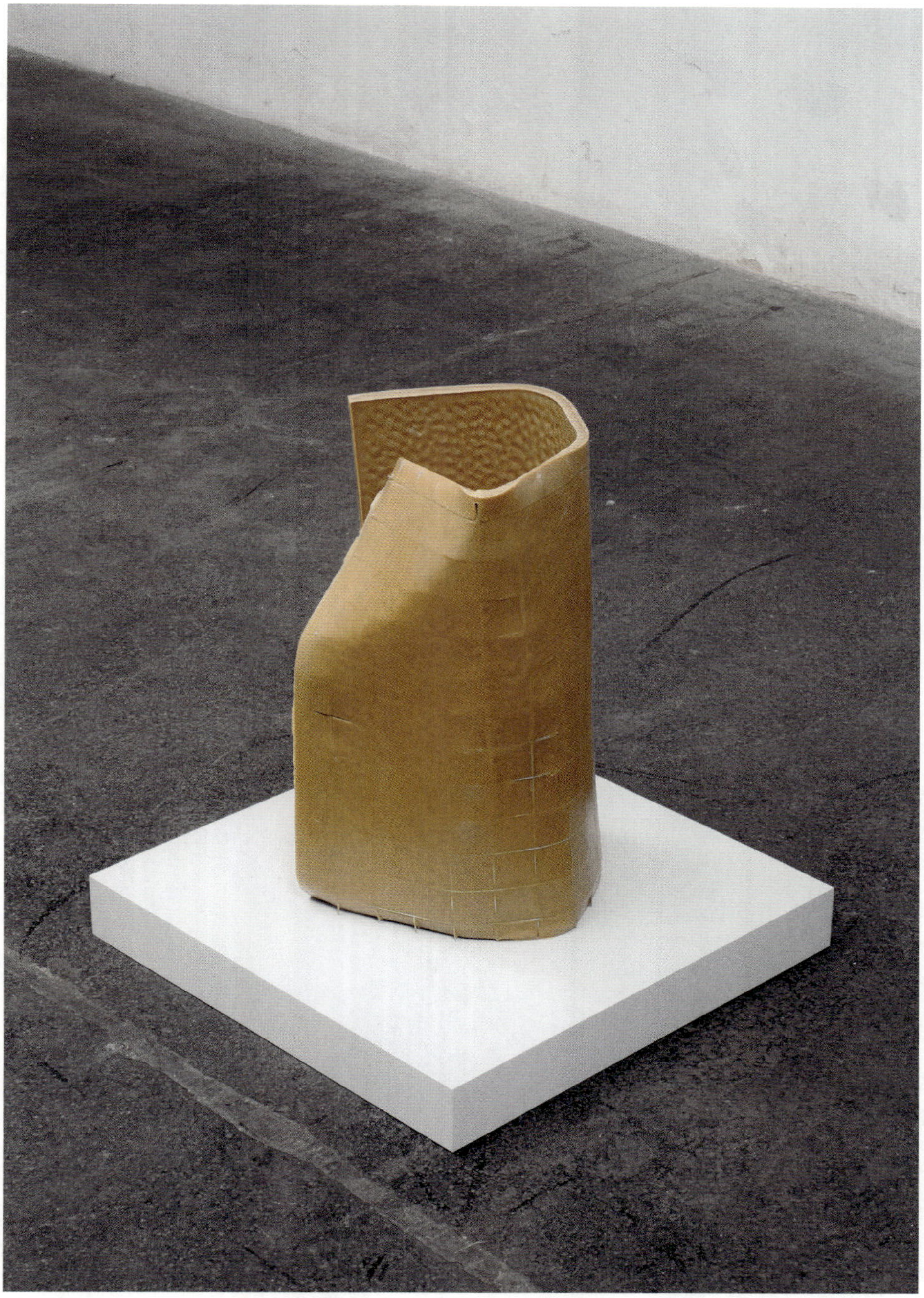

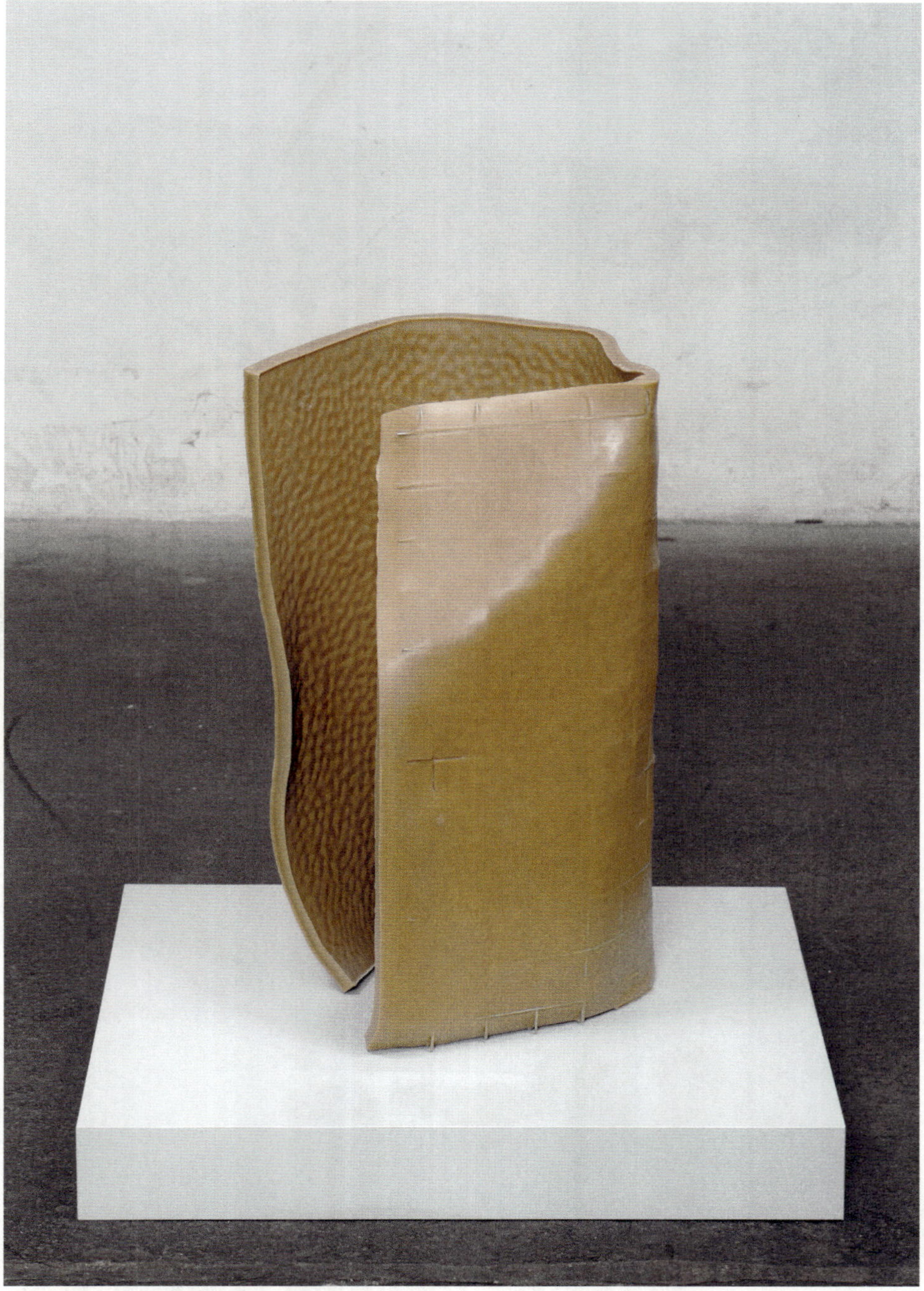

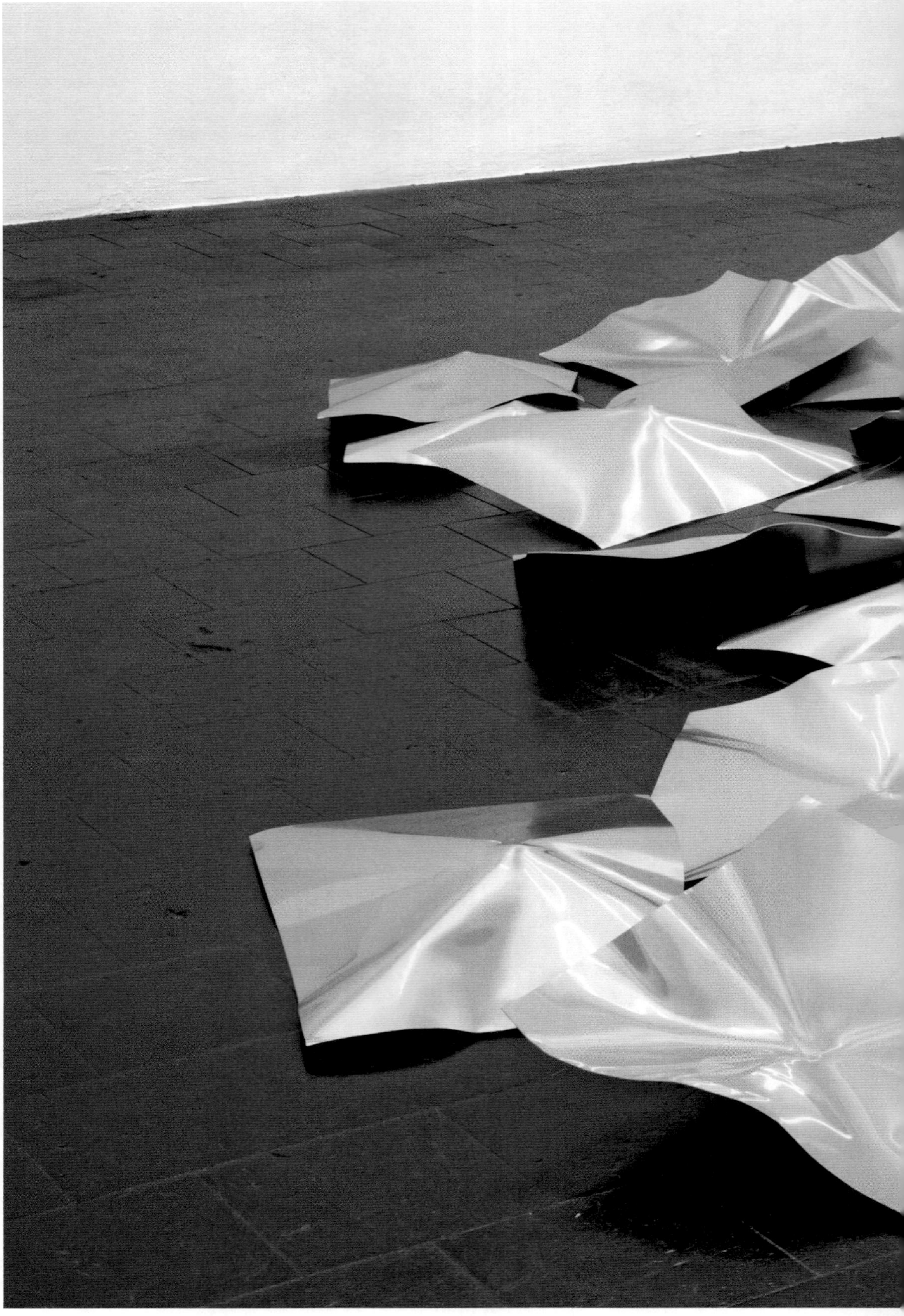

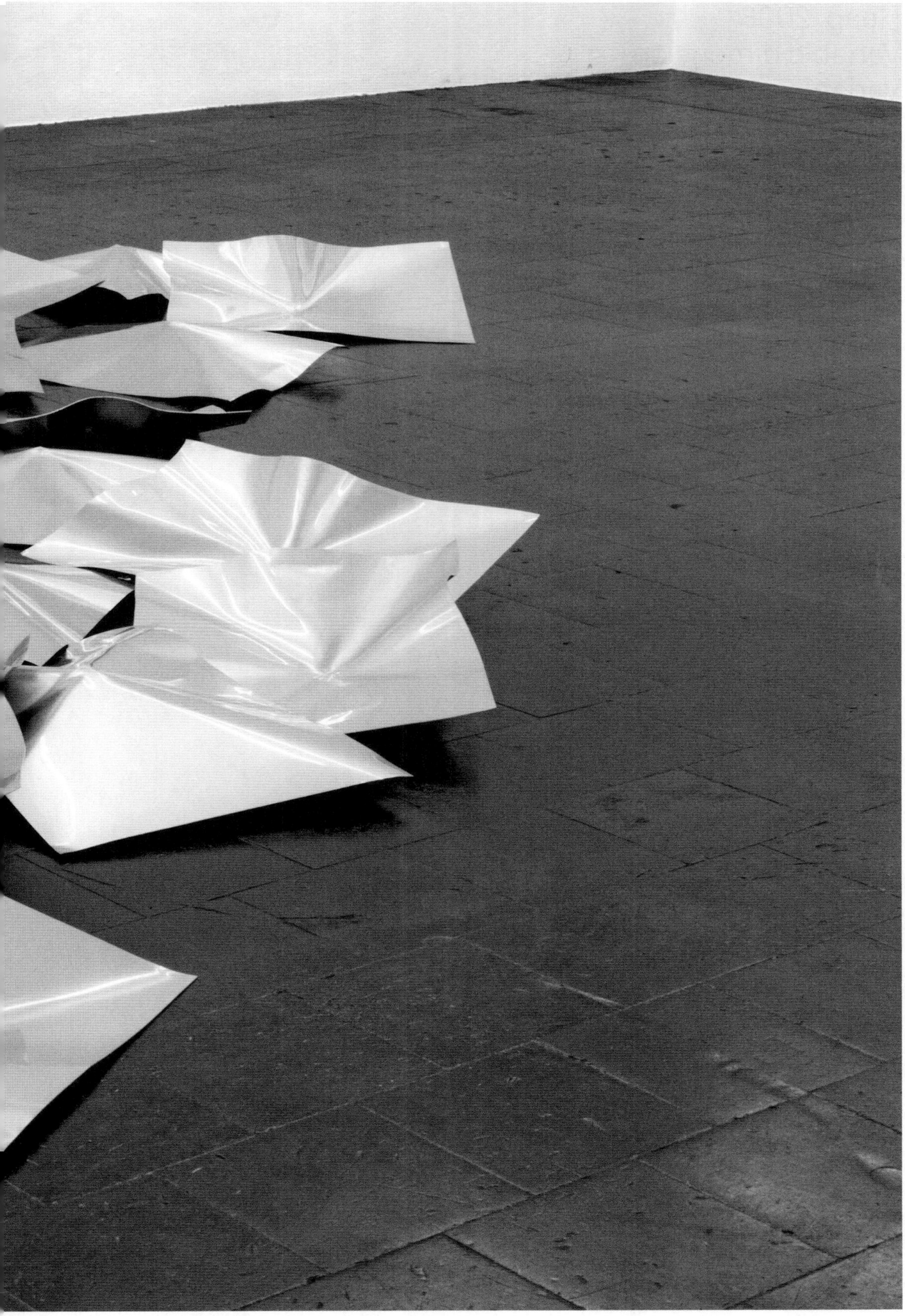

Heap, 2008
Variable dimension
Variable amount of aluminum sheets
13 x 49 x 66 cm each

Stack, 2008
29 x 66 x 65 cm
19 aluminum sheets
13 x 49 x 66 cm each
Lumber

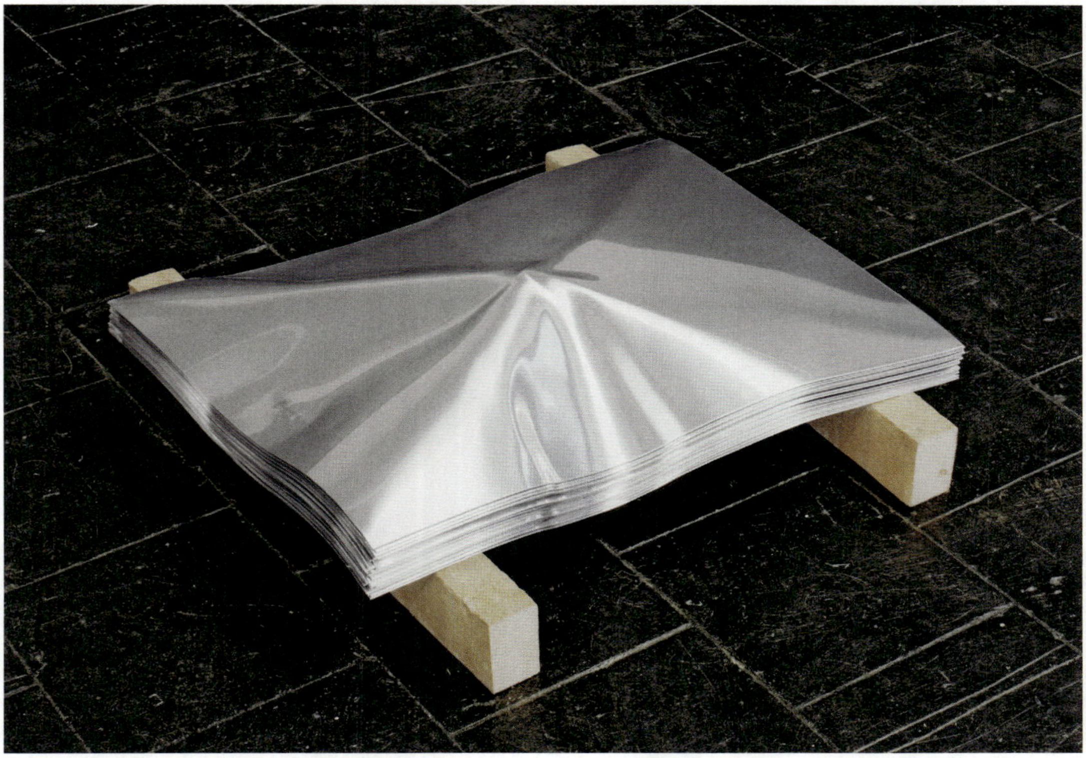

Untitled (rue Ramponeau), 2008
Lambdaprint
25 × 21 cm

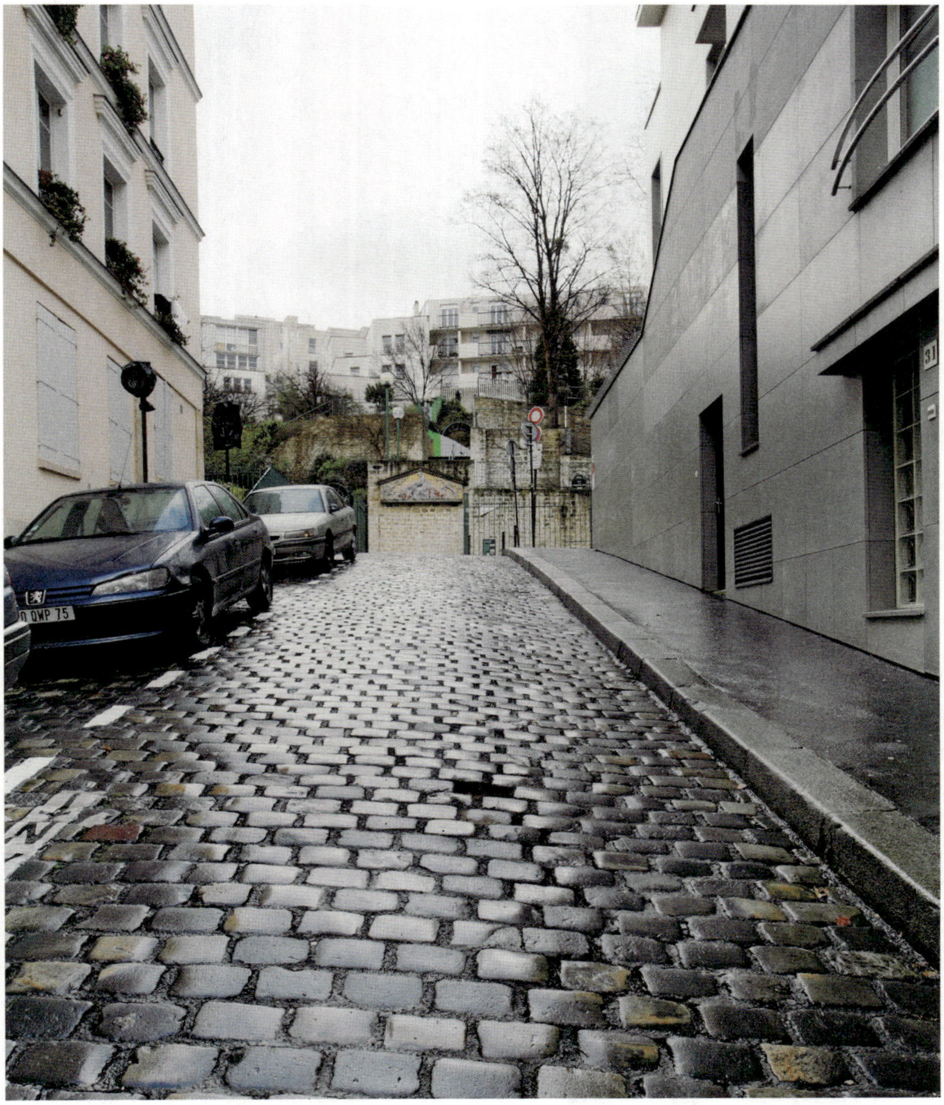

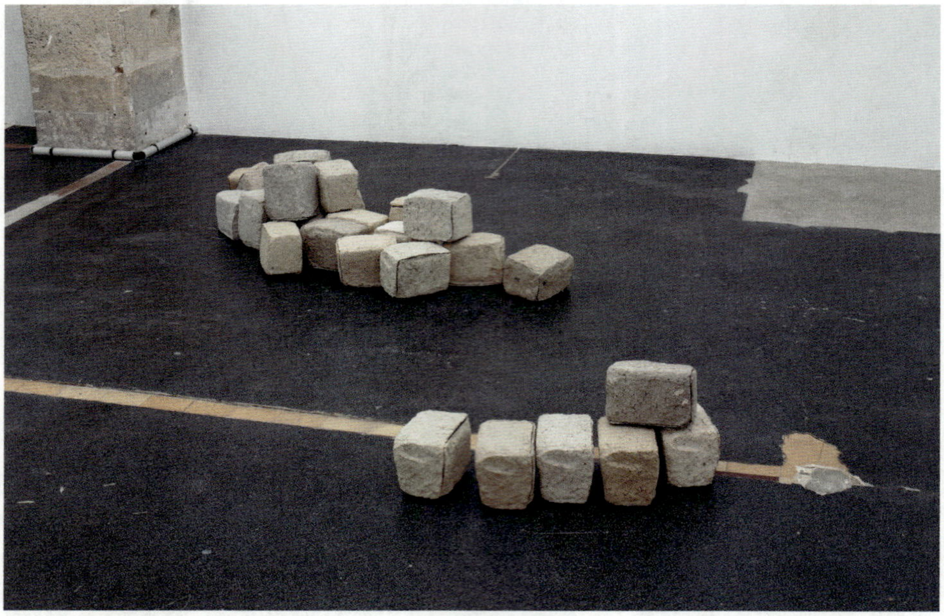

Untitled (Ramponeau), 2008
Papier-maché cobblestones made of historic paper
Dimensions variable
12 × 13 × 15 cm each

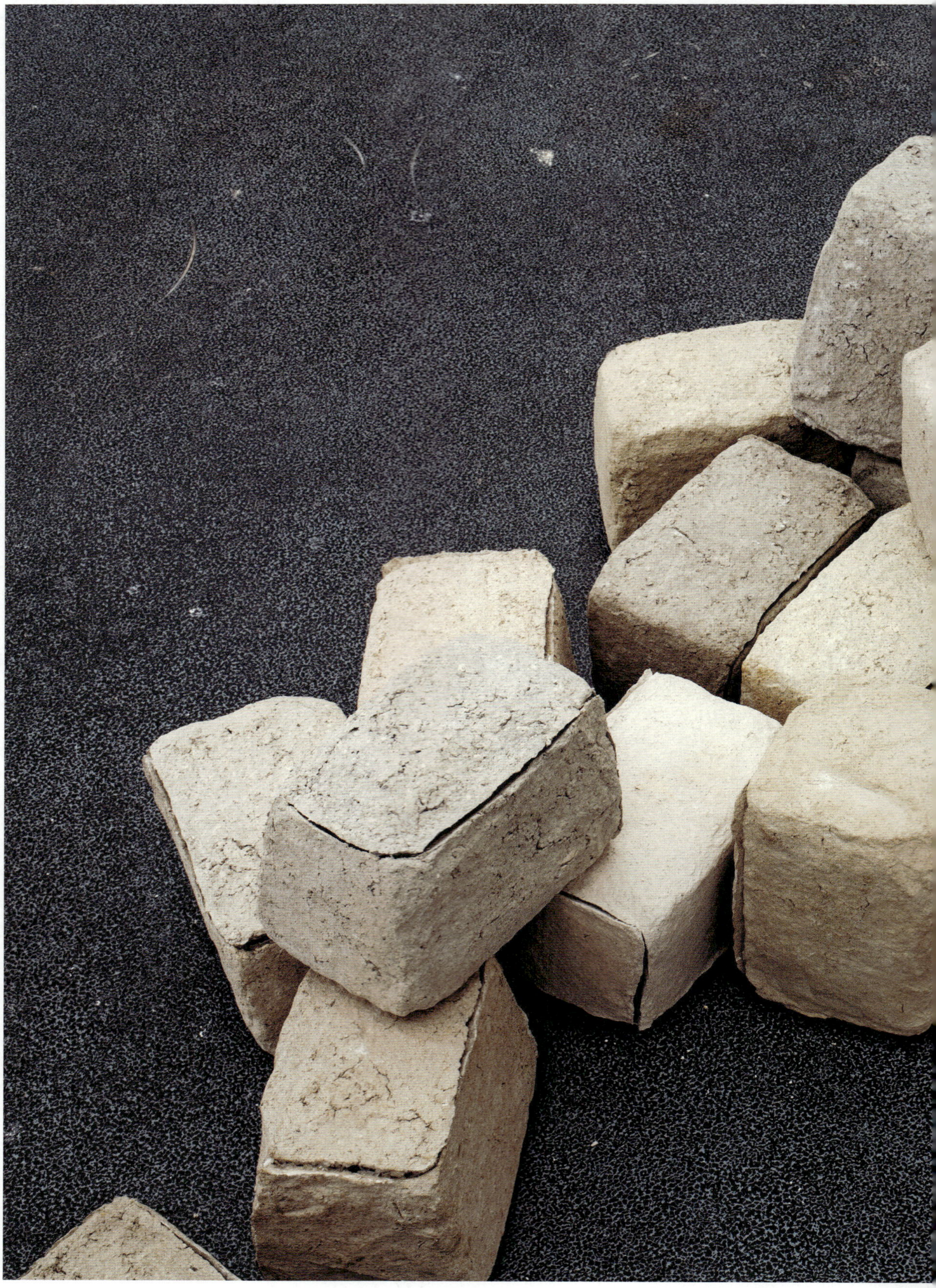

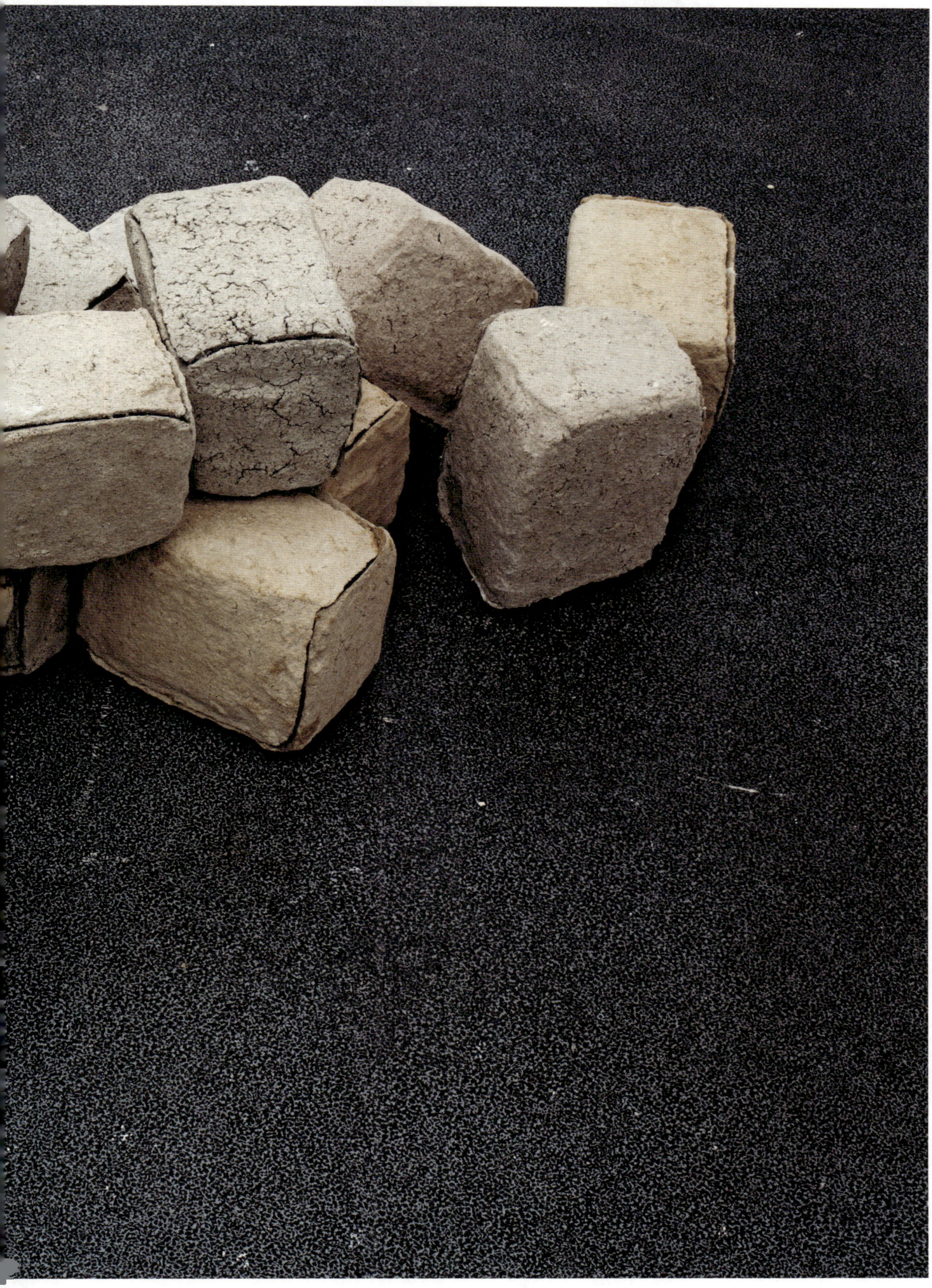

Untitled, 2008
Ripped books, cardboard box
38 × 51 × 24 cm

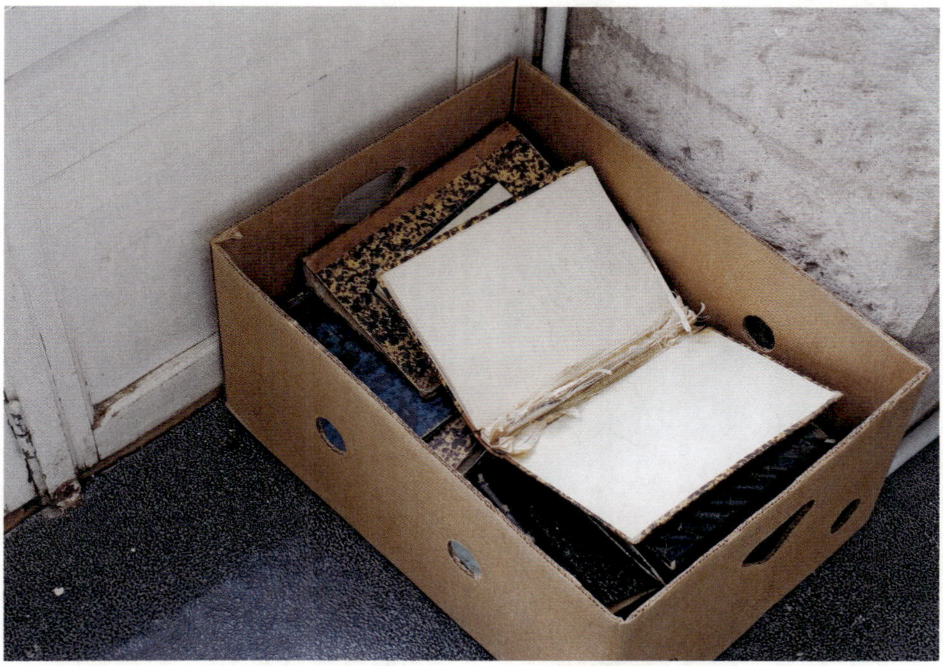

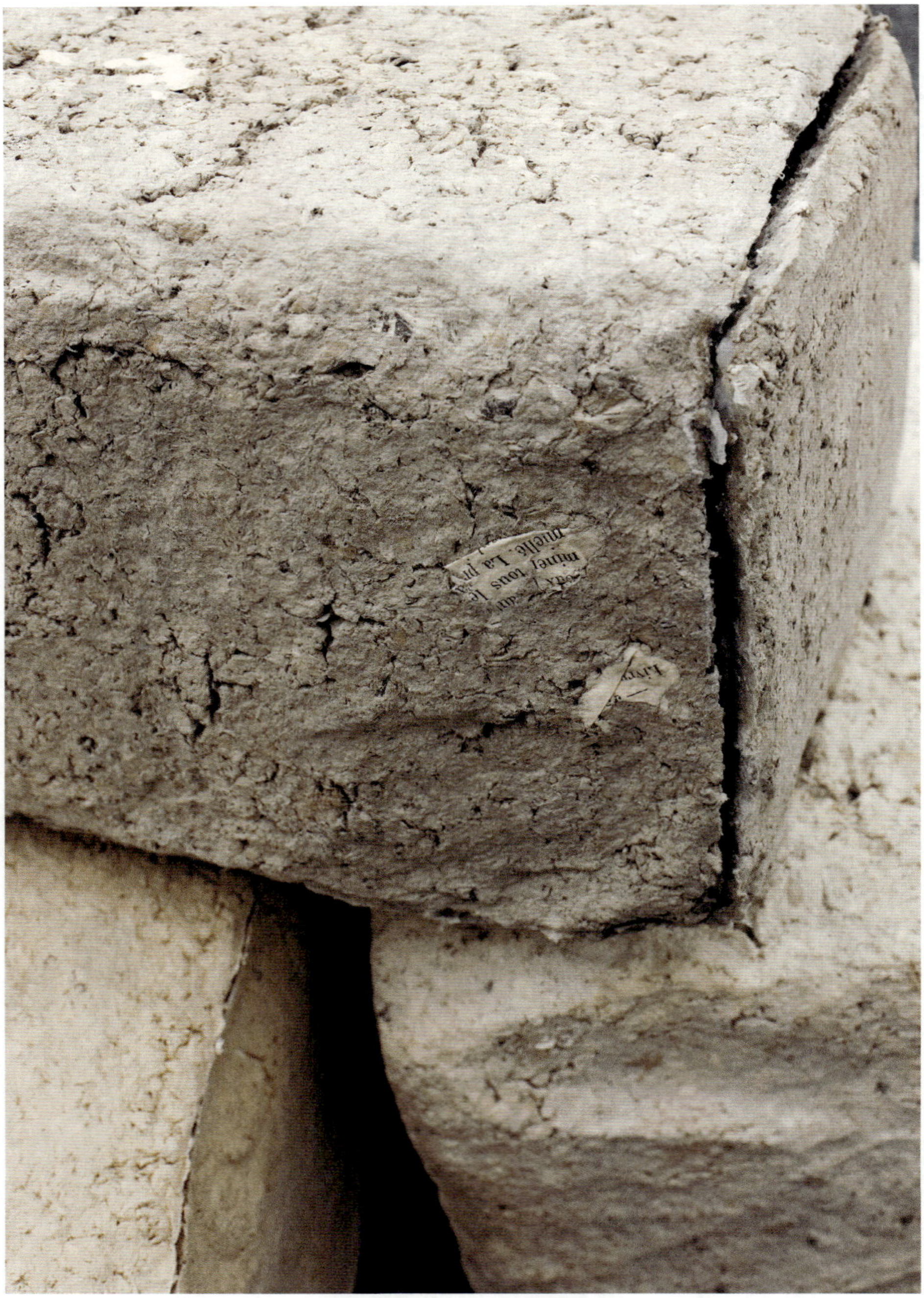

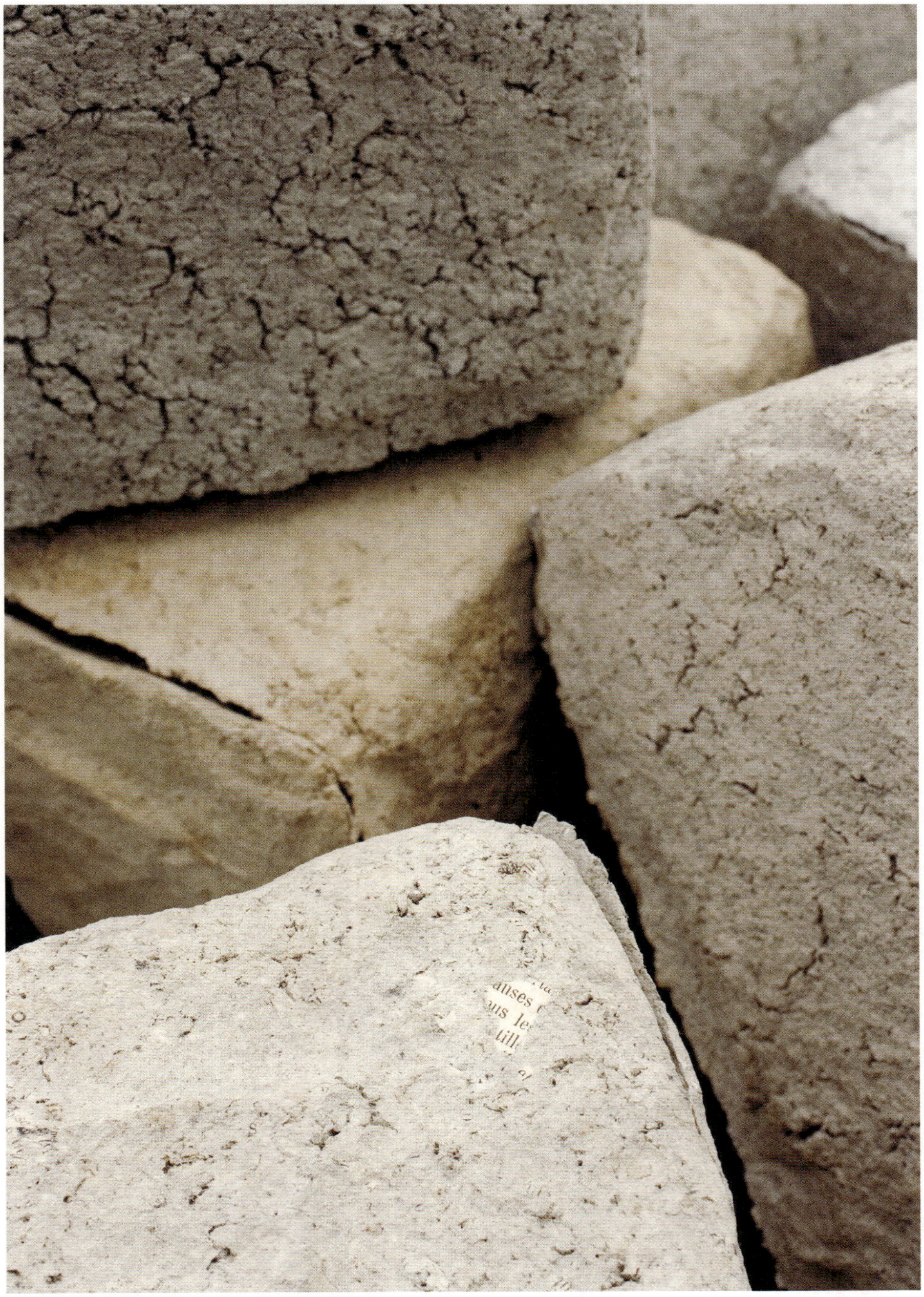

Trauma, 2008
Installation consisting of 7 doors
Dimensions variable

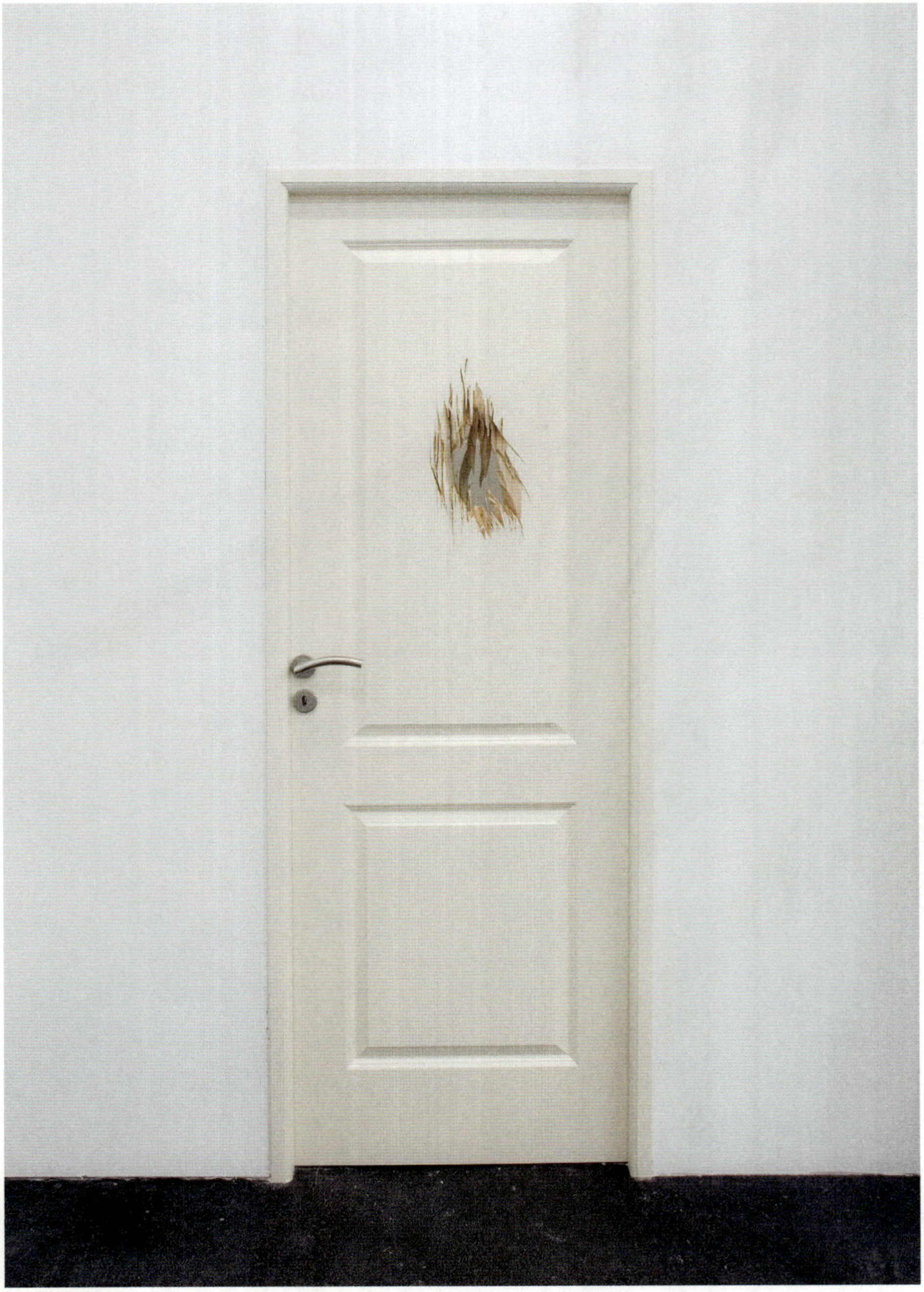

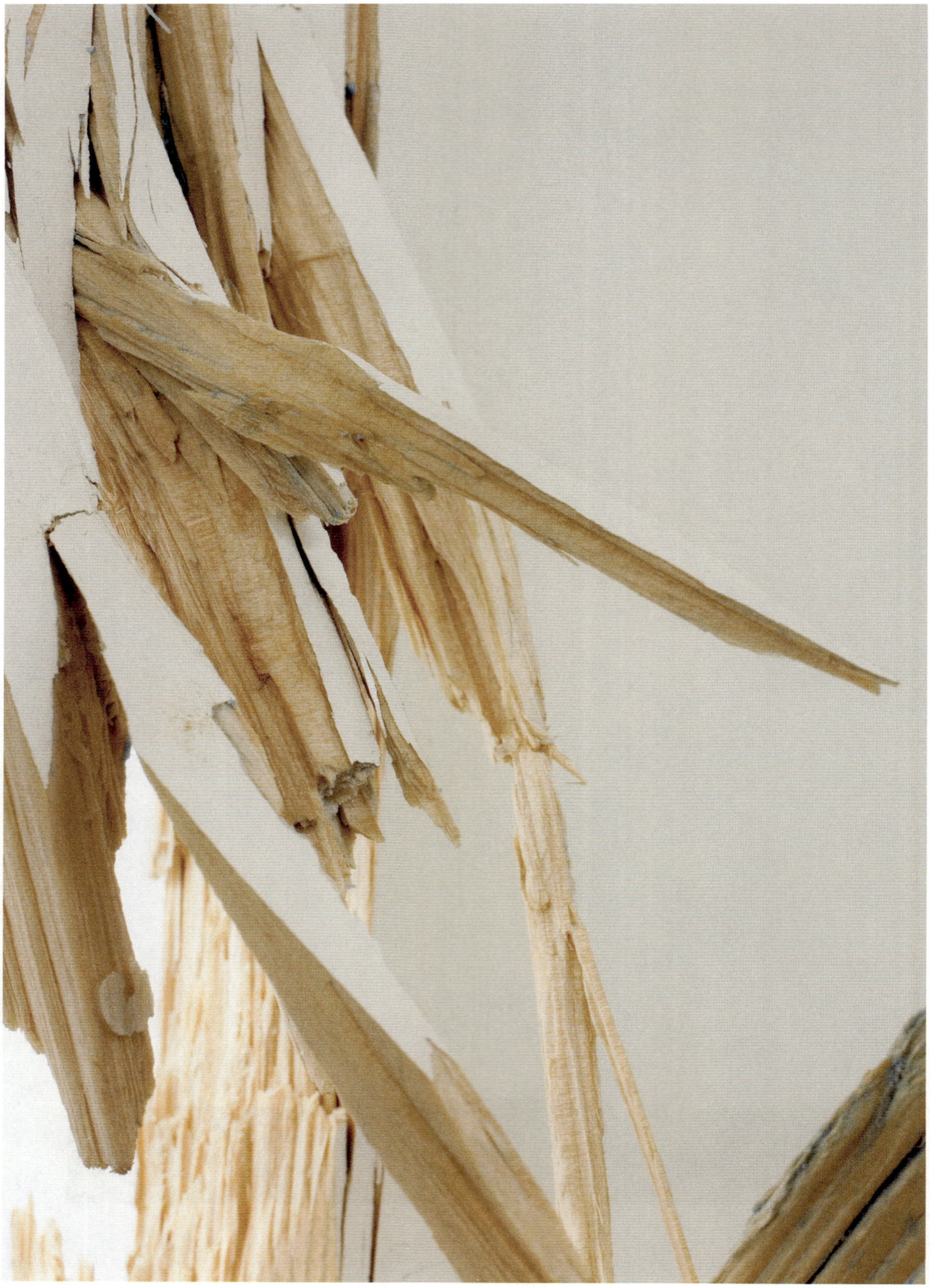

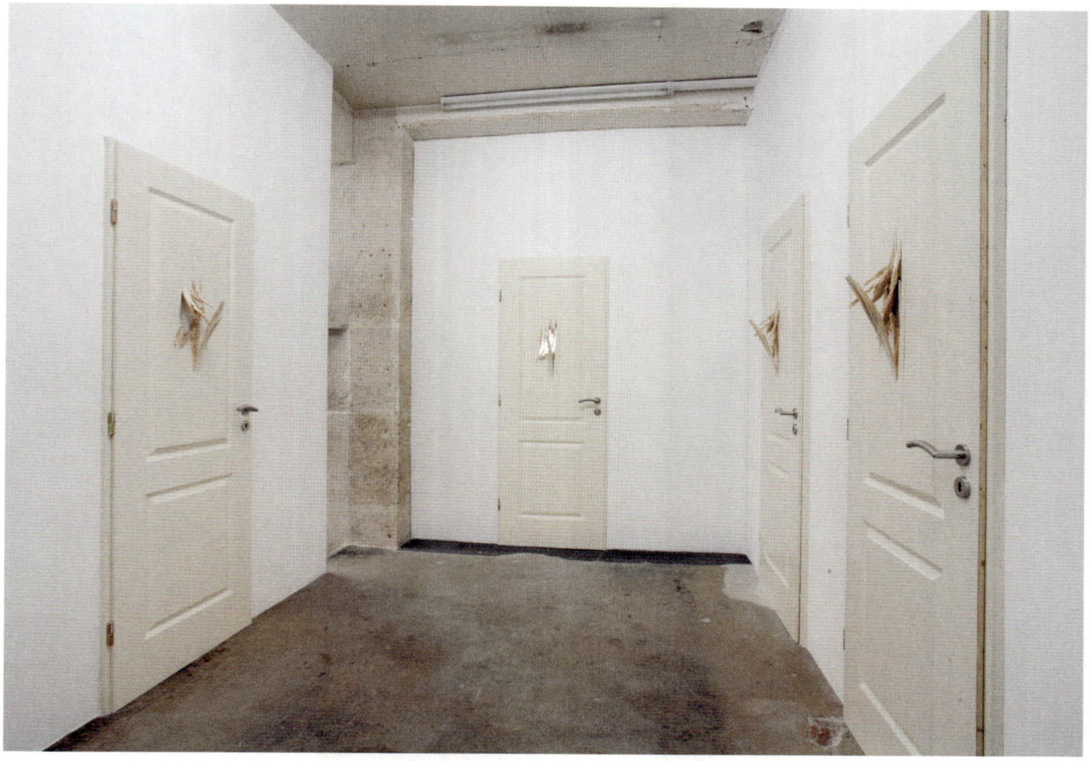

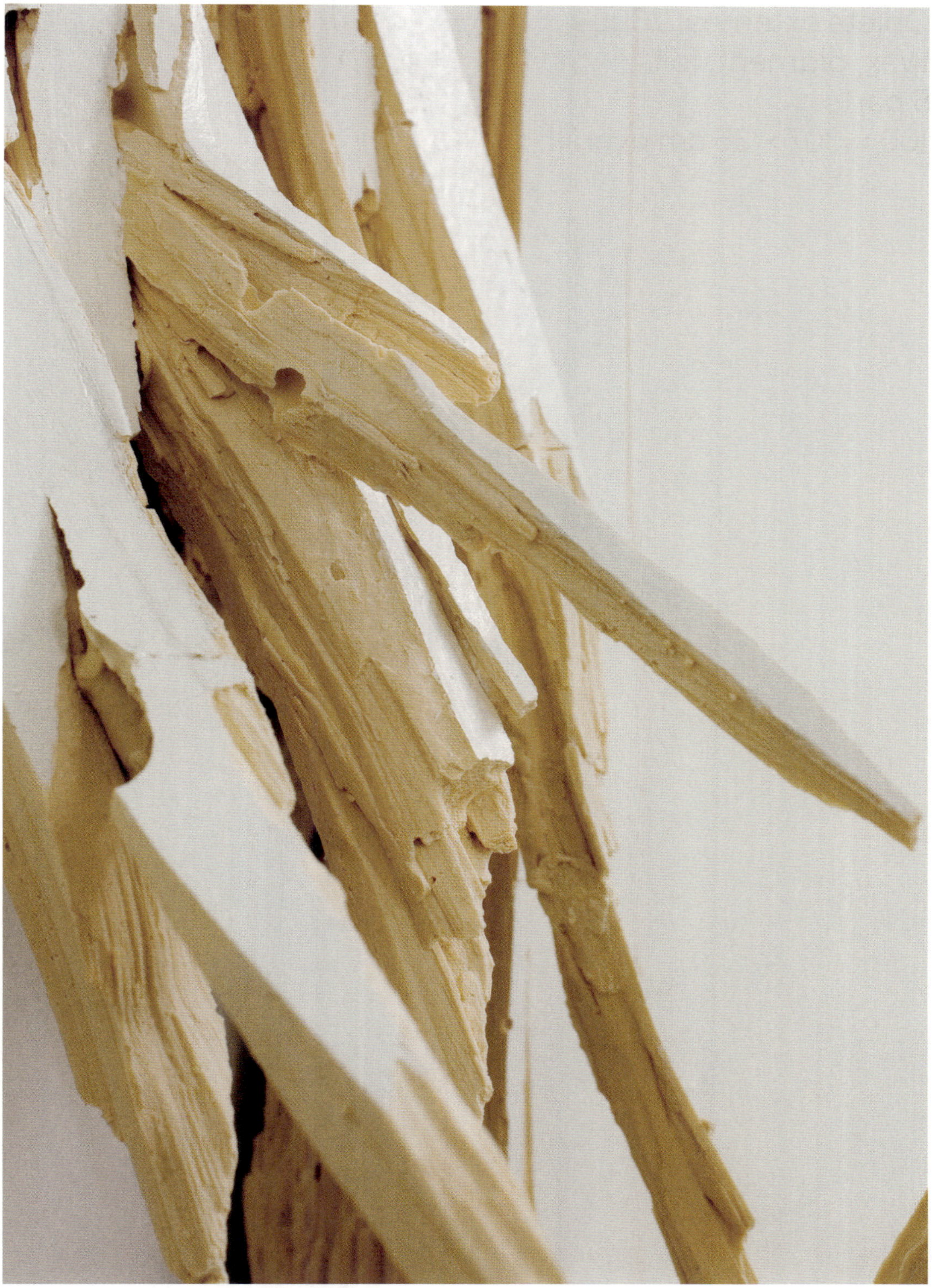

Objets externes, 2005
Wax, pigment, foil
5 parts
100 × 307 × 35 cm overall

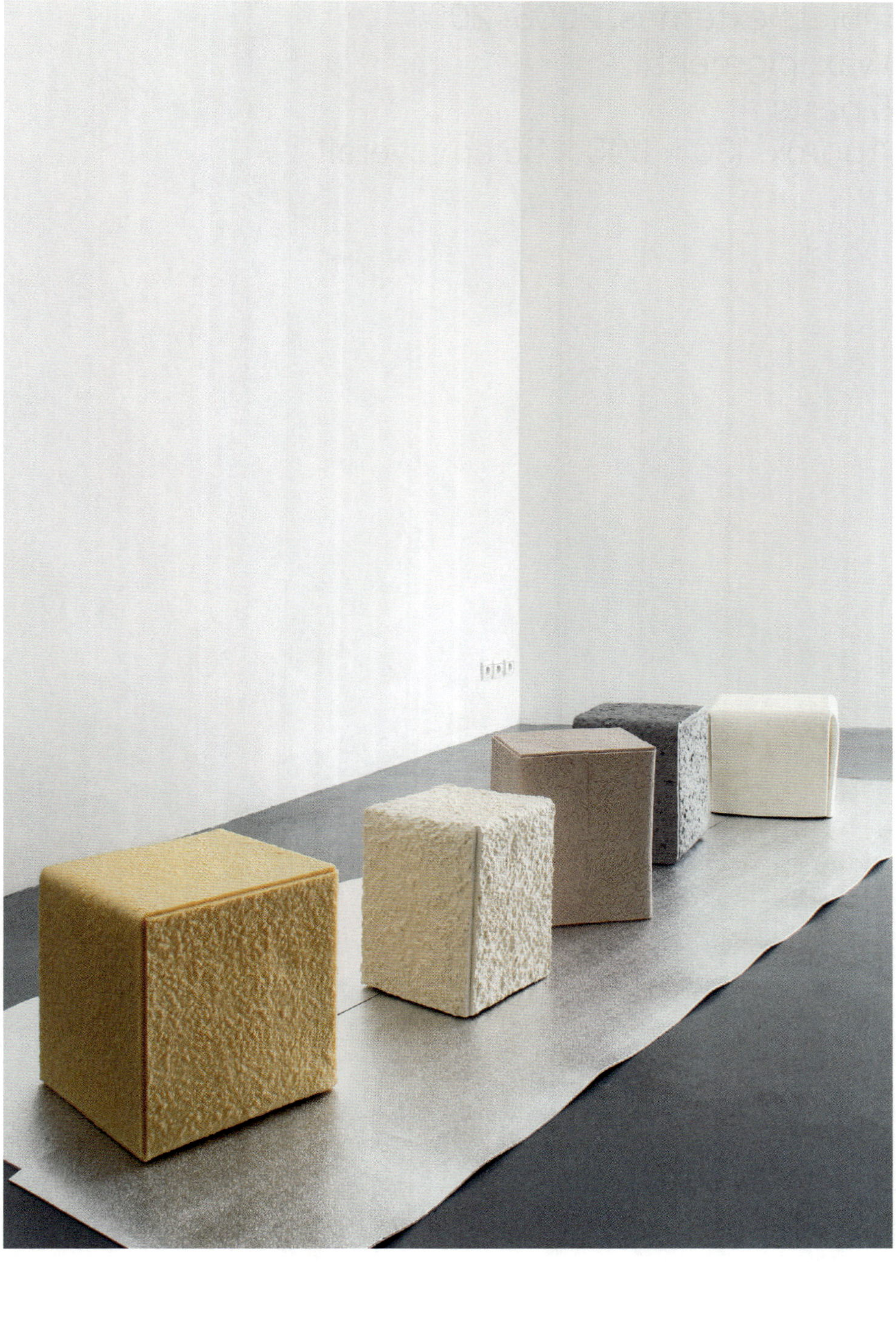

Objets externes, 2005–2007
Wax, pigment
5 parts
Approx. 130 × 300 × 35 cm overall

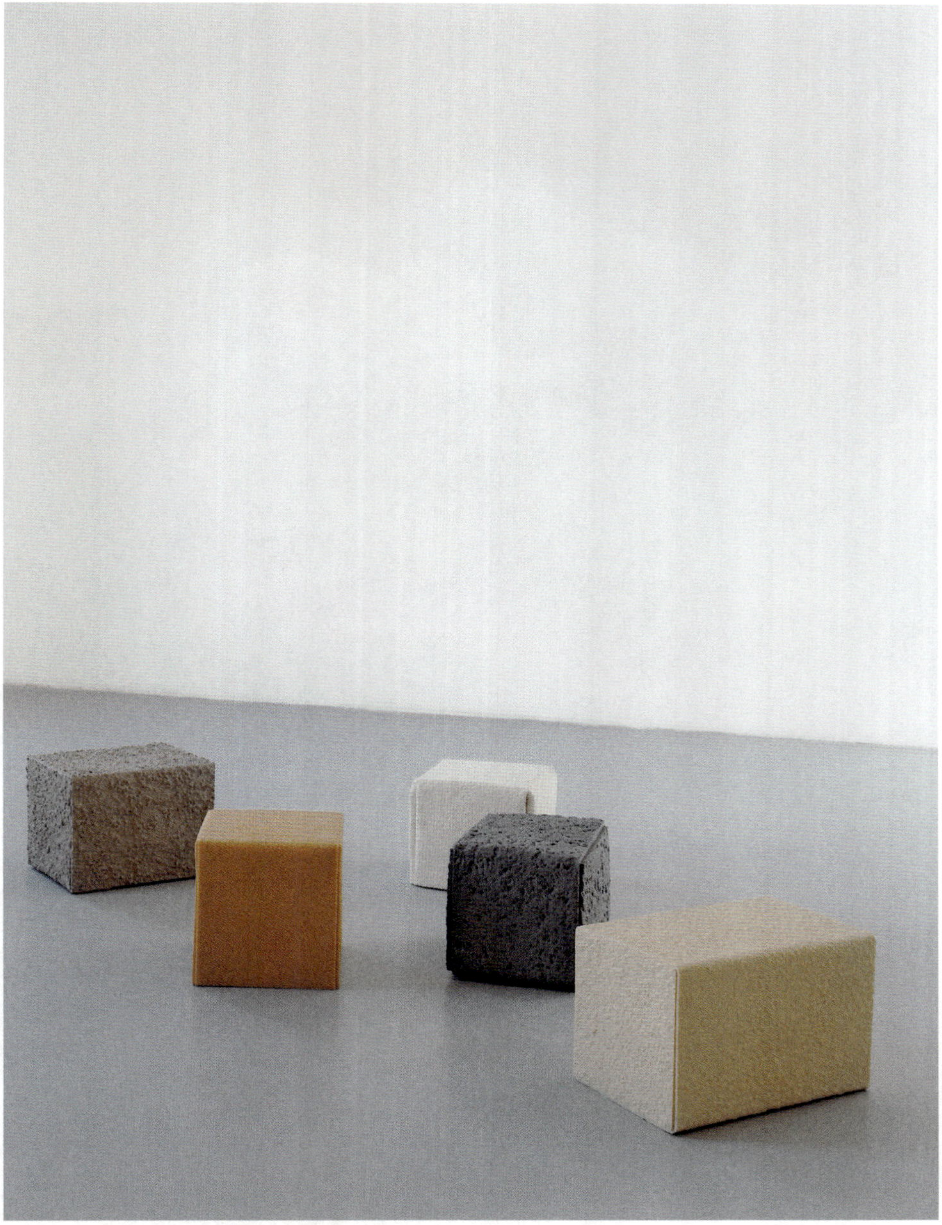

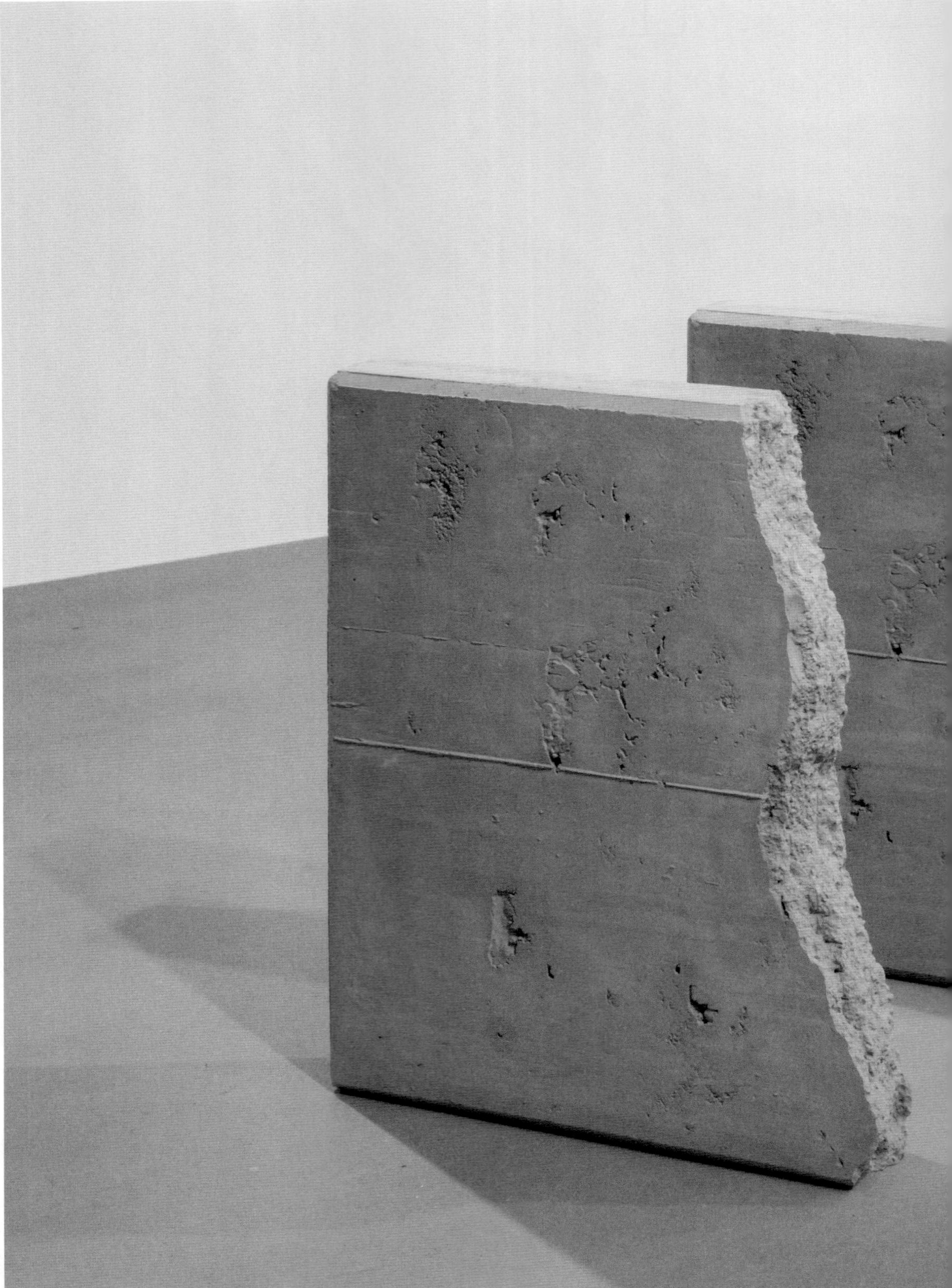

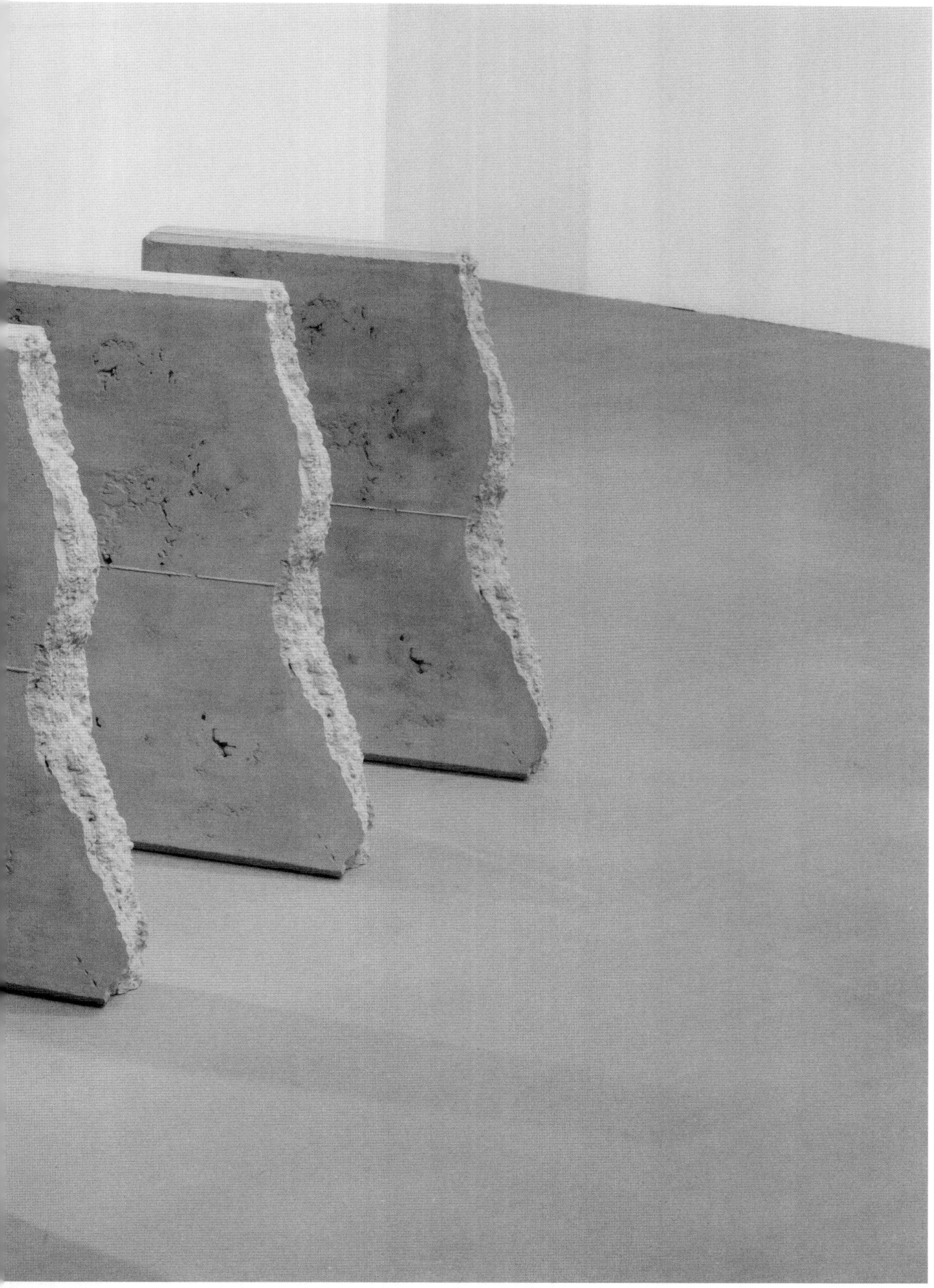

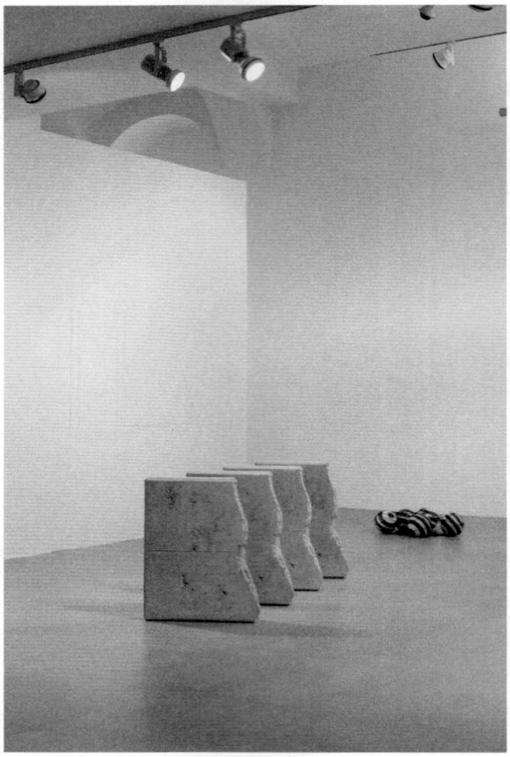

Untitled (Chunks), 2004
Sewacryl laminate
85 × 13 × 70 cm each
85 × 172 × 130 cm overall

Untitled (Gegenstücke), 2014
Concrete, steel, acrylic glass
127 × 145 × 30 cm

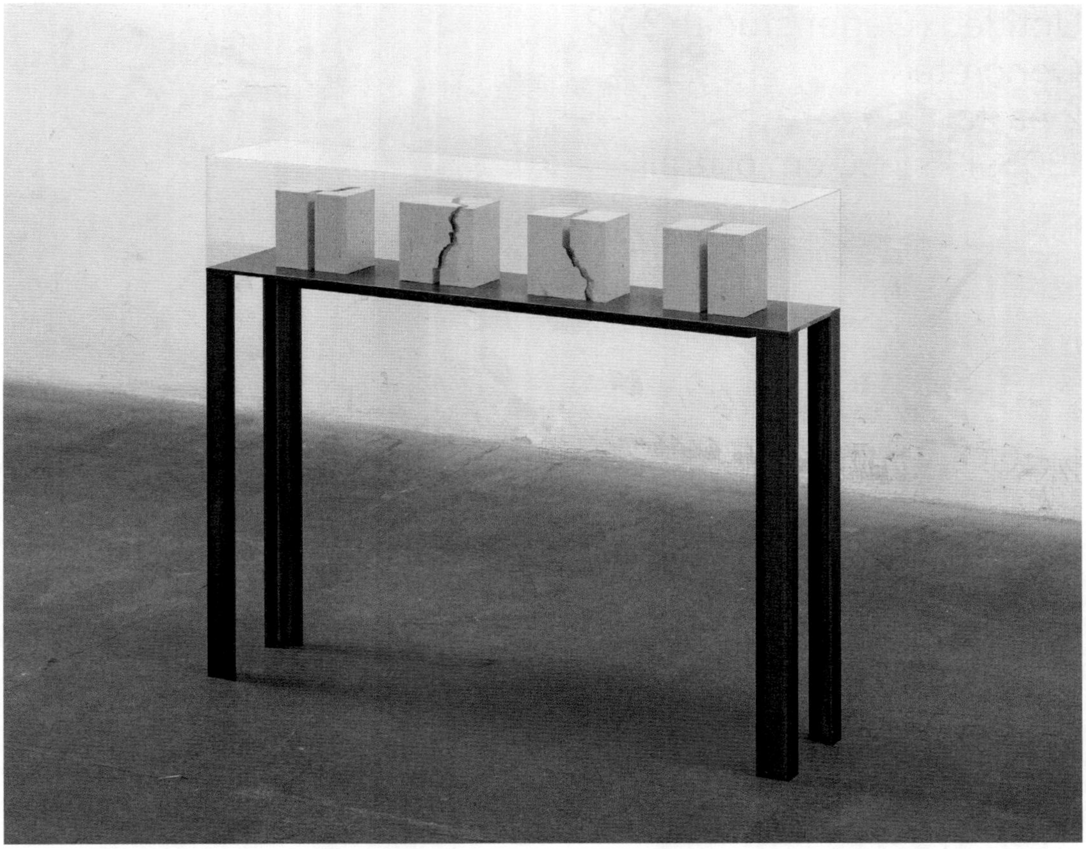

Untitled (Gegenstück), 2012
Concrete
2 parts
130 × 135 × 90 cm overall

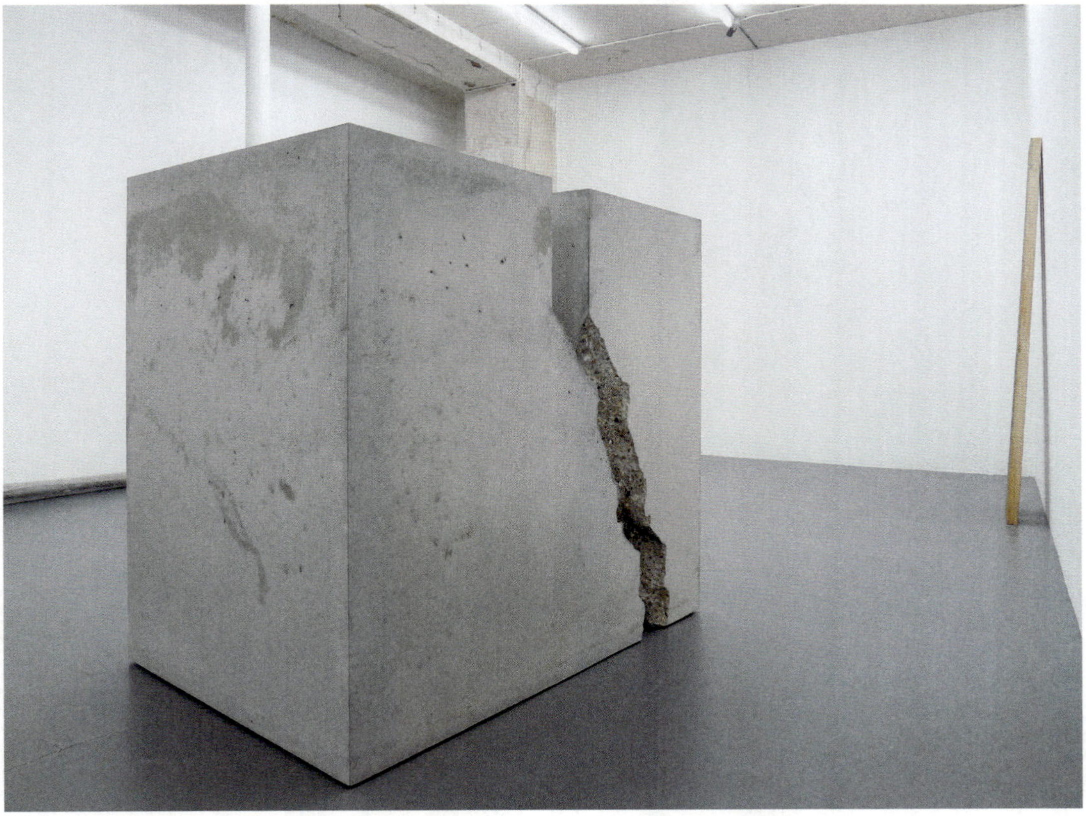

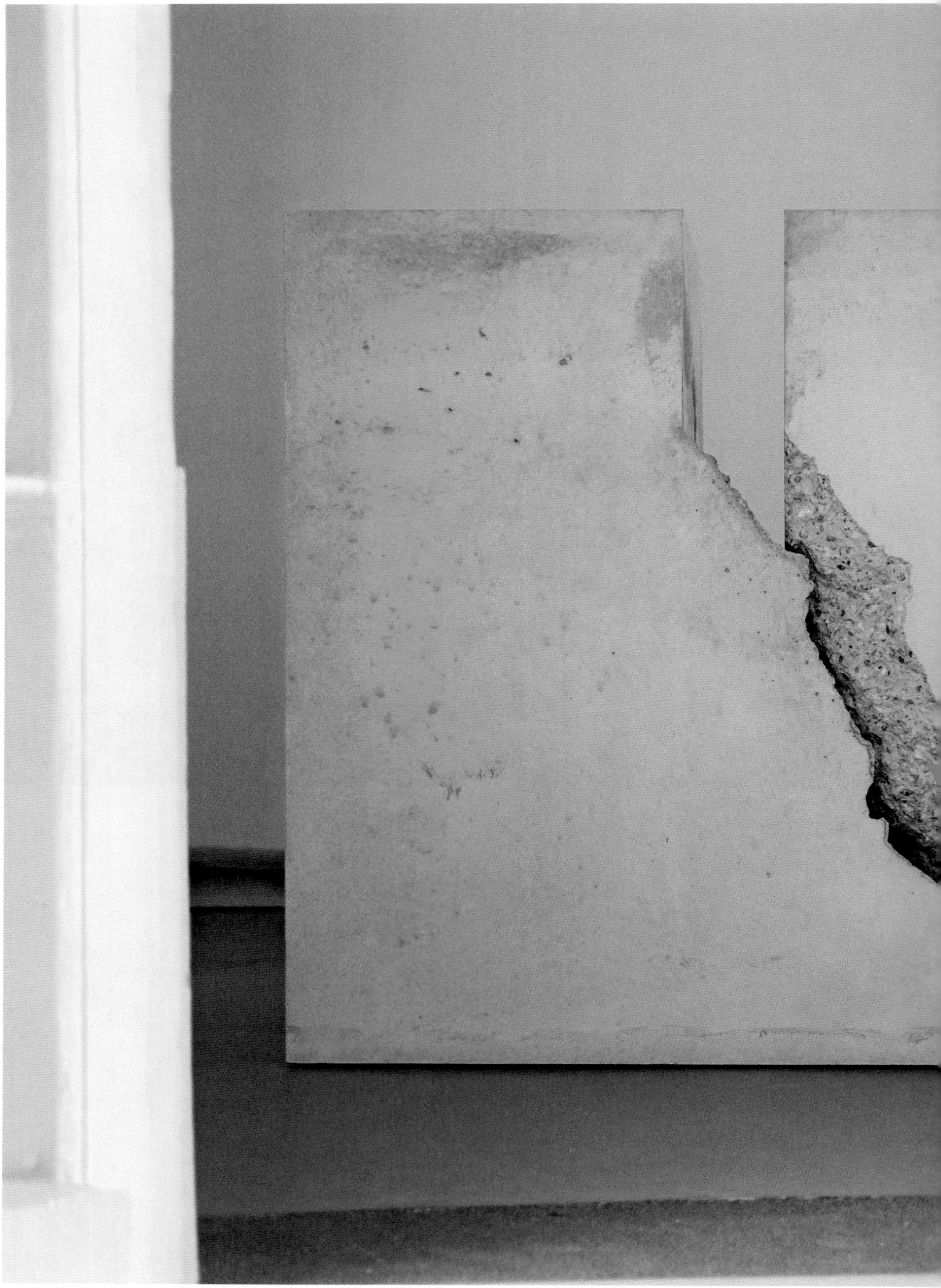

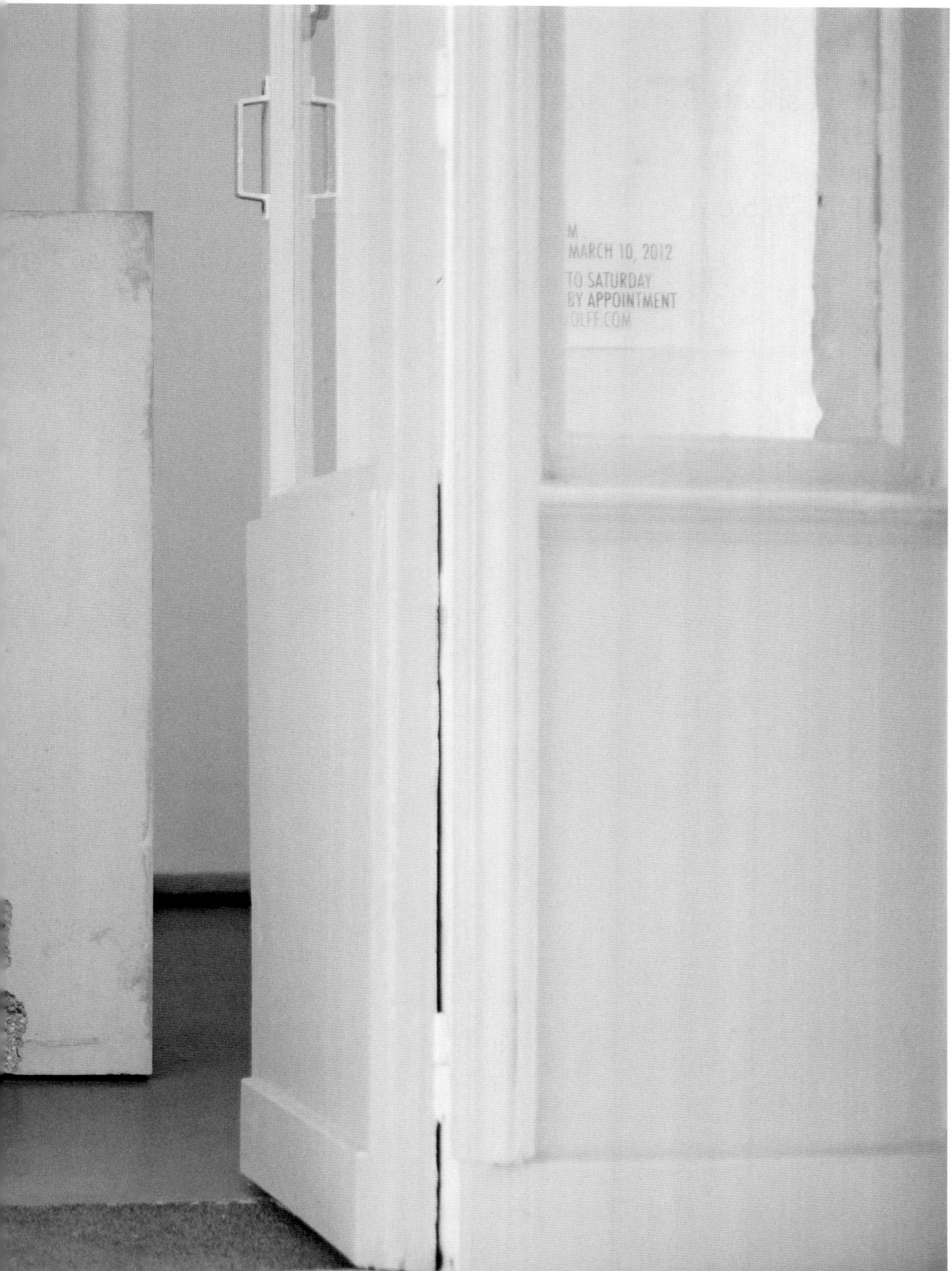
MARCH 10, 2012
TO SATURDAY
BY APPOINTMENT

Untitled, 2010
2 parts
16 contact sheets 8 × 10", framed
111,5 × 91 cm
Plaster cast
13 × 94,5 × 76,5 cm

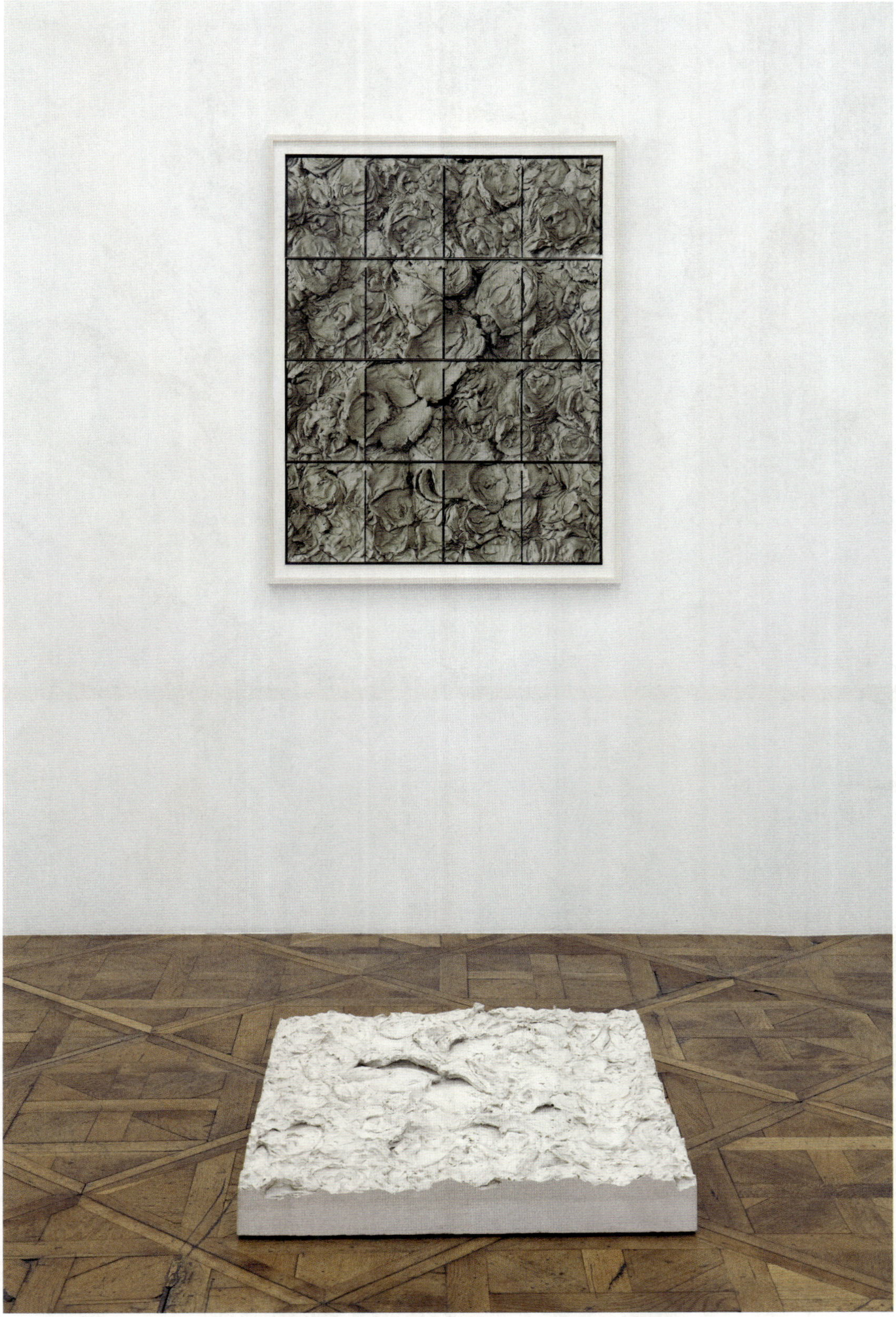

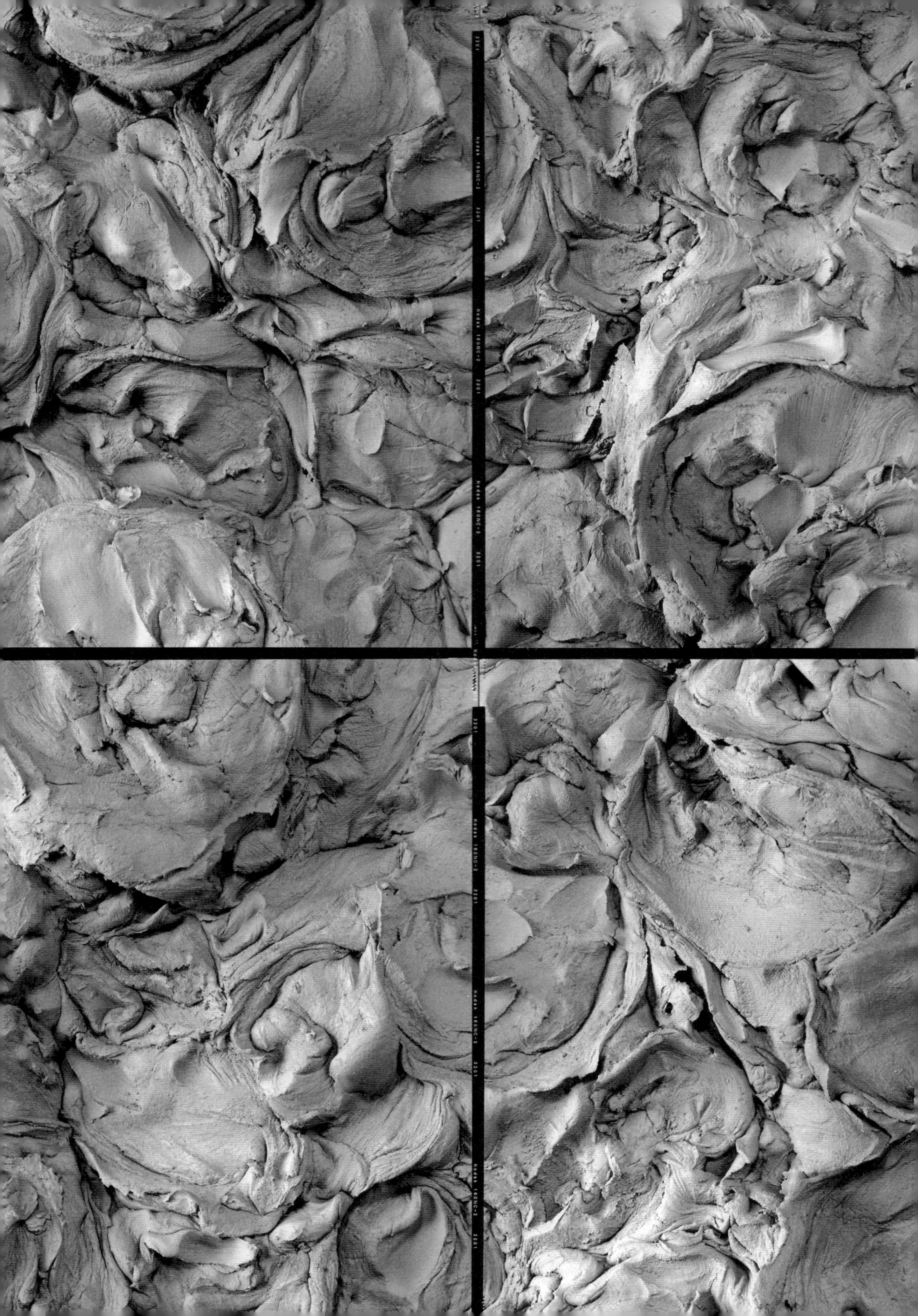
Kodak 160NC-2
2201

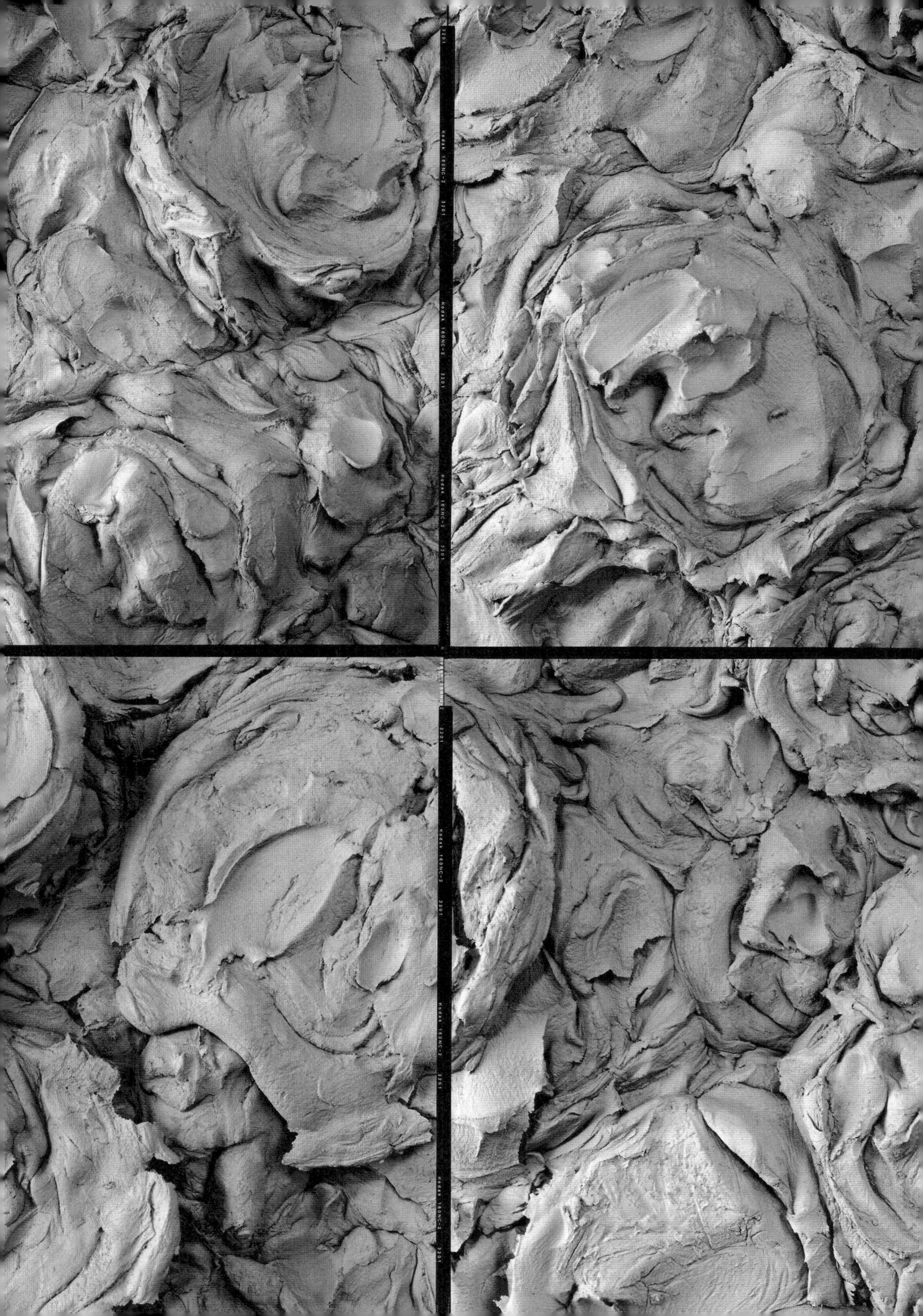

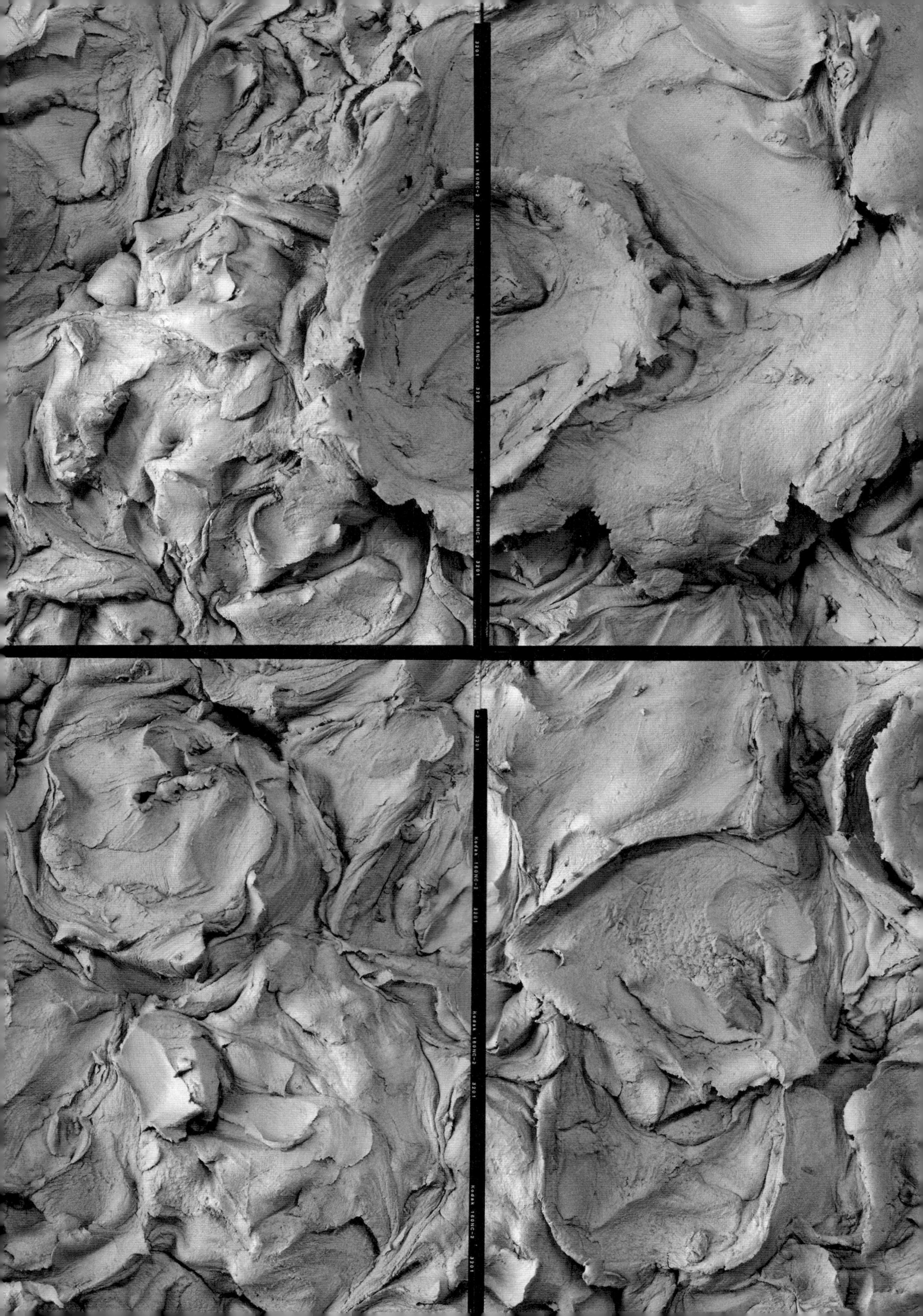

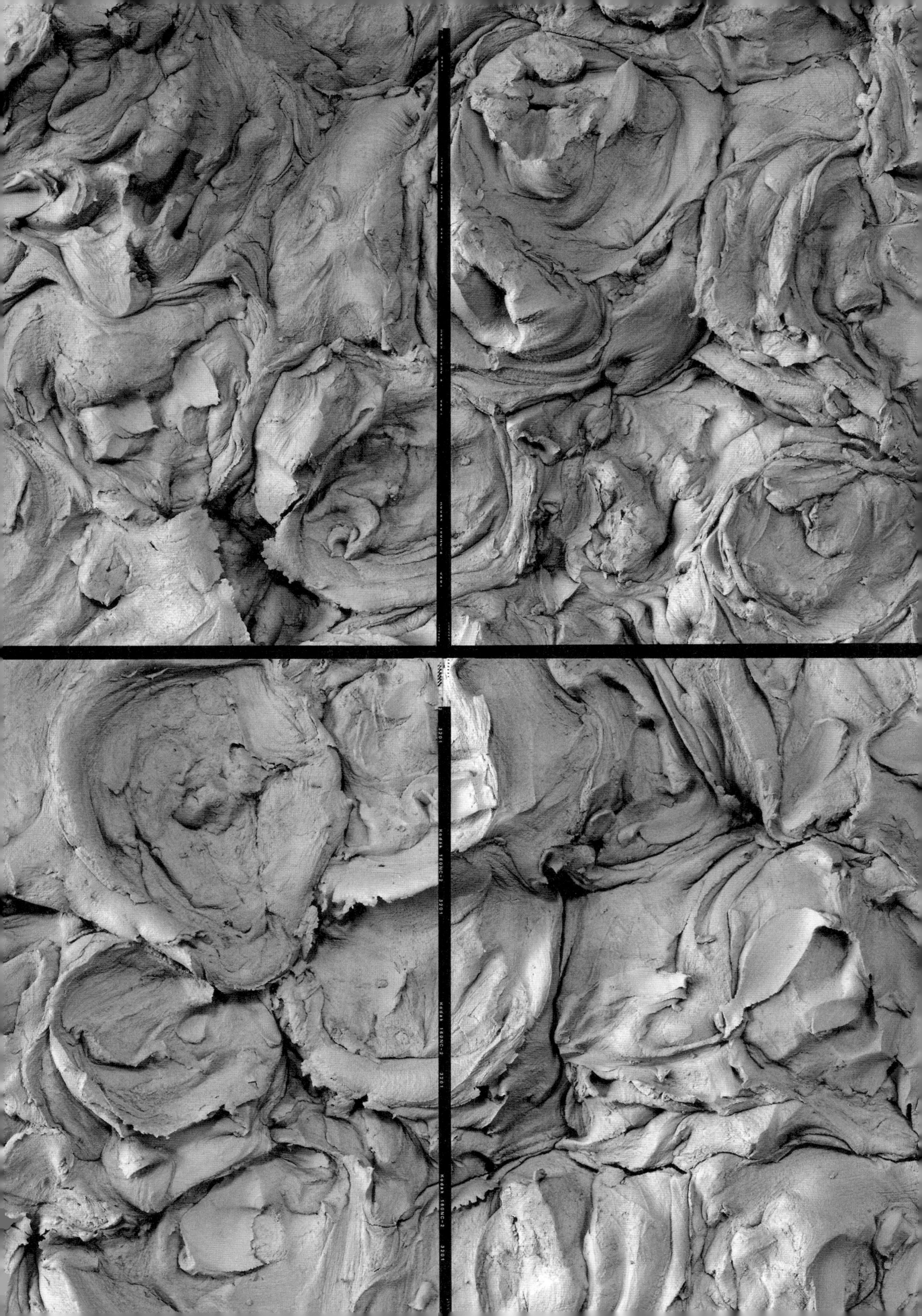

→ p. 40
not yet titled, 2015
1/5 parts
140 × 766 × 77 cm

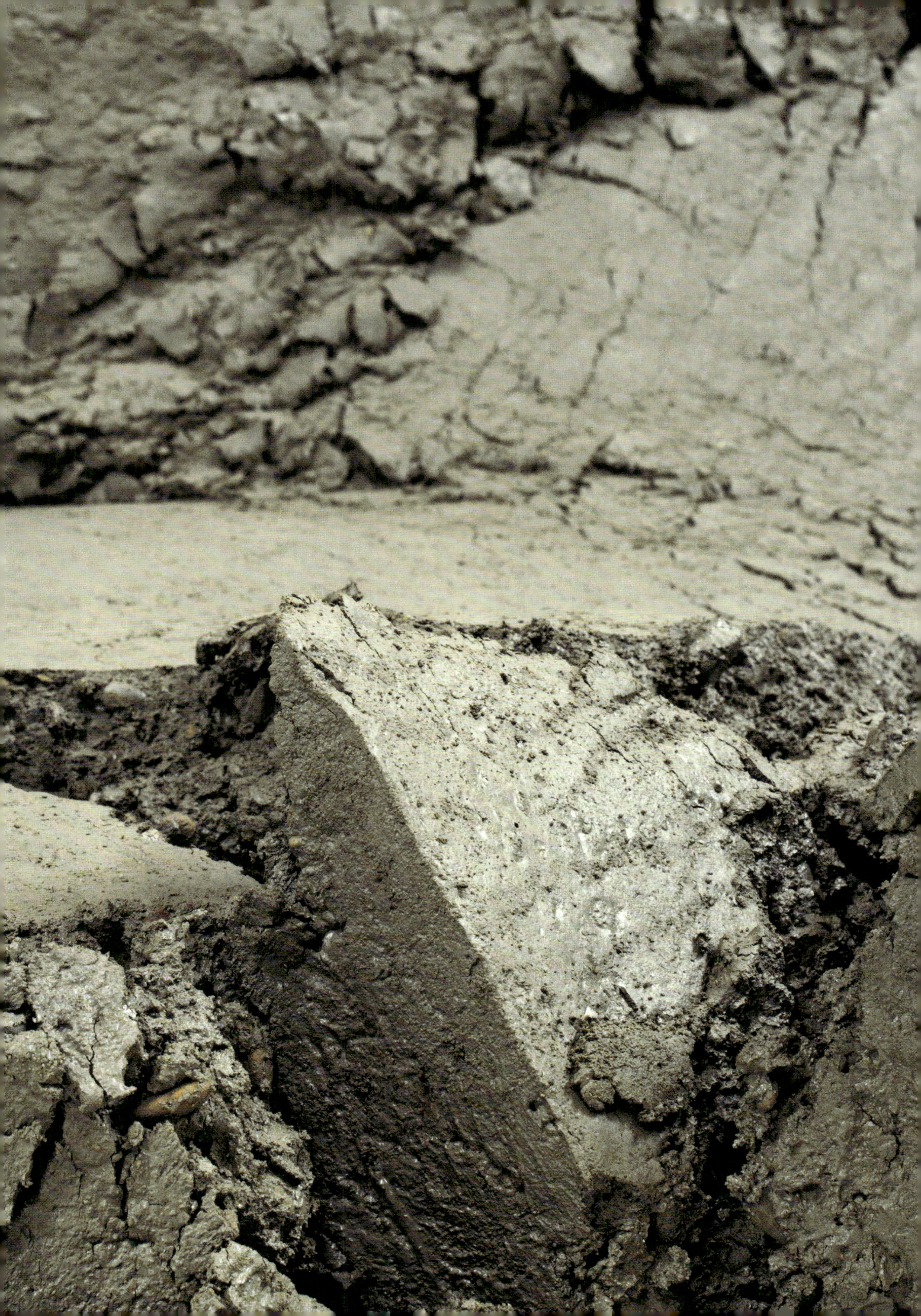

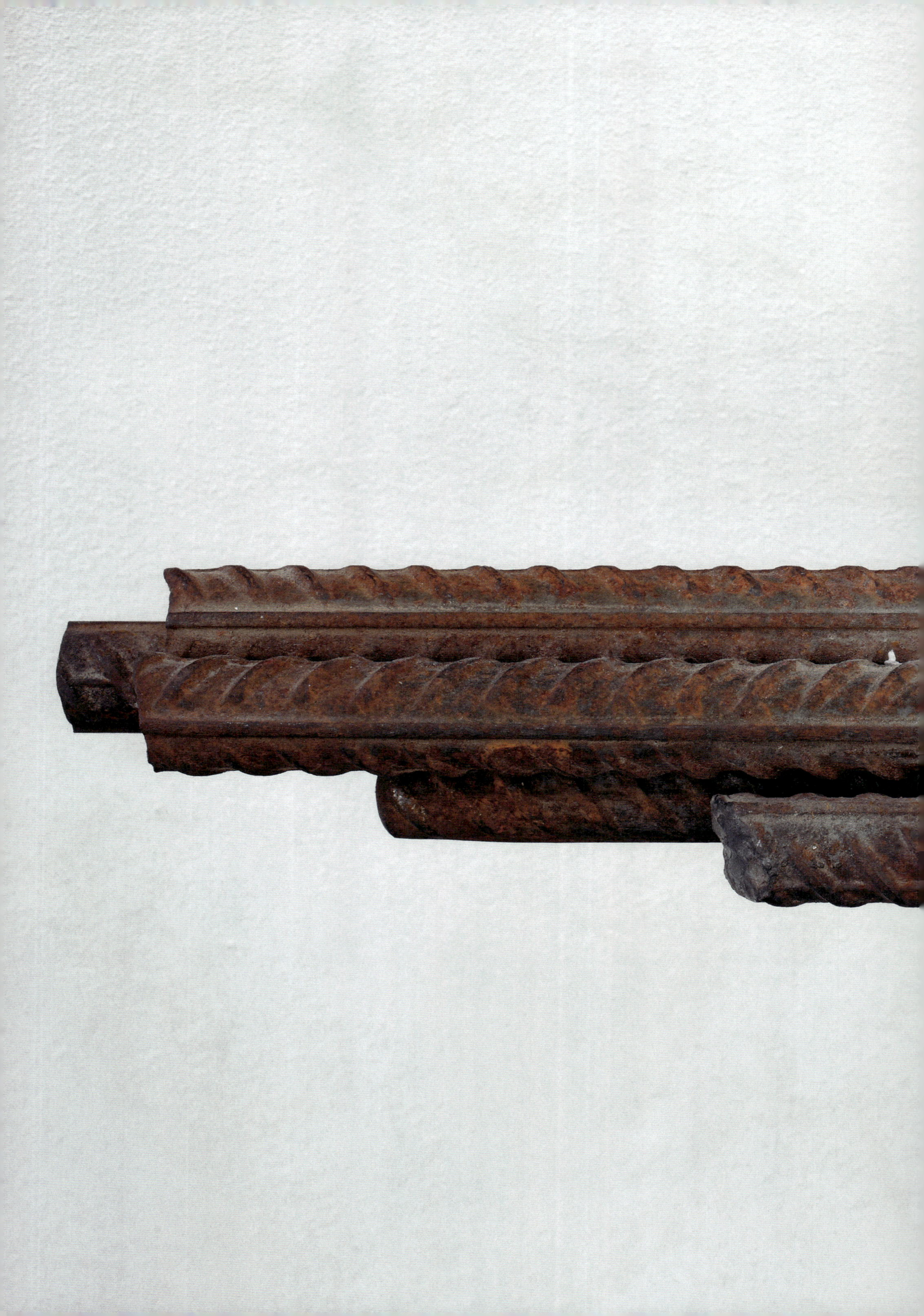

→ p. 102
Bündel, 2012
11 × 700 × 11 cm

→ p. 102
Bündel, 2012
11 × 700 × 11 cm

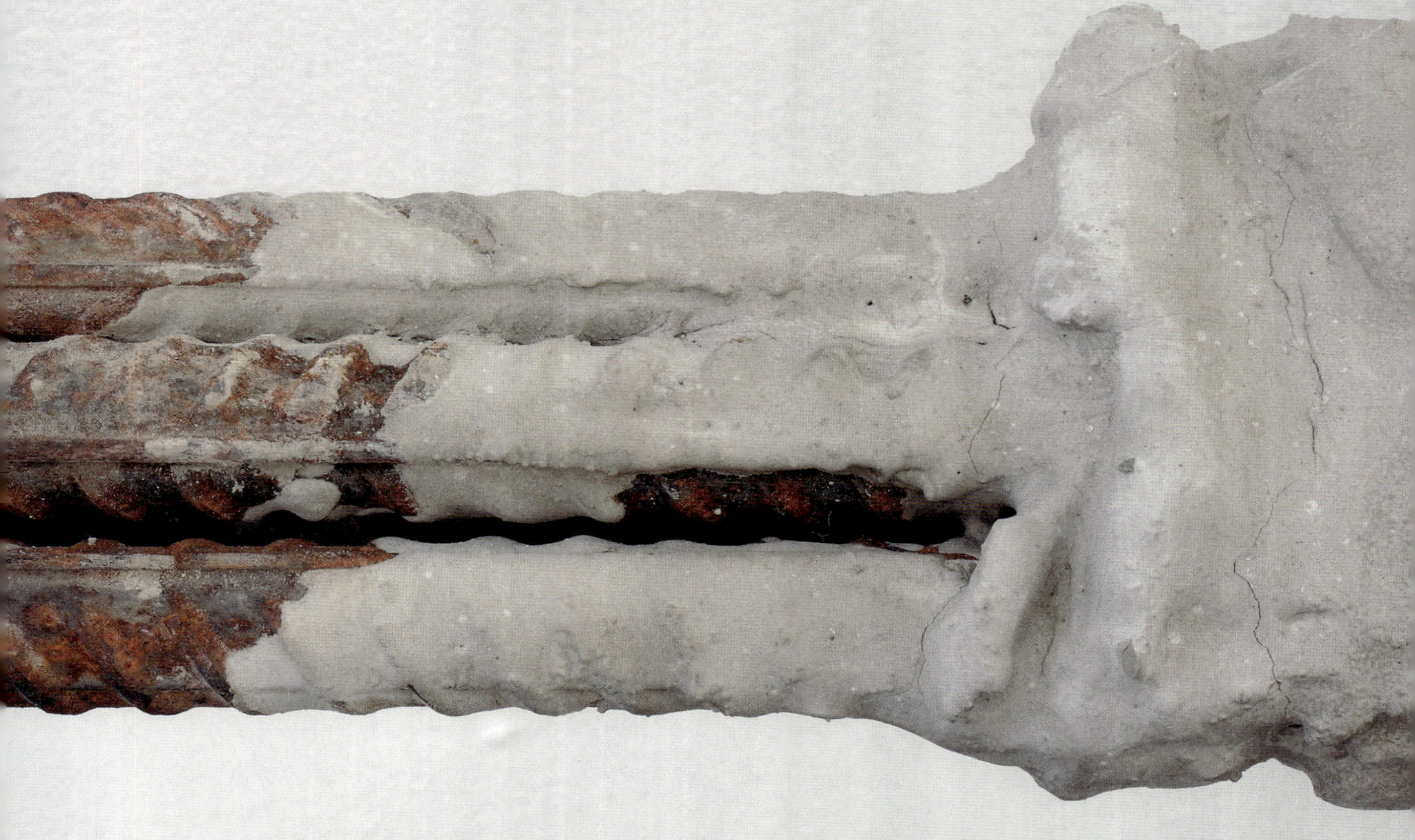

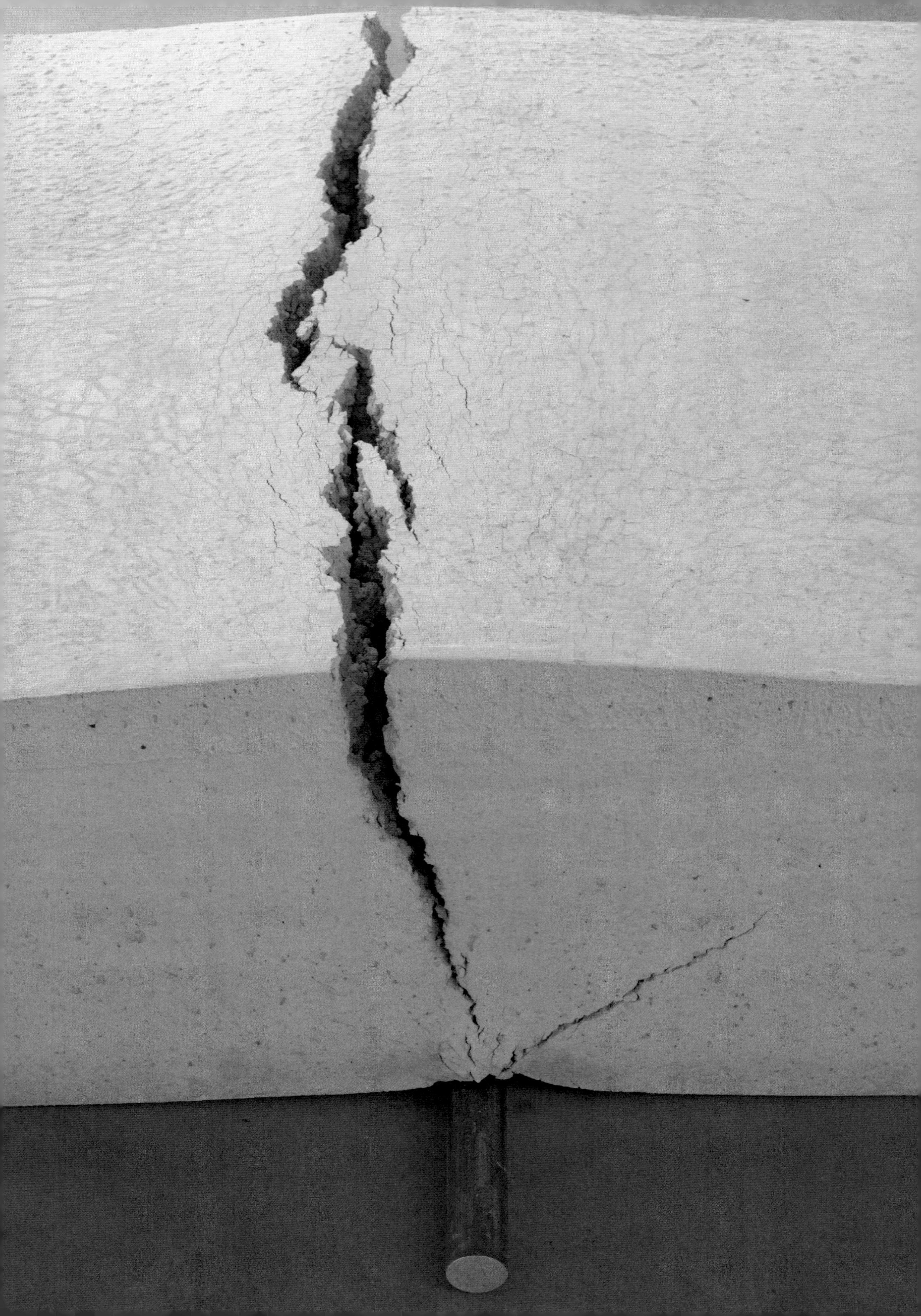

→ p. 48
not yet titled, 2015
53 × 107 × 141,4 cm

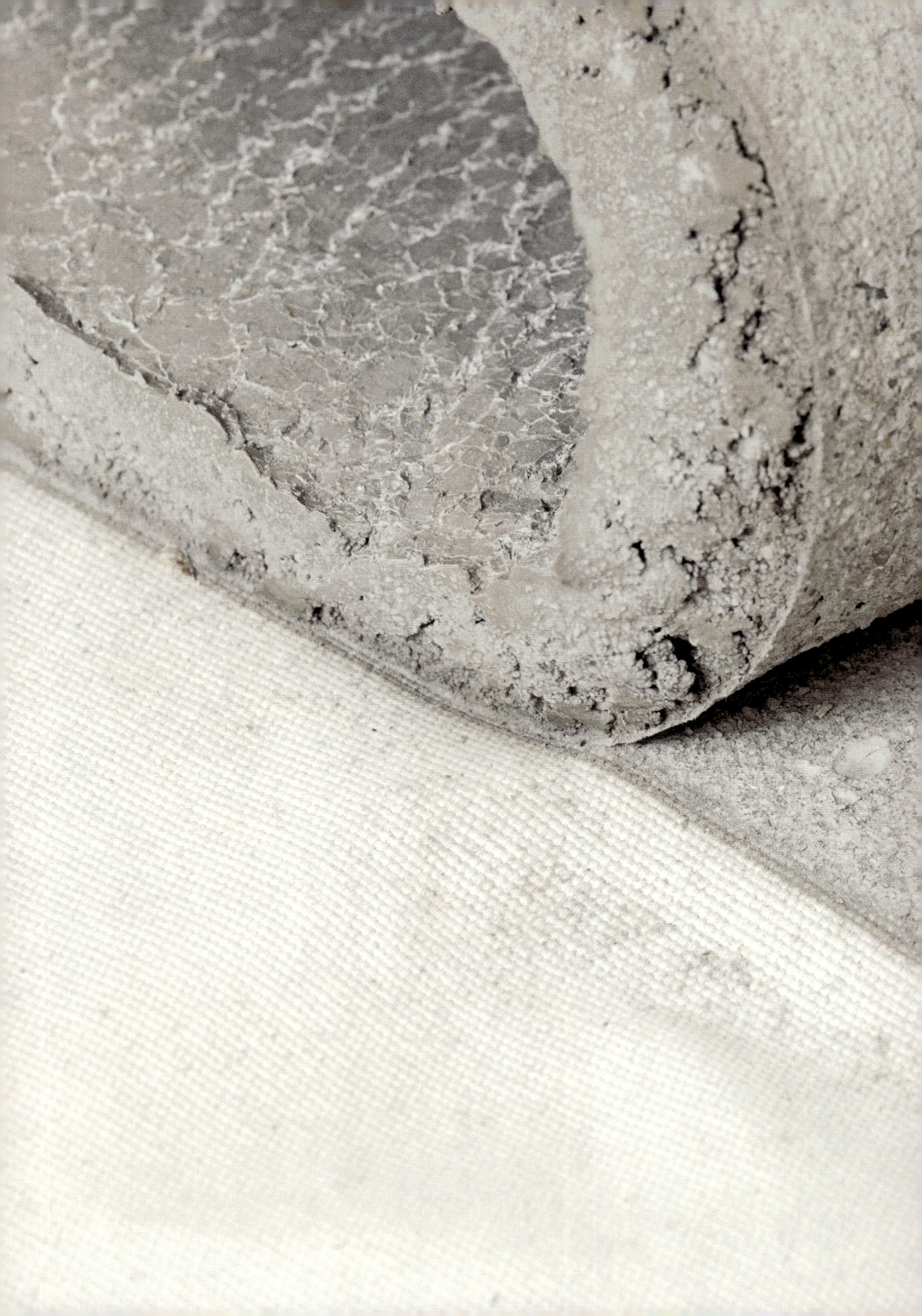

Methodology and Process: The Development of Christoph Weber's Comprehension-Driven Treatment of Material

Fiona Liewehr

In an interview preparatory to this article, Christoph Weber described his artistic development as a practice moving from "methodological comprehension" in earlier pieces to collaborating and struggling with one material: concrete. From their titles alone, the sculptures **Beton (gehoben)** (concrete [lifted]), **Beton (gefaltet)** (concrete [folded]) and **Beton (gerollt)** (concrete [rolled]) describe procedures that seem to defy the conventions of concrete's use. This archetypical twentieth-century building material is associated with fixity of shape, solidity, inalterability, hardness and resilience. Yet concrete is elegantly wrapped around reinforcement bars in **Bündel** (Bundle), protrudes from a tarpaulin hanging on a wall in **Beton (gerollt)**, bends pliantly around boards and steel plates in **Beton (gewickelt)** (concrete [wrapped]) and **not yet titled**, leans on the wall like an unsteady body in **bent inversion**; or as a frail sort of seesaw- or arc-shape balances on the floor in defiance of gravity's pull. The appearance of the artwork is both coarse and soft, solid and fragile, rigid and immovable — as if they are a congealment of time itself, clutching a moment and conserving an action to render it visible for the viewer. Thorough preparation of the mould and precise knowledge of the hardening process are critical for the final result. At the very moment when its state of matter shifts from viscous to solid, Weber lifts, overturns or folds the concrete and forces it into a shape for which the material was not intended. Happenstance is intentional, just as failure is a constant companion in the artist's experimental trials, albeit one he sees as constructive.

Christoph Weber is interested in processuality and the contextual shift created by the physical metamorphosis from the shapeless to the literally concrete, a transition during which he subjects the material to an extreme load test. The material, rather than submitting to total *a priori* control, dictates the artworks' shape by way of its physical properties and its production process. In his more recent concrete sculptures, Weber's performative procedures and the material's processuality are manifested in shapes that are practically "flash-frozen."[1]

1 Thomas Trummer, "Precariously Balanced Roughness," in *RES* (June 2013), p. 50.

→ p. 66
Beton (gefaltet), 2013
7,5 × 58 × 62 cm

Beton (gehoben) → p. 90
Beton (gefaltet) → p. 66
Beton (gerollt) → p. 92
Bündel → p. 102
Beton (gewickelt) → p. 58
not yet titled → p. 56
bent inversion → p. 82 / 98

Even if the focus appears to be placed on the artistic act and the near-infinite array of ways to shape concrete, Christoph Weber's work should by no means be classed as purely formalist. He is also permanently interested in semantic dimensions, in what he calls "methodological comprehension". He is vitally occupied by his search for a specific technique that can realise his concepts, for the criteria of when and why a particular artistic method or material must be brought into play. Accordingly, his point of departure is a conceptual analysis, the idea of an object that governs the choice of material and the process of execution, even if that process in turn — despite all artistic mastery — remains unpredictable.

Weber has said on several occasions that, for him, concrete is a material of violence, a symbol of destruction and occupation. Indeed his first works in concrete might leave viewers with precisely that impression. In **Contradiction**, reinforcement bars jut out dangerously into the room while serving, in their systematic neatness, as an almost melancholic "picture frame" for the exposed concrete square. In **Schade, dass Beton nicht brennt** (pity concrete doesn't burn) a concrete block that has been forcibly liberated from its casing using flame-throwers testifies at once to vulnerability and an almost sentimental, scenic beauty.

Christoph Weber's work always displays an innate dichotomy between construction and destruction, violence and tenderness, depression and hope. In the artist's own words, it has a distinct "laconic sadness"[2] to it. No sculptures convey this compound dichotomy better than a series of pieces that bear the common designation **Untitled (Gegenstück)** (counterpart) from 2010. In each piece, two monolithic concrete blocks stand facing one another, separated by a crack and appearing to have been broken apart from a single solid block. If one of the blocks is missing an enormous corner piece, its counterpart has a protrusion that matches it perfectly. Yet there are also smooth surfaces between the two blocks, revealing the absurdity of the fissure and thereby the artificial production process. First, one block was cast in concrete. After it hardened, a corner was broken off. Next, the resulting surface of fracture was moulded in silicone rubber and added to the mould of the second block, which was then poured. Both objects indicate that Christoph Weber's artistic practice not only accommodates the metaphors inscribed in the material, but also the material's unique consistency. As a type of artificial rock, concrete passes through various states of matter from liquid to solid, enabling it to be cast in a pre-determined shape or sculpted in its hardened state. Concrete allows for both "modelling," an additive process that creates a shape by affixing material, and "carving," a subtractive process that creates a shape by removing material.

2 In this connection, Weber also discusses literature, especially the work of Thomas Bernhard and Erich Kästner's metropolitan novel *Fabian*, for whose "laconic sadness" he feels a deep affinity. Cf. unpublished interview with Timothée Chaillou, January 2012.

Contradiction → p. 104
Schade, dass Beton nicht brennt → p. 74 / 78
Untitled (Gegenstück) → p. 150

→ p. 78
Schade, dass Beton nicht brennt, 2012
45 × 30 × 15 cm

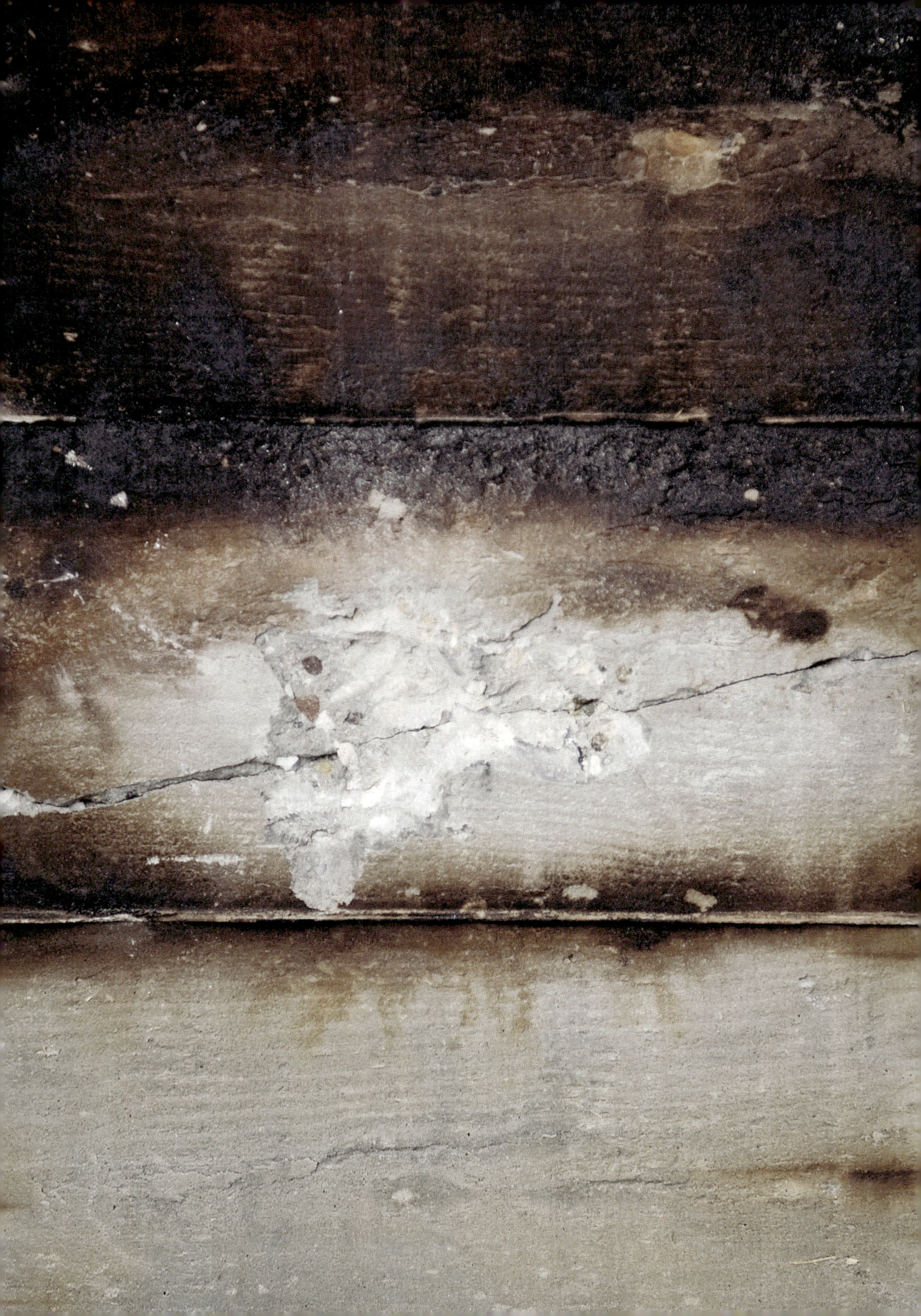

Weber's **Gegenstück** sculptures always follow the same procedure. Rational, calculated fabrication is followed by physical demolition, which in turn serves as a precondition for renewed fabrication. Construction enables deconstruction and the other way around. The capacity for human control remains crucial throughout. Christoph Weber would never abandon his process-oriented technique in favour of a purely mechanical procedure; unlike the Minimalists, he would never use mass-produced or made-to-measure industrial products. Although his sculptures are reminiscent of minimal art, they never deny the traces of their production conditions, the material's consistency always remains in view, and they never convey the Minimalists' rigid self-referentiality and chilly severity. Christoph Weber even creates the **Gegenstücke**, some of which weigh tonnes and are beyond human scale, by hand on his own. He only resorts to help from a crane and assistants when demoulding and repositioning them. In that sense, Weber is a completely traditional sculptor who processes his work.

Concrete was not always Weber's preferred medium for his sculptures, but they were always about "methodological comprehension," about materials as carriers of meaning, about questions of construction and deconstruction or, to put it broadly, about the inextricable entanglement of material, formal and semantic dimensions. Unlike his current concrete sculptures, Weber's earlier works do not put their materiality on display. Rather, the materials he uses are processed and transformed so as to metaphorically reference other materials or objects. While the earlier works suggested historical or socio-political implications, such implications are already inscribed in the concrete itself. This transformation from one material to another, with its own appearance and set of connotations, is now accomplished within one material and its states of matter.

In his installation **Untitled (Ramponeau)**, for instance, Weber arranges papier-mâché cobblestones modelled on one taken from the Rue Ramponeau in Paris, the location of the last barricade of the Paris Commune in 1871. By creating the papier-mâché exclusively out of books that predate the Commune, Weber not only inscribes the abstract objects into a tangible historical discourse, he poses questions about the interrelationship of fiction and reality, signifier and signified. The materials in **Objets externes** (external objects) undergo a similar procedure: he created silicone rubber moulds of building façades, used them to cast slabs in coloured wax, and folded the slabs into post-minimalistic-looking cubes.

Untitled (Gegenstück) → p. 150
Untitled (Ramponeau) → p. 126
Objets externes → p. 140 / 142

With the silicone moulding process, the precise surface textures of the façades were recreated down to the slightest detail, negotiating questions about the categories of public and private, outdoor and indoor. As the texture of some of the façades have since changed or been painted over, the objects can be seen as kind of time capsules that inscribe historical information from the past for the sake of the present and future, but also expose the specific material properties of change and evanescence.

The "comprehension" of a historical or personal experience depends on memory. In 1914, Sigmund Freud proposed "remembering, repeating and working through" as a method for coming to terms with a traumatic experience by re-presenting the past.[3] Jacques Lacan reinterpreted Freud's theory in 1953 and radicalised it by describing repetition as a symbolic act in contrast with memory, which he called an imaginary act.[4] Postmodern philosophy views repetition as a positive capacity of action, an act of differentiation; because an "again" never occurs at the same point in time, time is the differentiator. The act of repetition produces memory; the act differentiates itself from what was repeated and enables something different and new. The action itself is what differentiates.

In works such as **Untitled (Chunks)** or **Trauma**, Weber consciously endeavours to come to grips with the theme of repetition as a means of re-presenting repressed fears and memories. In both cases, the prerequisite of repetition is destruction. For **Untitled (Chunks)**, he created many deceptively realistic copies of a concrete block that he had violently broken apart. He lined up the new blocks, made of chalky grey plastic, in a precise row across the room. Although the installation might call to mind a defensive barricade, the exact repetition of its shape and spatial presentation gives the violent imagery an absurd overtone. This absurdity and artificiality is exposed more directly than in later sculptures, for it only references the material of concrete instead of actually being made of it. Likewise, **Trauma** plays with the bewilderment that comes from precisely repeating destruction several times over. Weber smashed into a door with an axe, meticulously moulded the splintered gash in silicone rubber, and affixed the replicas onto six identical doors. The arrangement of the identically broken doors around a closed room, which visitors can only glimpse through the hole in the original door, can be read as a reference to the destructive power of humans and the psychological trauma of both perpetrators and victims.

3 In 1914, Sigmund Freud coined the term "working through" in a short article as a psychoanalytic technique based on the assumption that remembering an unpleasant experience and repeating it are not enough to bring about a permanent change. See: Sigmund Freud, *Erinnern, Wiederholen und Durcharbeiten (Weitere Ratschläge zur Technik der Psychoanalyse, II)* (Remembering, Repeating and Working Through [More Suggestions on Psychoanalytic Technique, II]) (1914), in *Gesammelte Werke*, vol. 10 (Frankfurt: S. Fischer, 1946), pp. 126–136.

Untitled (Chunks) → p. 144
Trauma → p. 134

All of Christoph Weber's work grapples with reality, its representation and perception mechanisms, investigating nomenclature, conceptual patterns and socio-political systems of organisation. His art is intrinsically imbued with both semantic / conceptual and formal / material ambiguity and embodies an implicit dichotomy between deconstruction and construction. It is never only one or the other, but always both: unsettling and conciliatory, solid and vulnerable, aggressive and passive, coarsely unrestrained and elegantly sensual — and always human. Christoph Weber's path as an artist has taken him from contextual shifts by material transfer to his current exclusive use of concrete, within which he negotiates formal and semantic implications. One might posit that his treatment of materials has changed overall: While the act and repetition of destruction sometimes played central roles in his earlier work and can still be recognised in his scorched concrete sculptures and his bisected solid **Gegenstücke**, his more recent work seems to suggest a self-confident, almost playful treatment of the material. For Christoph Weber, concrete has become a matter of course. His struggle against the material has given way to a sense of play with(in) it. What remains constant is his practice of "methodological and processual comprehension", an act that, in its specific temporality, will never be an affirmative confirmation, but always a visualisation, a differentiation, an attempt.

4 In particular, see: Jacques Lacan, *The Seminar of Jacques Lacan: Book I: Freud's Papers on Technique 1953–1954*, ed. Jacques-Alain Miller, trans. John Forrester (Cambridge: Cambridge University Press, 1975).

Untitled (Gegenstück) → p. 150

→ p. 134
Trauma, 2008
Dimensions variable

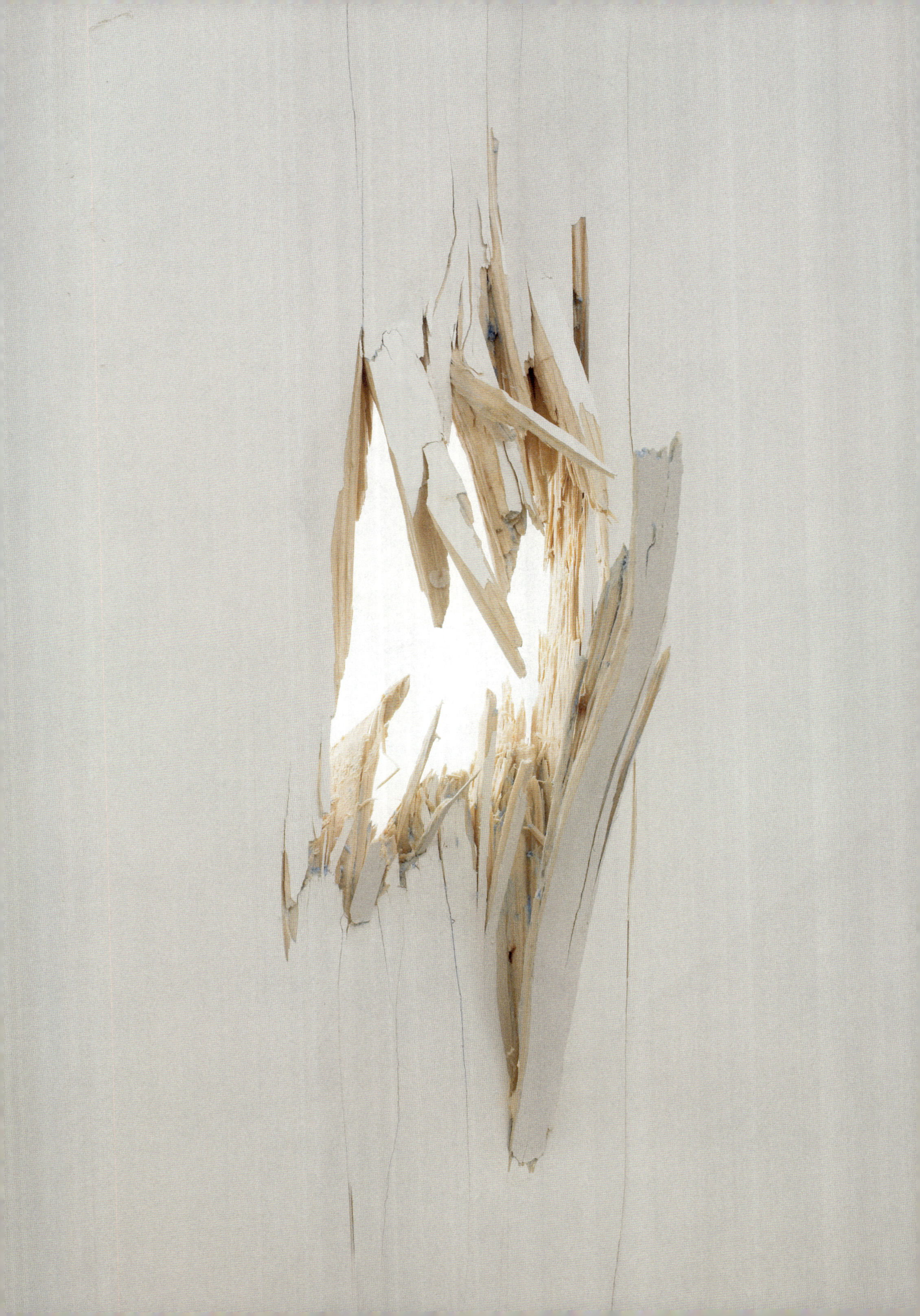

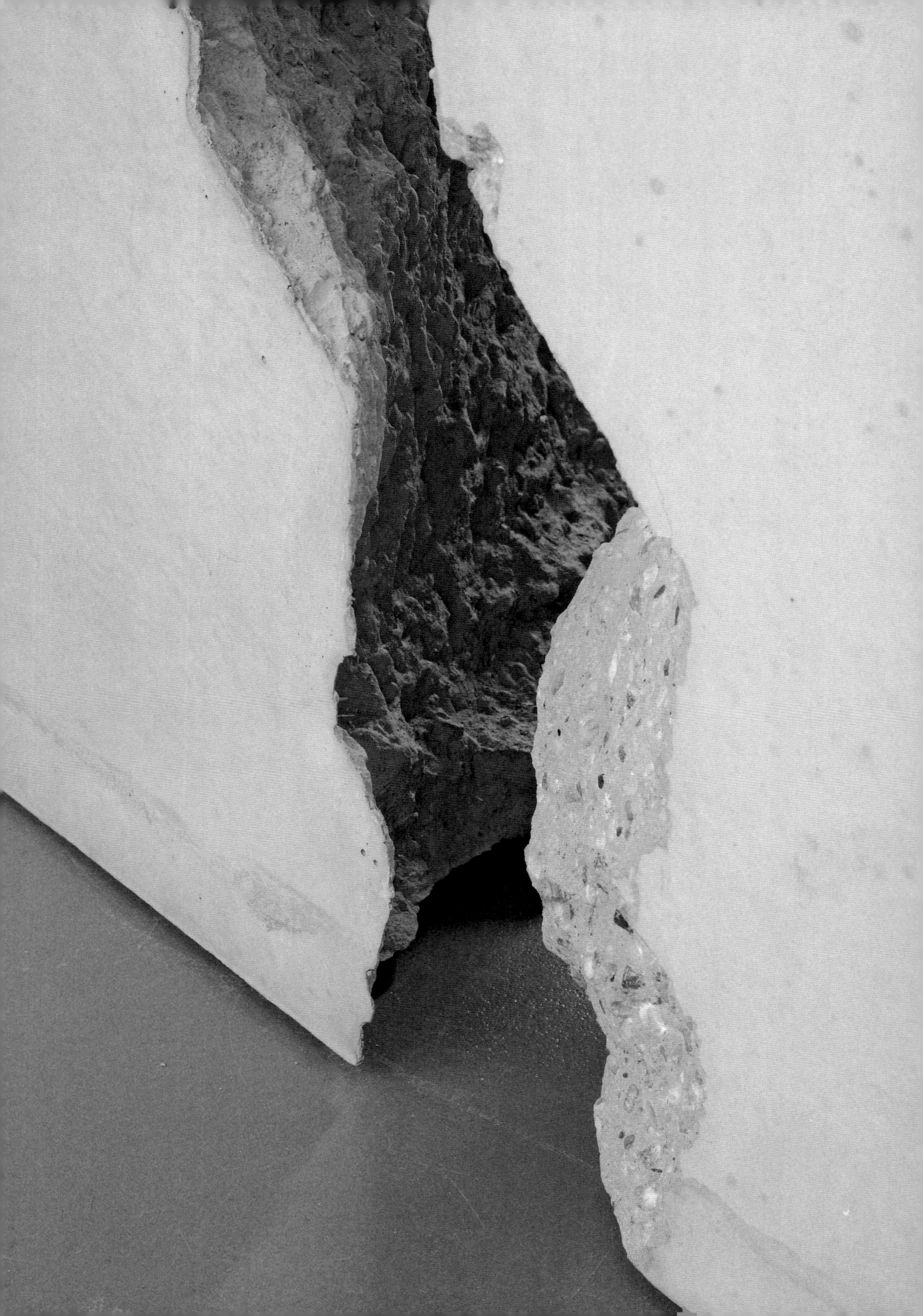

→ p. 150
Untitled (Gegenstück), 2012
130 × 135 × 90 cm overall

→ p. 142
Objets externes
2005–2007
Approx. 130 × 300 × 35 cm

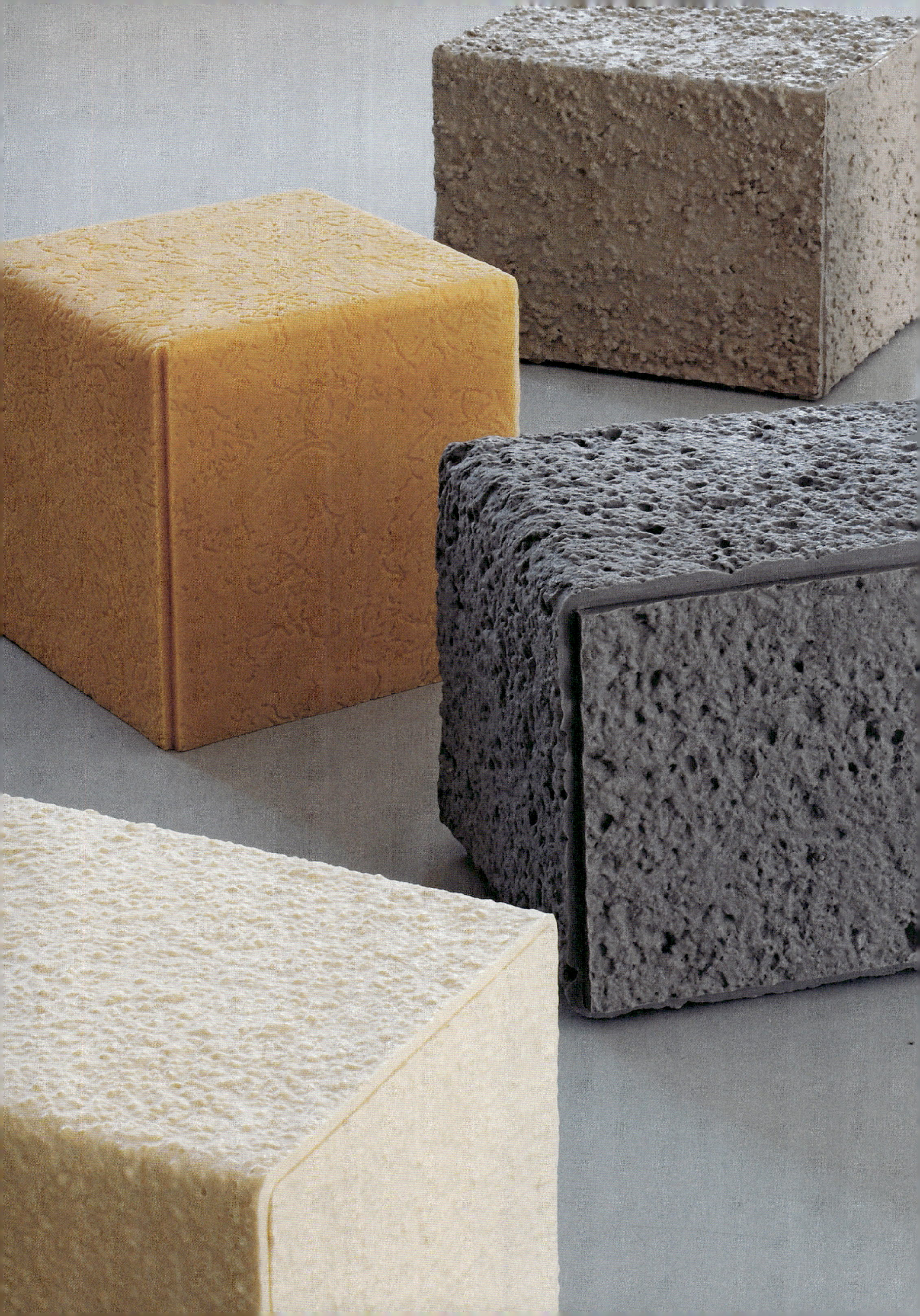

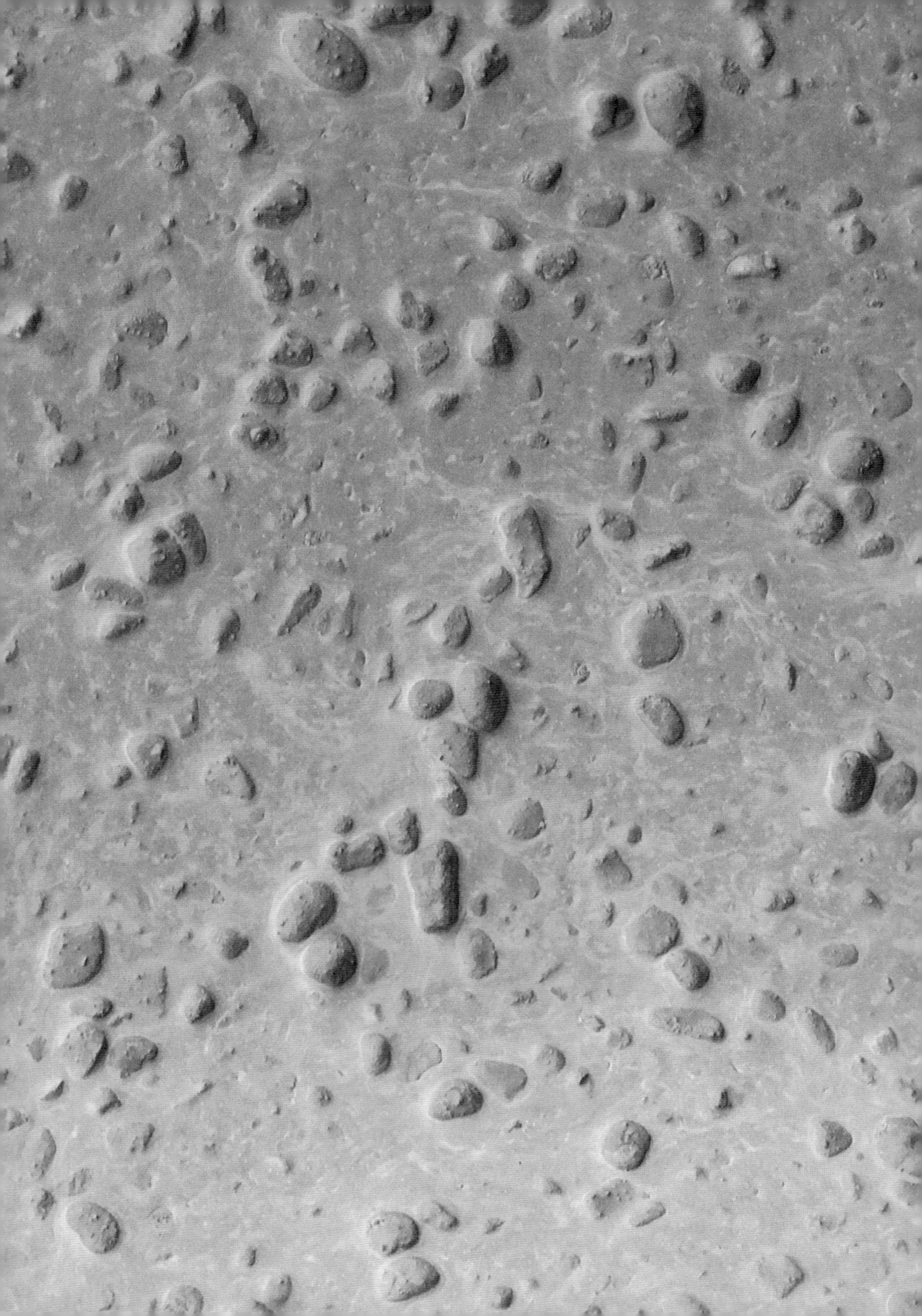

→ p. 82
bent inversion (seitlich stehend), 2012
36,6 × 115 × 0,7 cm

→ p. 96
unfold, 2011
1/2 parts
198 × 19 × 5 cm each

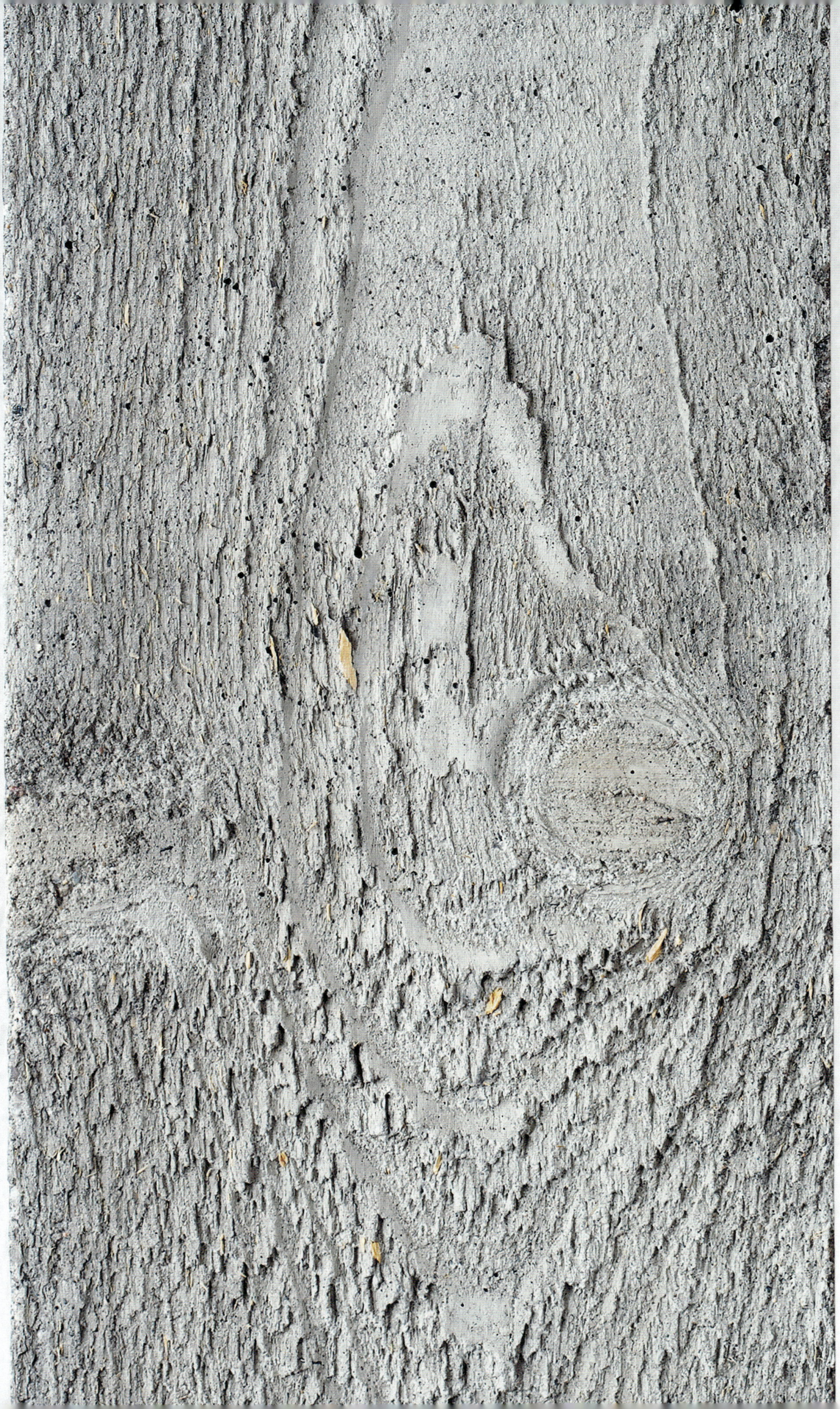

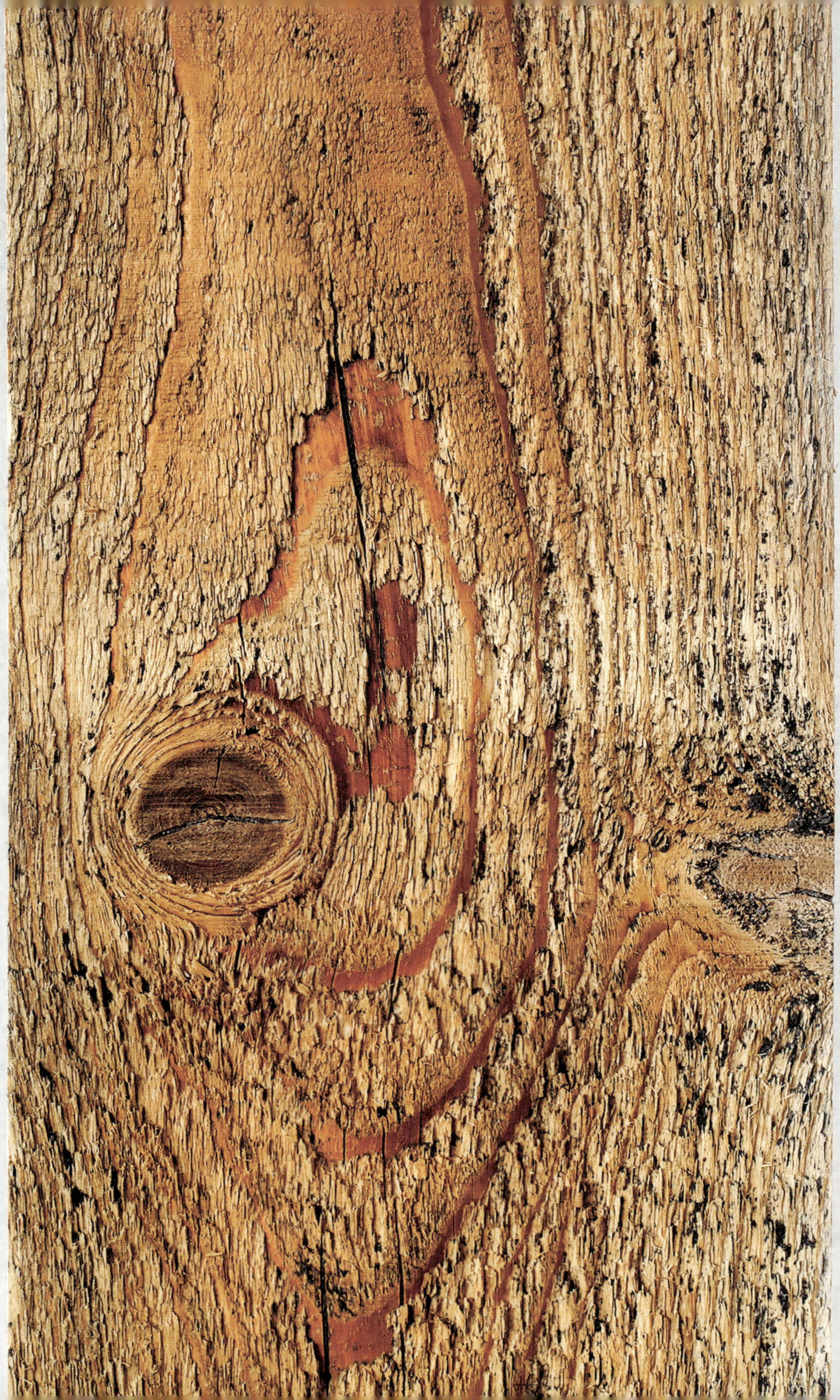

→ p. 96
unfold, 2011
2/2 parts
198 × 19 × 5 cm each

→ p. 126
Untitled (Ramponeau), 2008
Dimensions variable
12 × 13 × 15 cm each

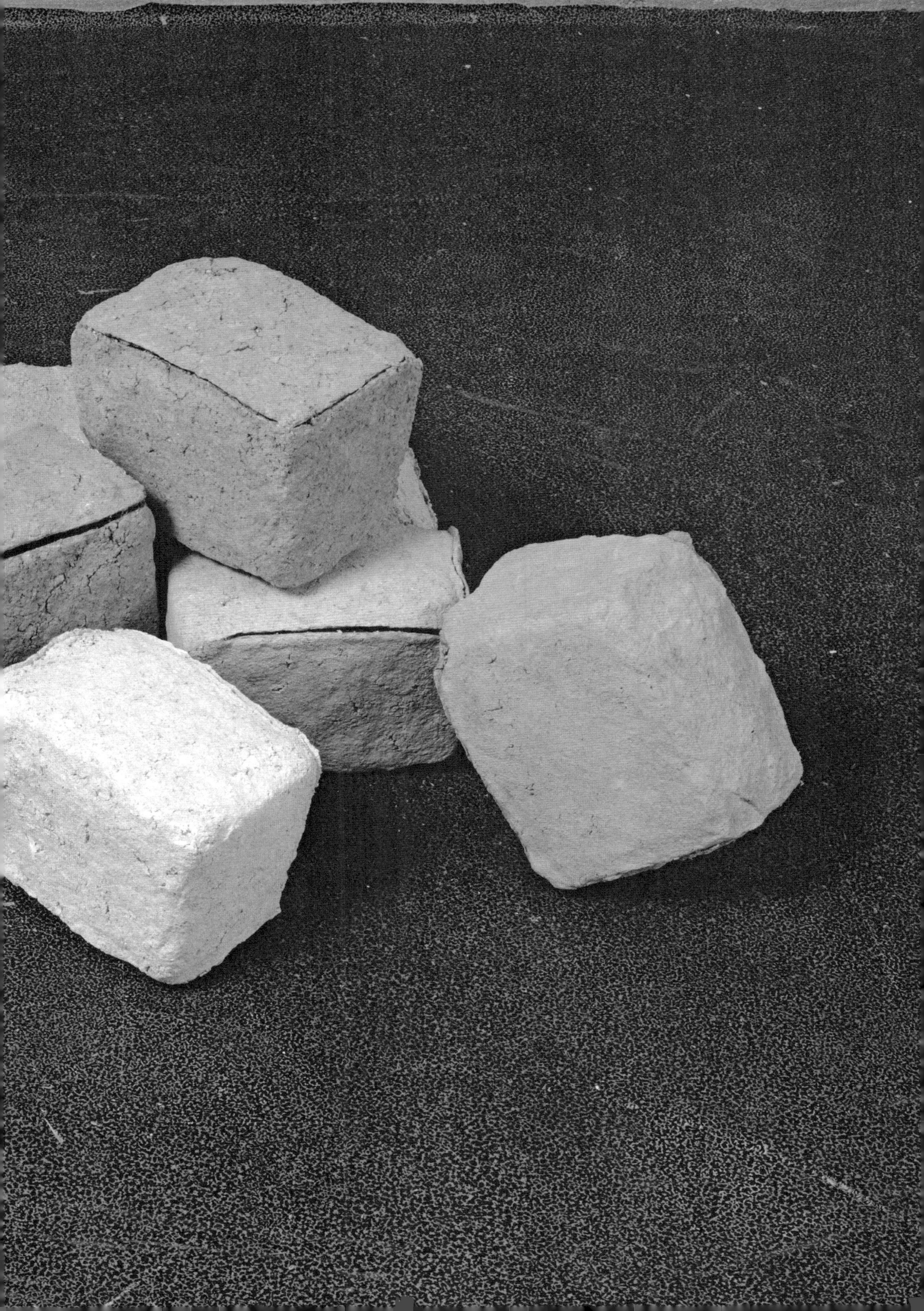

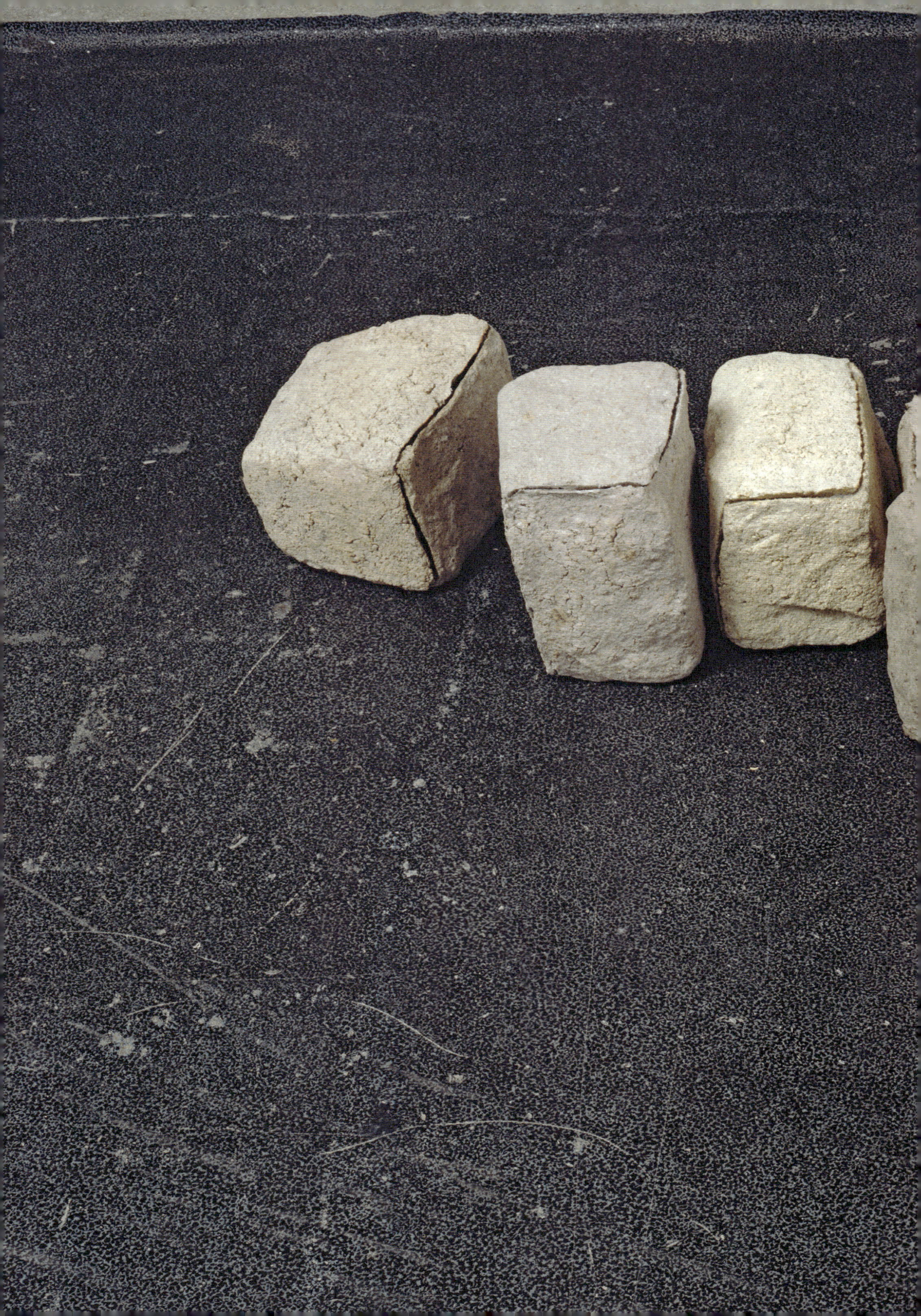

Papier-maché Cobblestones: On Christoph Weber's **Untitled (Ramponeau)**

Jens Kastner

I have no significant events to relate from the years 1870–71.
I divided my time between the field and the studio.

Paul Cézanne
(in a letter to Ambroise Vollard)[1]

How striking is it that the pioneer of modern art had nothing to report from this period.[2] 1871 was the year of an event in which, according to the Russian revolutionary and contemporary witness Pjotr L. Lawrow, "socialists of all persuasions worked not to implement some particular programme or isolated dogma, but rather to take every opportunity to bring about the historical conditions for a conscious struggle of the proletariat against its oppressor."[3] This event was the Paris Commune.

But Cézanne was focused on his own work,[4] a stance that was emblematic of the artist's role in the newly autonomous field of art, which separated the radicalism of artistic production from any kind of emancipatory politics. Their reconciliation has been sought ever since. Not that connections between politics and art have been absent from the modern age: They have indeed endured throughout this period in both social and artistic terms, and 1871 was itself a crucial point of reference for politically oriented art. Even then, well-known artists such as Gustave Courbet and Camille Pissarro were expressing sympathy for the rebels and paving the way for what became a fluctuating history of "art interlinked with

1 Cited in Ulrike Becks-Malorny, *Paul Cézanne, 1839–1906. Pioneer of Modernity* (London: Taschen Verlag, 2007), p. 19.
2 Thanks to Tom Holert for his critical and helpful comments on this text.
3 Pjotr L. Lawrow, *Die Pariser Kommune. Geschehnisse – Einfluss – Lehren* [1880] (Unrast: Verlag Münster, 2003), p. 182.
4 That this process of concentration is not the exception but, because it is so focused on the processes of shaping and perception crucial to art, the recognised rule. "There is no doubt," writes the art historian Herbert Read on Cézanne, "that what we call the modern movement in art begins with the single-minded determination of a French painter to see the world objectively." Herbert Read, *A Concise History of Modern Painting* [1959] (London: Thames & Hudson, 2006), p. 13.

→ p. 126
Untitled (Ramponeau), 2008
Dimensions variable
12 × 13 × 15 cm each

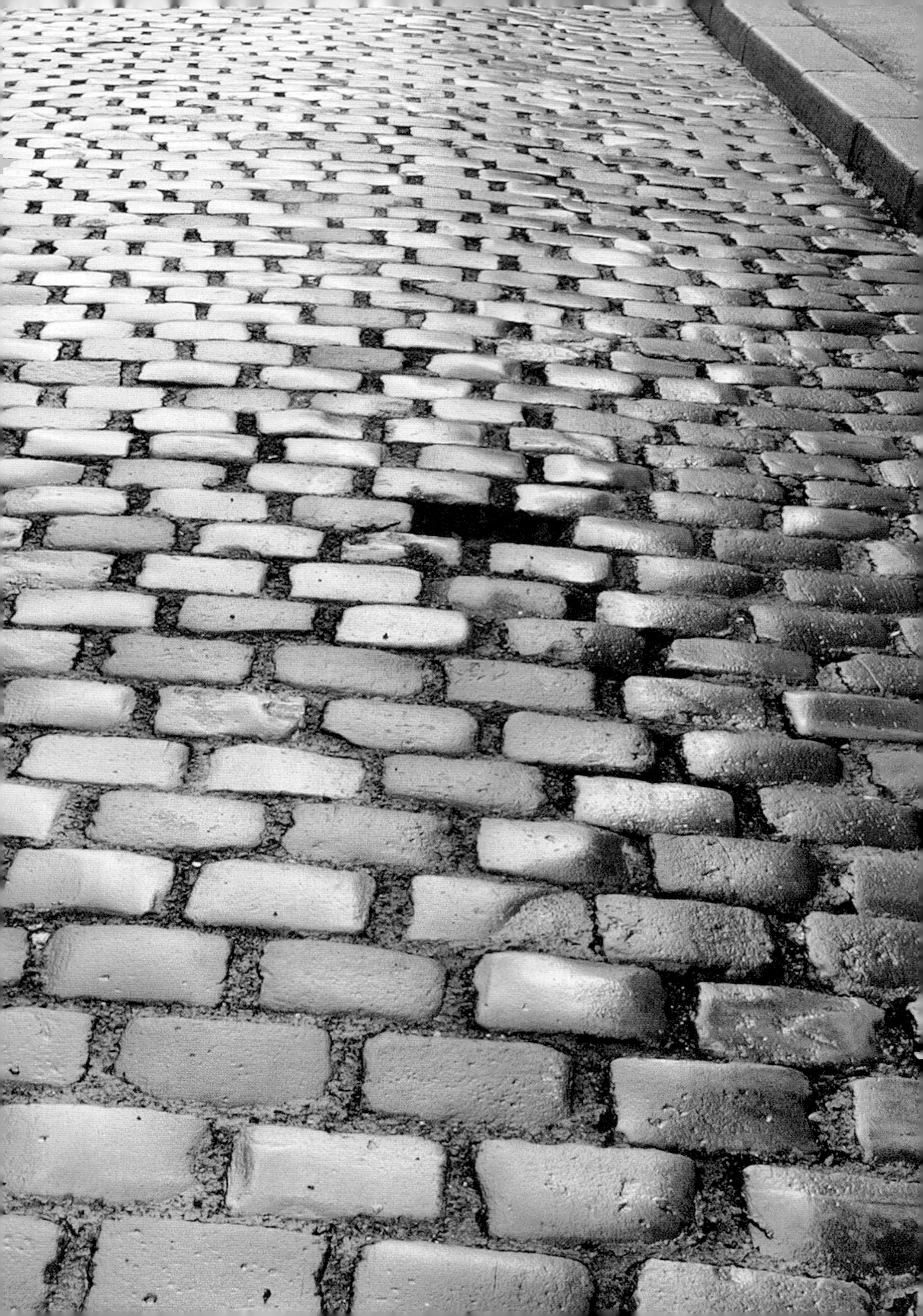

revolution."[5] Nevertheless, whether its engagement is expressed through its themes, contents, or simply the positions adopted by those who make it, the need to justify the involvement of art in politics is as old as "art" itself.[6]

Any political engagement requires a certain dialogue with notions of artistic autonomy. Christoph Weber is one of many artists to have entered into this exchange, and the resolve with which he has made this step is clear from **Untitled (Ramponeau)**: a work which goes back to the first moment in which the separation can be said to have occurred. The "pioneer of modernism" may have chosen not to see the social and political struggles of this time, but the significance of the moment has continued to be recognised "in every language of the civilised world."[7][8]

When Weber made his heaps of papier-mâché stones, reproduced from a cobblestone, which he took from the rue Ramponeau, the site of the Commune's last barricade in May 1871, he did so using books that were around at the time. Snippets of text can be discerned in the papier-mâché's grey-brown sheen: The stones cannot hide the fact that they are made from the wrong material.[9]

In one sense, these piles of papier-mâché stones touch base with other works of Weber's in which the question of material is raised; the usage it permits, what it has to say. Weber's buckled, folded, and tilted concrete is of course provocative and shows no respect for the grandiose sense of stability that has made it, together with glass and steel, a symbol of economic progress as well as a reference point for art. Stones made of paper might also induce the same surprise and unfamiliarity as that of folded concrete, but insofar as they prompt broader reflections on the artistic processes involved in selecting, using, and giving value to things, these papier-mâché cobblestones do more besides.

5 Gerald Raunig: *Kunst und Revolution. Künstlerischer Aktivismus im langen 20. Jahrhundert* (Vienna: Turia + Kant 2005), p. 7 and 63ff. See too the exhibition organised in 2007 by Charles Esche and Will Bradley in the Tate London and the Vanabbemuseum Eindhoven and the accompanying publication on the relationship between art production and social change is considered in relation to the Paris Commune, Charles Esche and Will Bradley eds., *Art and Social Change. A Critical Reader* (London: Tate/Afterall, 2007).

6 See for example Helmut Draxler, "The Curse of the Good Deed / The Claim to Autonomy and the Suspicion of Ideology in Political Art," in *Texte zur Kunst no. 80* (December 2010), pp. 100–103.

7 Pjotr L. Lawrow: *Die Pariser Kommune*, op. cit., p. 181.

8 Weber has also made *Untitled (copper engraving, 1631)* with the same historical and material accuracy: copper strips in the form of modified clouds of smoke are mounted on the wall along the lines of a caricature from a 1631 leaflet. Such leaflets were first produced during the 30 Years' War, and, because of the then high rates of illiteracy, were heavily reliant on visual elements.

9 A photograph of the street with the missing stone and a box of old books no longer or never read also form parts of the work.

Untitled → p. 130
Untitled (rue Ramponeau) → p. 124

→ p. 124
Untitled (rue Ramponeau), 2008
Lambdaprint
25 × 21 cm

Unlike his concrete works, Weber's cobblestones are not made from cheap materials like sand, but from what Pierre Bourdieu would describe as valuable "objects of cultural capital"[10]: old books. An educated audience would normally be shocked at their destruction, but any sense of outrage is allayed here simply because they are turned into art.[11] Weber's powerful paper stones raise several questions of legitimation: In what context and conditions do materials have worth? They also demonstrate the contingency of this kind of legitimisation. Things that are valuable one day for one person can be worthless the next or to someone else. This is not, of course, completely arbitrary; norms and institutions underwrite the relative permanence of value. But the principle is clear: Enduring value has to be produced by meanings developed in the course of social struggle. This is not just the kind of struggle that pitches cobblestones against police truncheons, but the struggle to establish legitimate perspectives, the worth and significance of values, norms, and meanings, and so a common notion of the social dynamic.

This struggle for meaning is exactly where artistic production and street protests meet, even when they are playing by very different rules.

Art is governed by rules, which were already implicit in Cézanne's desire "to see the world objectively" (Read), and have been further refined by attempts to purge art of subjective expression and coded narration. Modern art has moved away from representation to give the nature of materials an increasingly decisive role (in the production of "good art"). It is a game, which has often assumed more of an analytical than a playful character: a matter of running through all the possible permutations. When Carl Andre lined up his 137 firebricks end to end on the floor, (*Lever*, 1966) it was not to allow them to be decrypted or decoded, but so that they could be experienced as materials in space.[12] Such an apparent and decisive purification of art from all its extrinsic elements remain ambivalent in their effects. The involvement of audiences (in the experience of the space, for example) always tends to return to the question of the social and cultural orders to which they belong. Existing patterns and grids

10 Pierre Bourdieu: "The forms of capital," [1986] in J. Richardson ed., *Handbook of Theory and Research for the Sociology of Education* (New York: Greenwood, 1986), pp. 241–258.

11 This is not so easily achieved when old cars are turned into art, as in Nam June Paik's *32 cars for the 20th century: play Mozart's Requiem quietly* (1997) because car-lovers value artistic transformation less than book-lovers do. Nevertheless, Paik, like Weber, draws attention to the precise shift between spheres of recognition, legitimation, and valuation, that a celebrated work like the diamond-studded skull by Damien Hirst (*For the Live of God*, 2007) deals with far less consistently because it leaves its materials unchanged. The diamonds can be sold again as diamonds, but books and the cars cannot.

12 Because art, in Andre's programme, "is a direct experience with something in the world," Carl Andre, interview by Willoughby Sharp, *Avalanche 1* (Fall 1970), p. 24.

→ p. 130
Untitled, 2008
38 × 51 × 24 cm

(of thought and perception) are not to be disrupted by the decoding and processing of information, but by the experience of the material in its space: No matter how free it is of metaphysical clutter, this is an art that still seeks to shake up established notions of presentation and representational art.[13] In its effects, this strand of radical artistic experience, at least as embodied by Carl Andre, encounters that other tradition of politically engaged art in which "painters build barricades" (Ludwig Rubiner).[14]

These refined perspectives also brought new insights to bear on the very rules of politics. Collective protest was no longer simply a logical reaction to poverty and injustice, but now included an enormous range of motives related to the discrepancy between the state of the world (or one's own situation) and how it could or should be lived. It has certainly become clear that social movements function as producers of meanings that far exceed the articulation of their concrete demands[15] to encompass meanings, definitions, and classifications that affect the whole social space. In the 1960s, the cultural dimension, understood as practices and processes of producing meaning and significance, was central to the sociological reception of new social movements, as well as to the actual conflicts in which they were involved. The actual conflicts themselves backed this focus on the cultural dimension: Whereas the Commune's piles of cobblestones were intended as means of resistance and defence, the barricades erected during the legendary events of 1968 were more aesthetic than strategic. Even then, however, as Carl Douglas has shown, the barricades were also about the erection of moral defences and the "communal construction"[16] of a visible collective subject. Far from military defences, "the barricades erected in Paris during the night of May 10–11, 1968, were an historical quotation," writes Ingrid Gilcher-Holtey in her analysis of the movement.[17] "Built by schoolchildren and students aware of their significance at the time of the Commune and during the liberation

13 Carl Andre, who invited the public to walk on his work and experience it in a bodily sense, was in this respect quite pleased to see his art having such ambivalent effects. Although he sought to rid artistic production from all non-artistic elements, he was at the same time—as Julia Bryan-Wilson suggests—"at the forefront of an abstract, politically committed art practice". Julia Bryan-Wilson, *Art Workers. Radical Practice in the Vietnam Era* (Berkeley: University of California Press, 2009), p. 49.

14 Ludwig Rubiner, „Maler bauen Barrikaden“ in *Künstler bauen Barrikaden. Texte und Manifeste 1908–1919*, ed. Wolfgang Haug (Darmstadt: Sammlung Luchterhand, 1988) pp. 81–86.

15 See for example Stuart Hall, "Signification, Representation, Ideology: Althusser and the Post-Structuralist Debates," in *Critical Studies in Mass Communication*, vol. 2, no. 2 (June 1985), pp. 91–114.

16 Carl Douglas: "Barricades and Boulevards: Material transformations of Paris, 1795–1871," in *Interstices. Journal of Architecture and Related Arts*, no. 8 (2007), pp. 31–42, here p. 39.

17 Ingrid Gilcher-Holtey, *'Die Phantasie an die Macht'. Mai 68 in Frankreich* (Frankfurt am Main: Suhrkamp, 1995), p. 240.

→ p. 130
Untitled, 2008
38 × 51 × 24 cm

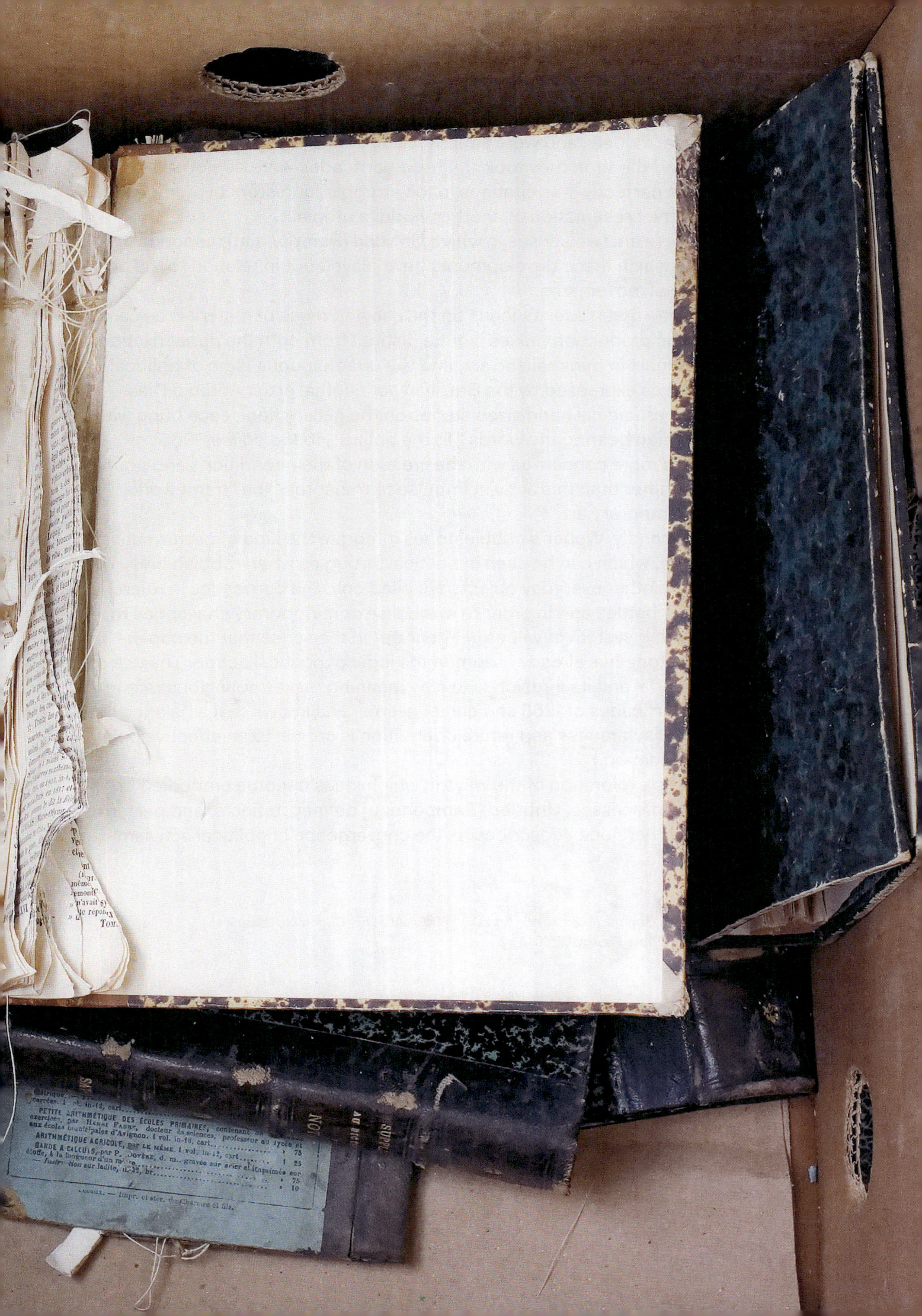
PETITE ARITHMÉTIQUE DES ÉCOLES PRIMAIRES, contenant
docteur ès sciences, professeur au lycée et
ARITHMÉTIQUE AGRICOLE, par LE MÊME. 1 vol. in-12, cart.
BANDE A CALCULS, par P.
gravée sur acier et imprimée sur
Impr. et stér. de

of the city from the German occupation, they evoked the memory of these historical models, and were entirely made in their image in terms of their goals and the form they took."[18] These barricades were deployed simply—perhaps perfectly—as citations in the struggle for historical memory as well as the presentation of another world, a utopia.

There are two senses in which **Untitled (Ramponeau)** responds to the ways in which these developments have played out in relation to the arts and social movements.

In the first place, its focus on the use and reuse of materials as central to artistic production makes it quite distinct from both the purist fixation on materials in minimalistic art, and the unambiguous logic of political activism as expressed by the Brazilian conceptual artist Antonio Dias. When Dias laid his hand sized stones on the gallery floor, each hung with a small sign bearing the words "To the police" (*To the police*, 1968). Weber is more concerned with the creation of their conditions and possibilities rather than this activist impulse to transgress the "frameworks of contemporary art."[19]

Secondly, Weber's cobblestones integrate the kind of performative recycling, which can be seen in political struggles when rubbish bins, cars, and other everyday objects are piled onto the barricades in reference to earlier battles and in order to symbolise contemporary challenges to the existing system of values. ("Integrate" in the sense that the papier-mâché stone has already assumed the logic of political action: The use of the material and its infusion with new meaning makes conscious reference to the barricades of 1968 and earlier events, and knows that a balance of historical awareness and future orientation is crucial to an effective political imagination.)

In its exploration of the ways in which ideas become embodied in material processes, **Untitled (Ramponeau)** defines, reflects, and performs what has here been described as the convergence of political activism and art.

18 Ibid.

19 Tom Holert, *Übergriffe. Zustände und Zuständigkeiten der Gegenwartskunst* (Hamburg: Philo Fine Arts, 2014), pp. 9ff.

→ p. 126
Untitled (Ramponeau), 2008
Dimensions variable
12 × 13 × 15 cm each

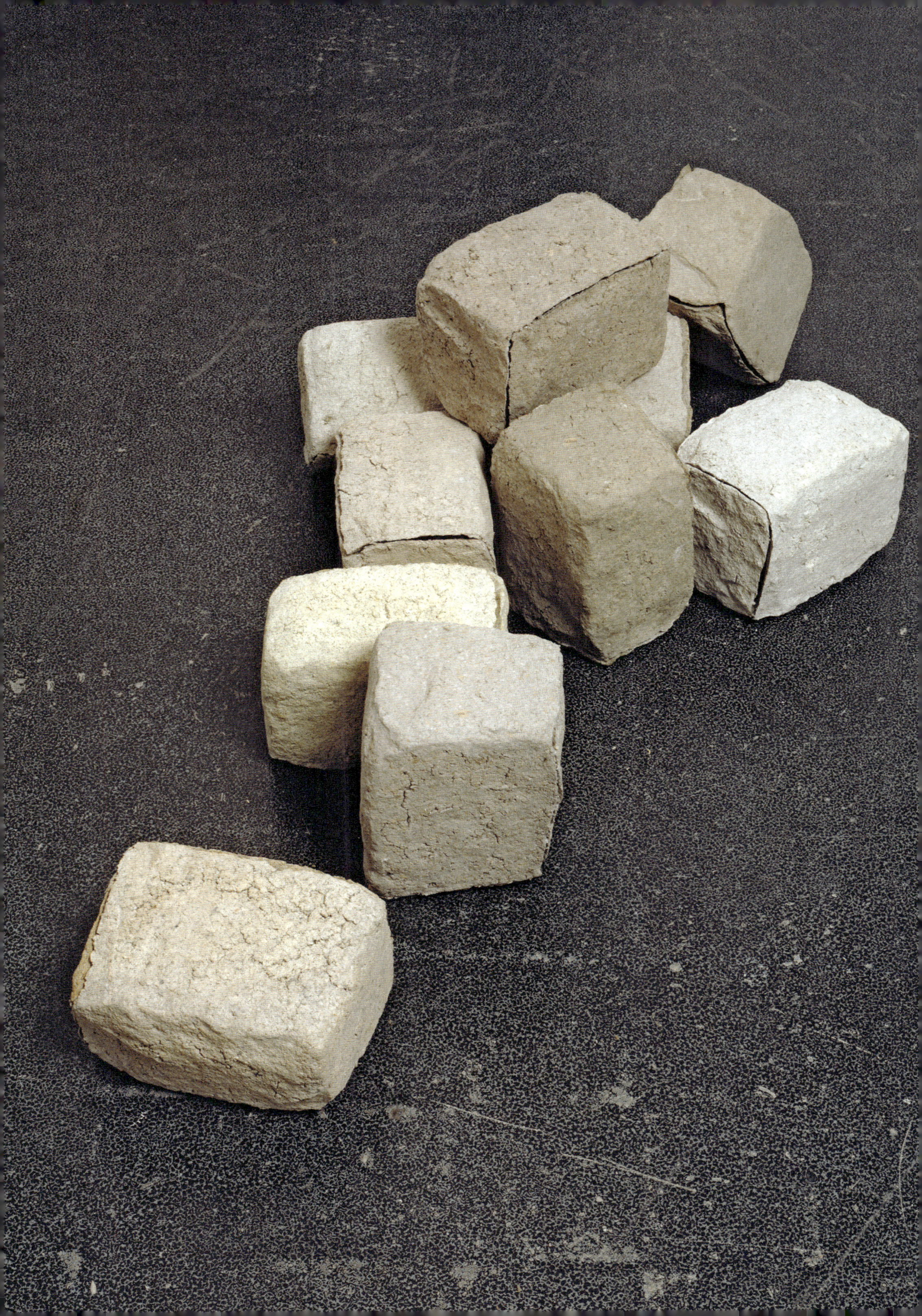

Moulds / not yet titled
(pinhole camera
stop-motion setup)
35 × 43 × 37 cm

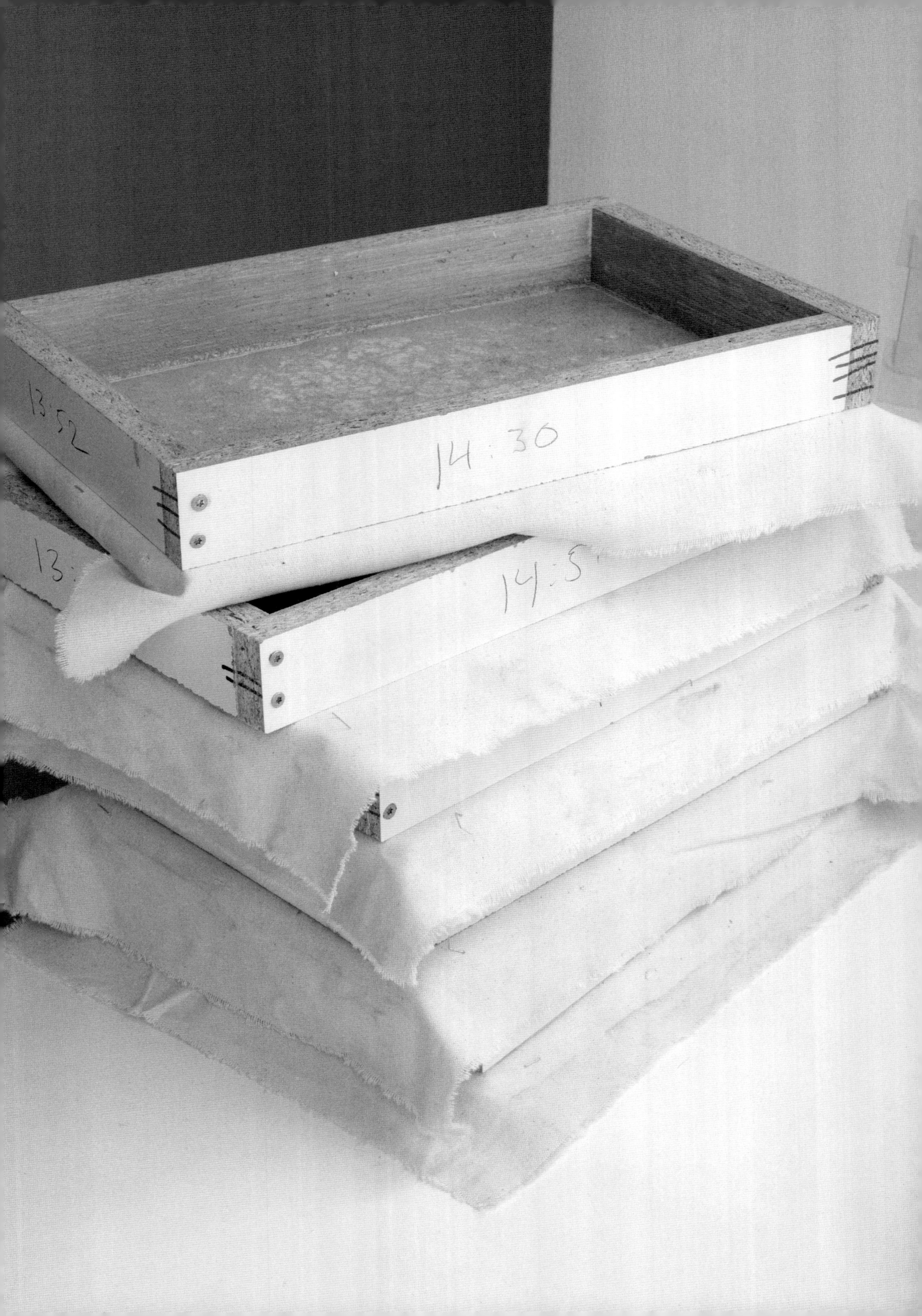
13:52
14:30
13:
14:5

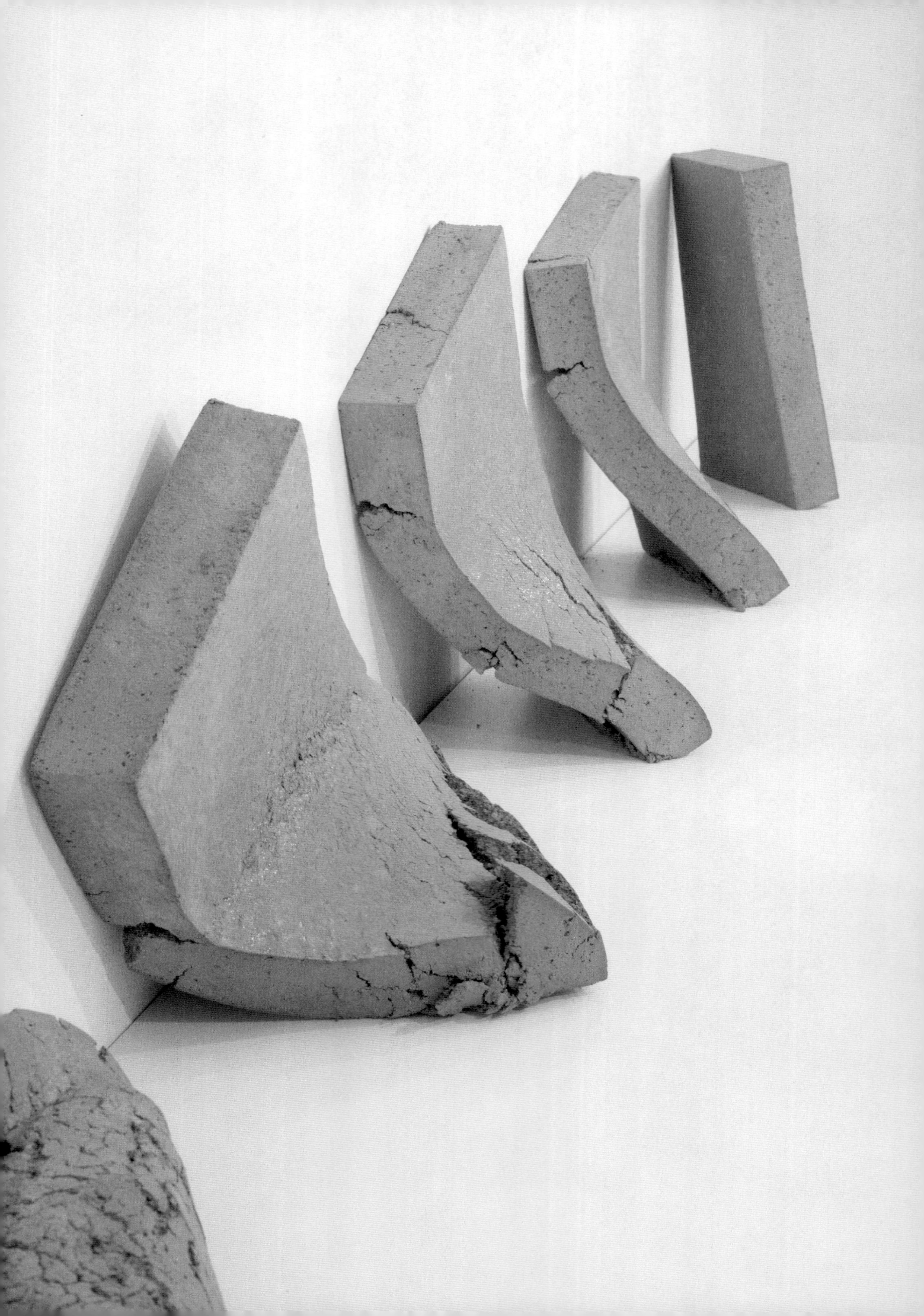

The Obscure in the Concrete: Reflections on **not yet titled** (pinhole camera stop-motion setup)

Andreas Duscha & Christoph Weber

An analogy exists between two things if they are similar in one property even if they differ in other properties.

What happens when the production conditions of one medium are transferred to another that is subject to entirely different rules? Do photography and the concrete pouring process share only one commonality — the fact that both procedures involve positives and negatives — or can other similarities be found? Can the essence of concrete casting, whose constituent factor is time, be replicated in a photographic image? How would such replication affect the image? These questions are what gave rise to our collaborative art project **not yet titled (pinhole camera stop-motion setup)**.

The focus was on the idea of using these processes as mutual constraints. In an experimental design of sorts, we sought to test what would occur if specific factors of different media were applied in comparable fashion. One central factor in our undertaking was time. The length of time that concrete spends curing in the mould plays the most critical role in its solidity. In **not yet titled**, Christoph Weber lengthened the curing time incrementally, as if producing a series of bracketed photographs. The resulting five objects, lined up in sequential order, are reminiscent of the early movement studies of Eadweard Muybridge. A movement is split up into five autonomous images that, when taken sequentially, comprise a depiction of consecutive motion. With concrete casting the piece with the shortest curing phase slumps inward, yielding the most to gravity, and resists its moulded form. Progressively longer curing times produce greater stability, with the last concrete slab being almost perfectly formed. Therefore, the material's capacity for manipulation — its resulting solidity — is defined by time. At first it is as malleable as wax in a warm hand; later it resists any and all intervention.

Scale models / not yet titled (pinhole camera stop-motion setup)
36 × 206 × 20 cm

not yet titled → p. 40

Time (in relation to aperture and the film's light sensitivity) enables the photographer to not only represent reality indexically, but to shape and manipulate it, inscribing the artistic vision into the image and bending it to the photographer's will. As exposure time increases, the image becomes harder and harder to manipulate until it goes black, erasing itself and eluding any further processing. When reduced to the bare materials, a piece of black photo paper and a fully hardened chunk of concrete are the respective end points of irreversible processes.

What happens if the factor of time is carried over from one medium to the other? What if the different lengths of time Christoph Weber allowed his concrete pours to cure before demoulding them were used as exposure times for the five photographs of those very objects? This draws a relationship between data points that are actually independent, an exercise comparable to the intellectual game invented by the main characters of Umberto Eco's novel *Foucault's Pendulum*. These characters regularly profess connections between utterly unconnected facts and details, assembling a set of circumstances that can stake its claim on reality due to the acceptance of others.

For his motion sequences, Eadweard Muybridge used up to thirty-six adjacent cameras that were set off in turn. Given that Muybridge's very short exposure times were unnecessary for our enterprise — the objects were already in a "frozen" state — pinhole cameras were a logical choice. As a variation of the camera obscura (dark chamber) as opposed to an everyday camera, the lens of a pinhole camera consists of a tiny hole. Its reduction to the simplest and most basic camera design gives it the greatest scope for adaptation to specific, personalised needs. The cameras were built to the exact size of the moulds, making the image surfaces congruent with the sculpture's original dimensions before deformation. Particleboard was used for both the pinhole cameras and the moulds, uniting their form so that only their function diverged.

Inside a pinhole camera, the photographic subject is projected in an upside-down mirror image on the back wall opposite the pinhole. This is developed on a light-sensitive surface (photo paper) as a negative, which in this case we used without inverting it into a positive. This is where the aforementioned analogy to the concrete pouring process was brought to bear, for the moulds also constituted the objects' negative form before their manipulation. The pinhole camera's small aperture dramatically increases the depth of focus, making this the ideal close-up shot. But it also requires long exposure times, which allowed us to directly match the successively increasing curing periods.

Pinhole cameras,
floodlights / not yet titled
(pinhole camera
stop-motion setup)
65 × 212 × 52 cm

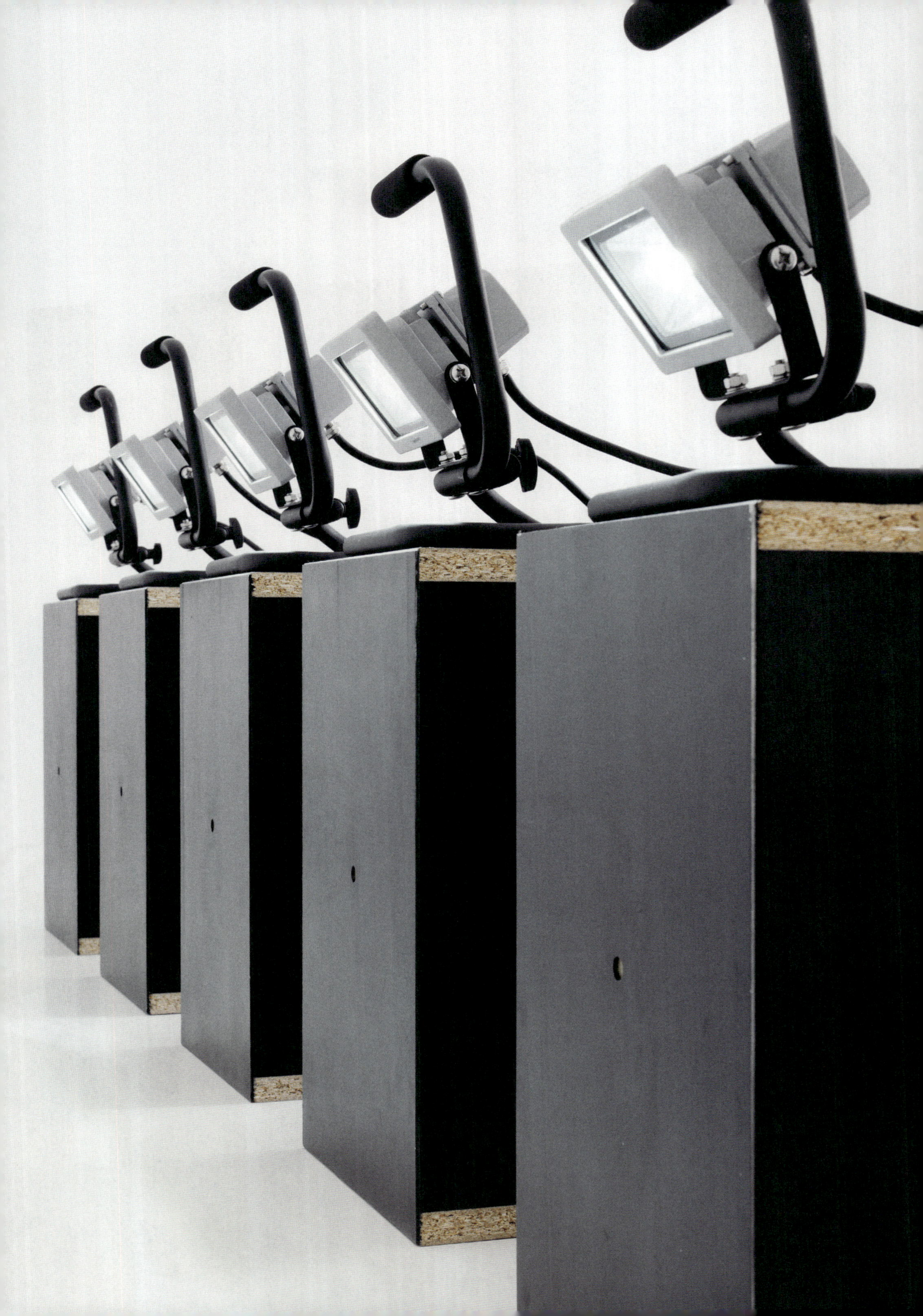

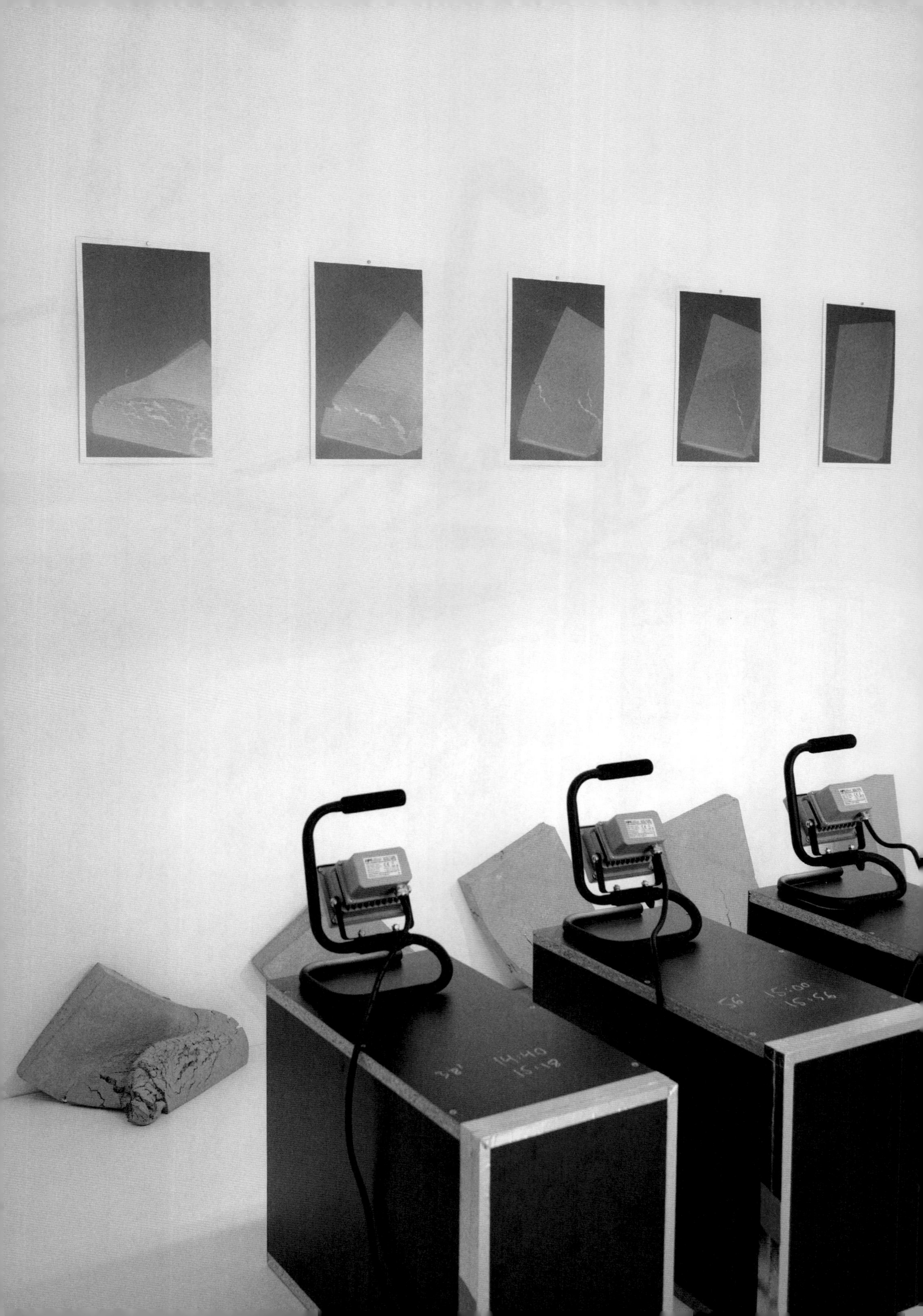
38' 14:40
15:18
56' 15:00
15:56

In this project, the pinhole camera serves as an epistemological apparatus because it performs the photograph's status as a "made" object rather than producing a mere likeness. The scissor-like interrelation of the object represented and the object representing is multifarious: The formal alignment of the mould and the camera, followed by the long exposure time, transferred the process of the object's emergence into a photographic "distillate" of both the photographic image and its individual creation process. Beyond depicting the object, the result simultaneously inscribes its history.

not yet titled
(pinhole camera
stop-motion setup), 2015
Collaboration with
Andreas Duscha
165 × 250 × 125 cm

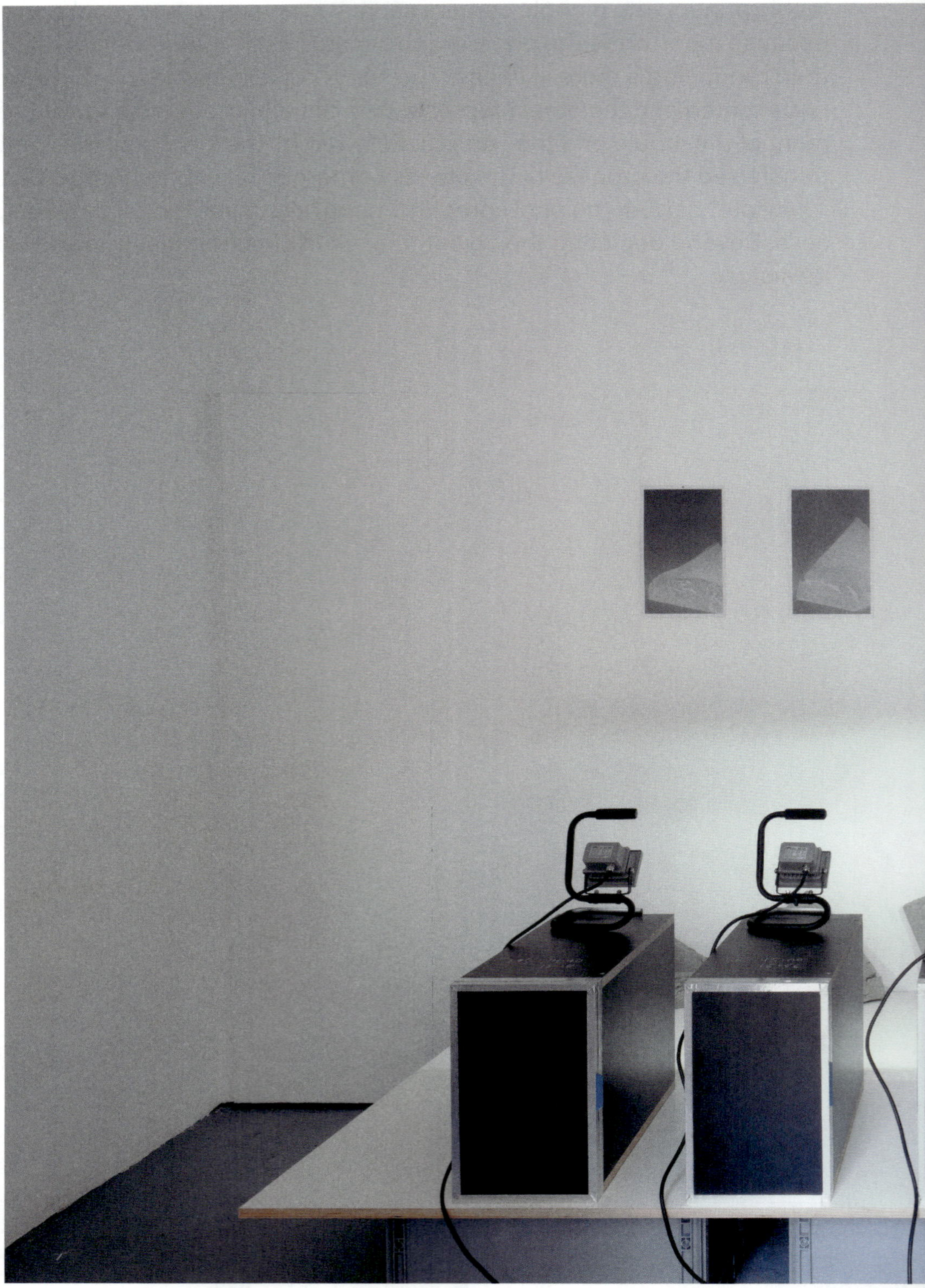

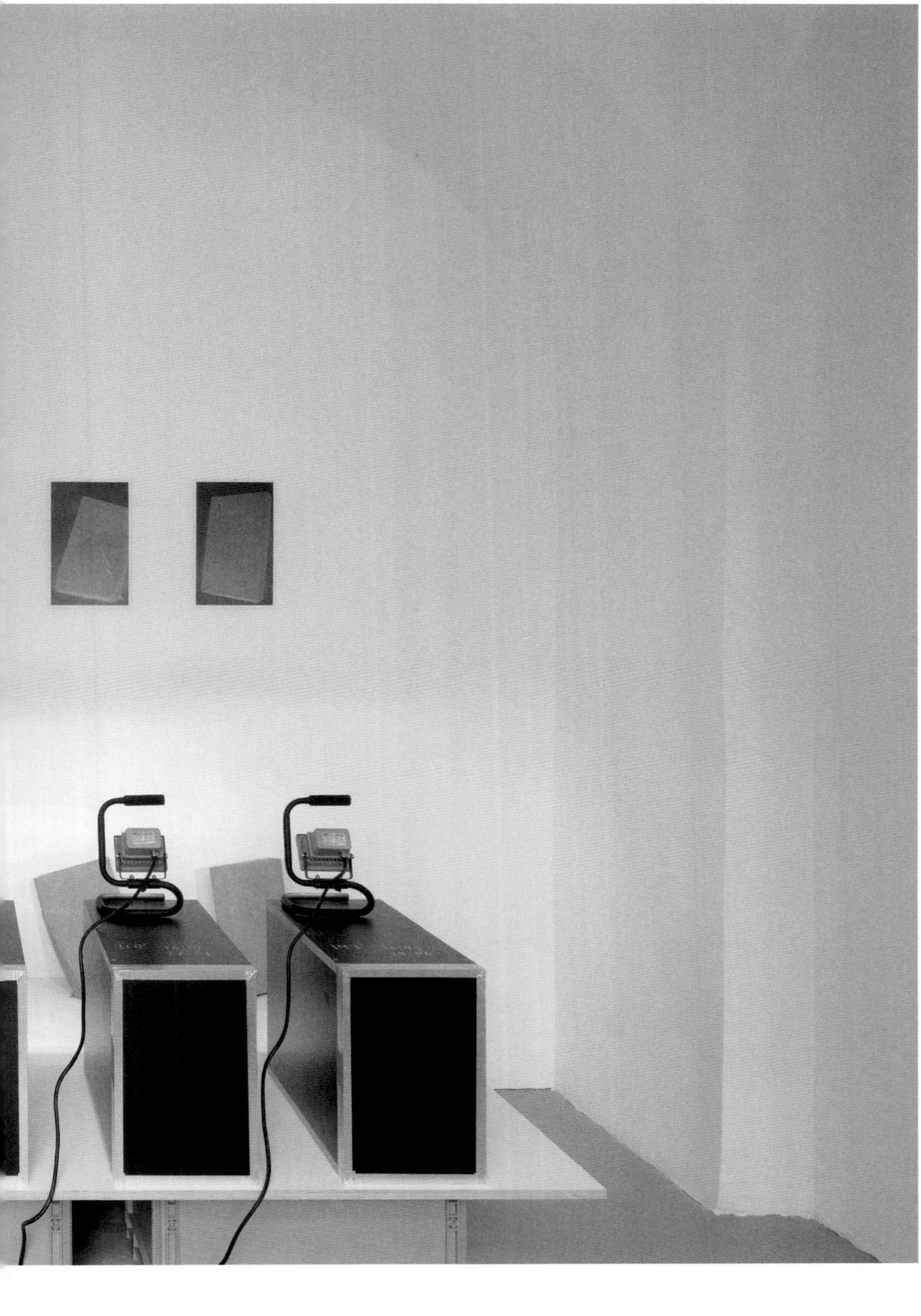

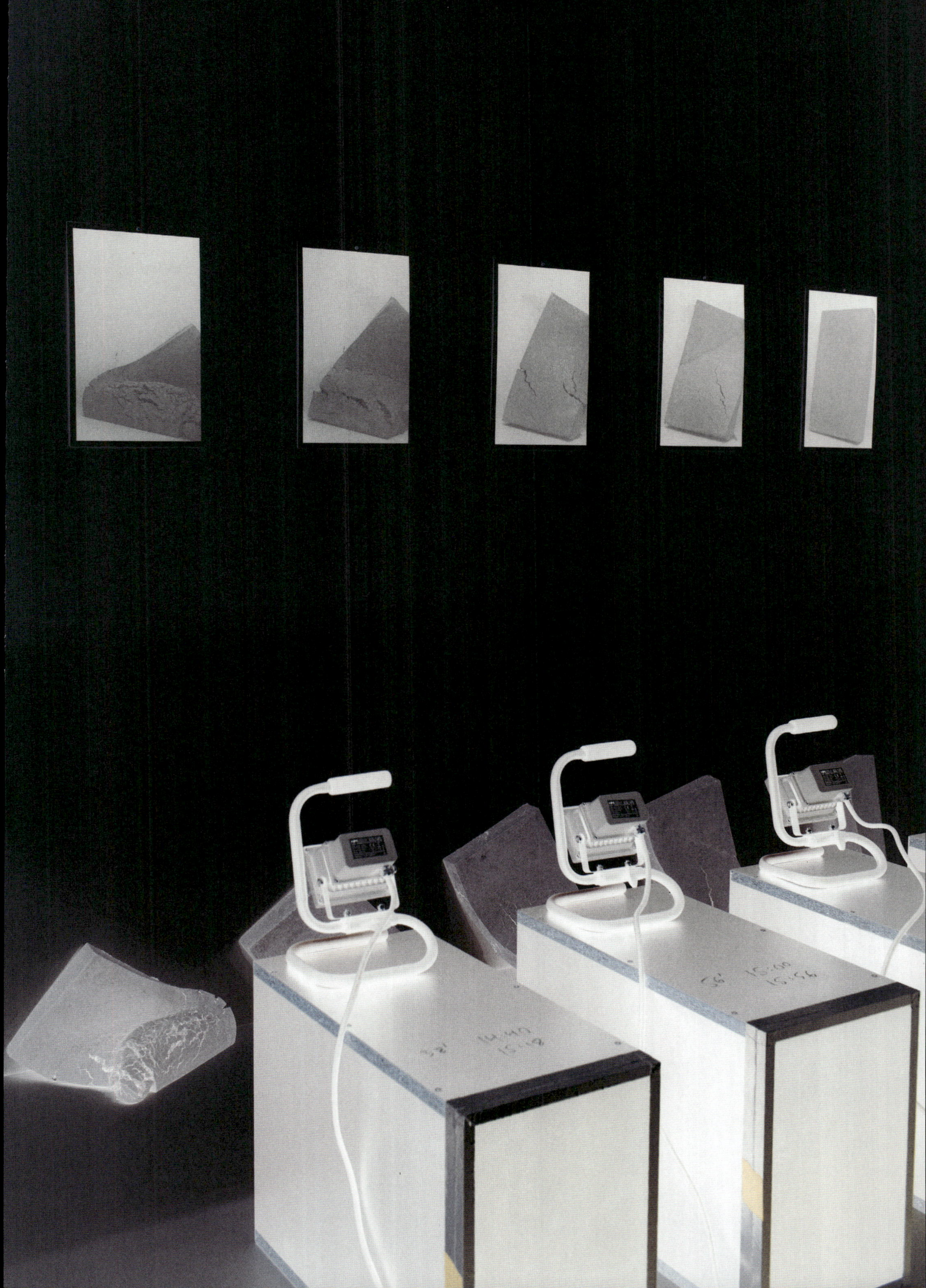

Beton (gehoben) → p. 90
Beton (gerollt) → p. 92
Beton (gewickelt) → p. 58
not yet titled → p. 60

Skulpturale Körper: liegend, hängend, abwickelnd ...

Versuche einer Situierung von Christoph Webers plastischem Schaffen

Konrad Bitterli

Beton, Beton, Beton
Beton, Beton, Beton, Beton
Waschbeton,
Mischbeton,
Fein-Stahl-Fertig-Beton.
Wir baun uns a haltbare Welt,
die in fuchzgtausend Jahr aa no hoit.

[...]

Wartungsfrei, sauber, keimfrei und schön,
ma ka si glei gar net gnua an ehm sehng
am Misch-Beton, am Stahl-Beton,
am Fein-Wasch-Klar-Sicht-Beton
Beton, Beton, Beton,
Beton, Paradies aus Farbig-Beton.

Gerhard Polt. *Beton*

Der Kontrast könnte größer nicht sein zwischen dem neoklassizistischen Interieur des altehrwürdigen St. Galler Museums und Christoph Webers roher Betonskulptur: Mächtig, beinahe unverrückbar, und dennoch zerbrechlich liegt sie auf dem feinen Parkett und „besetzt" den lichten Ausstellungsraum. Ihre lagernde Form scheint in einer gewaltigen Bewegung des Sich-Aufwickelns und Abrollens in sich zusammengefallen und abrupt auseinandergebrochen. Wuchtige Verwerfungen ziehen sich quer über ihre Oberflächen, verzweigen sich in zahlreiche feinere Bruchstellen, während von der Seite betrachtet körnige Betonausbrüche zwischen den Wülsten hervorquellen bzw. auf der anderen die Faltung als elegante Abwicklung erkennbar bleibt. Trotz feingliedriger Ausdifferenzierungen der Form erscheint die Skulptur geradezu selbstverständlich, beinahe lapidar, als hätte sich eine einzige kräftige Bewegung gewissermaßen in Beton verfestigt, die Spuren einer wuchtigen Geste, wie im Moment festgehalten.
Im Grunde handelt es sich um eine liegende, mehrere Zentimeter dicke quadratische Betonplatte in industriellem Grauton, welche der Künstler während des Aushärtens auf einer Seite angehoben hat, als ob er den zähen Baustoff sanft falten wollte. Exakt diesen Moment der Transformation, des extremen Belastens des Materials und des nicht vollends kontrollierbaren Kippens von einer bestimmten Form in eine andere provoziert der Künstler und hält ihn gewissermaßen in der finalen Skulptur fest. Auf der „Rückseite" bildet der Prozess eine regelmäßig geformte Rundung aus, während von vorne betrachtet das Material aufgrund seines Eigengewichts in sich zusammenfällt, wobei die entstandenen Verwerfungen mit der Gesamtstruktur verbunden bleiben. Zu sehen ist die in Beton festgehaltene Geste mit eleganten Wölbungen und abrupten Abrissen, Ausfaltungen und Bruchkanten; gedanklich nachvollziehbar sind der Prozess der Entstehung, die Geste des Anhebens, der Beginn der „Faltung", der prekäre Moment des Kippens durch die Materialüberlastung sowie die Kraft des Zusammenbrechens: im übertragenen Sinne also Momente der Konstruktion wie Destruktion, die gleichermaßen am künstlerischen Schaffensprozess teilhaben.

Not yet titled betitelt der Künstler augenzwinkernd seine Bodenskulptur und verweist dabei auf jenen entscheidenden Moment des Bestimmens in der Titelgebung wie Formfindung. Letztere wird in der gedanklichen Rekonstruktion unmittelbar einsichtig. Man könnte seine Skulptur mit ihren Platten, Faltungen und Verwerfungen als beschleunigte Versuchsanordnung, als künstlerisches Modell für tektonische Vorgänge in unermesslichen Zeiträumen (miss)verstehen, gewissermaßen als Simulation erdgeschichtlicher Phänomene. Einzig der Werkstoff verweigert sich einer derart einseitig naturhistorisch motivierten Lektüre, verweist Beton als funktionales Material und bautechnologische Sprache unmissverständlich auf industrielle Fertigungsprozesse in Architektur und Städtebau und steht geradezu exemplarisch für die Versprechungen der Moderne. Deren Utopie einer neuen Gesellschaft und deren urbanistische Visionen währten indes nicht lange: Beton, selbst wenn so innig besungen wie von dem deutschen Kabarettisten Gerhard Polt, verbindet man heute mit Nichtorten im innerstädtischen Raum, unwirtlichen Wohnbauten in den Agglomerationen, Resträumen zwischen Verkehrsinfrastrukturen oder generell der Verschandelung der Landschaft. Gelegentlich findet der Begriff als Metapher Verwendung für jene Endzeitstimmung, wie sie in der „No Future"-Haltung der Punkbewegung der späten 1970er Jahre anklingt, wo „Beton" für die Verkrustung der überlieferten gesellschaftlichen Klassenstruktur und des bürgerlichen Establishments steht, zumal Befestigungs- oder Bunkeranlagen bekanntlich aus ebendiesem Material erstellt werden.[1]

Werkstoff: Traditionen und Eigenschaften

Künstlerische Werkstoffe sind folglich nie einfach wertneutrale Materialien, sie verfügen über eine ihnen eigene Metaphorik, die den entstehenden Dingen eingeschrieben bleibt, genauso wie die Geschichte ihrer Anwendung und ihre kunsthistorischen Traditionen in jedem neuen Werk stets „mitschwingen". In der bildenden Kunst fand Beton nicht selten in architektonischem Zusammenhang Verwendung, zum Beispiel als „Kunst am Bau" in modernistischer Architektur, während sich die Baukunst ihrerseits dank der scheinbar grenzenlosen Möglichkeiten des „Béton brut" gleichermaßen skulptural ausformte. Dass Betonskulpturen in der Gegenwartskunst auf diese Traditionen zurückverweisen, erstaunt insofern wenig. Das geschieht indes in durchaus distanzierter Form, in den turmartigen Beton-Stelen von Isa Genzken (*1948) beispielsweise oder den skulpturalen Interventionen von Manfred Pernice (*1963). Letzterer greift in seinen „Betongüssen" die Formensprache realisierter Architekturen auf und transformiert isolierte Elemente in eigenartig hybride Objekte, deren Zweckbestimmung unsicher bleibt. Andere Künstler scheinen dem Werkstoff selbst bei klassischer Anwendung unerwartete Formen abzugewinnen: Lutz / Guggisberg (*1968 / 66) schaffen klein- bzw. mittelformatige Betonskulpturen, denen eine geradezu surreale Verspieltheit eigen ist. Kilian Rüthemann (*1979) wiederum trägt den dünnflüssigen Werkstoff im Spritzverfahren auf Wände auf und realisiert damit monumentale Raumzeichen, wobei er die Haftfähigkeit des profanen Baumaterials in der weißen Zelle des Ausstellungsraumes erprobt.

Christoph Weber faszinieren die Qualitäten des Werkstoffs: seine spezifische Formbarkeit, die Verarbeitung und das darin angelegte Gestaltungspotential. Es sind insbesondere der Prozess des Aushärtens und die Möglichkeit, dabei im richtigen Moment formend einzugreifen, die sich der Künstler im Gegensatz zu den Genannten für seine Werke zunutze macht. In diesem Sinne setzt er das Material Beton verschiedensten Kräften aus, hebt es an, legt es um, lässt es auseinanderbrechen .... Diese Bewegungen bleiben in der vollendeten Skulptur stets sichtbar: Das Werk ist gleichsam eingefrorener bzw. ausgehärteter Prozess. Selbst wenn es wie **not yet titled** auf den ersten Blick mächtig wirken mag, kommt nie der Eindruck von Monumentalität auf. Dennoch evoziert die Skulptur jene Metaphorik von Gewalt und Macht, die dem Werkstoff gleichsam inhärent ist. Allein, in den vom Künstler ausgelösten formalen Prozessen des Faltens und Einbrechens konserviert, erweitert er solche überlieferten Vorstellungen um entscheidende Momente wie Verletzlichkeit oder Fragilität und verdichtet seine Skulpturen zu inhaltlich vielschichtigen Metaphern zwischen Macht und Ohnmacht, Erschaffen und Zerstören ....

Rückblick: Prozesse in der Kunst

Op Losse Schroeven. Situaties en Cryptostructuren und *Live in Your Head. When Attitudes Become Form* hießen 1969 die beiden epochemachenden Ausstellungen im Stedelijk Museum Amsterdam bzw. in der Kunsthalle Bern. Zusammen mit der drei Jahre zuvor konzipierten Ausstellung *Eccentric Abstraction* in der New Yorker Fischbach Gallery haben sie wesentlich dazu beigetragen, einem erweiterten Skulpturbegriff zum Durchbruch zu verhelfen. Dieser überwand die neutrale Form und rigide Strenge der Minimal Art. Die sogenannte Postminimal Art stellte eine bewusste Abkehr von den Positionen eines Donald Judd dar und brach mit dem traditionellen Verständnis des Kunstwerks als Artefakt – zugunsten von eher prozesshaften Ansätzen. Zudem ergänzten Künstlerinnen und Künstler wie Eva Hesse, Richard Serra oder Keith Sonnier den Kanon der Werkstoffe um bislang unerprobte Materialien wie Neon, Latex, Polyester, Fiberglas, u.a.m., die sie stets in ihrer Materialität sichtbar zu machen suchten. „Anti-illusionistisch" wurde diese Kunst genannt, indem sie die Beschaffenheit der Werkstoffe und die Spuren des Schaffensprozesses nicht leugnete, sondern im Gegenteil gezielt nutzte. Nicht zuletzt zeichnete sich die Postminimal Art durch die erfrischende Art und Weise aus, wie Werke sich zum Raum verhalten: Sie kommen aus der Wand, hängen von der Decke, verspannen die Wände, besetzen den Durchgang .... Gleiches lässt sich vierzig Jahre später von Christoph Webers Skulpturen behaupten: Auch sie baumeln von der Decke, lehnen sich an die Wand, hängen ebendort, liegen auf dem Boden oder besetzen den Raum wie **not yet titled**. Bei letzterer verwandelt der Künstler die minimalistisch-strenge Form einer Betonplatte durch einen gezielten Prozess in eine letztlich nicht vollends kontrollierbare Form und führt im Werk gleichsam die Überwindung der gestrengen Ästhetik der Minimal Art vor.

Im Raum zeitgenössischer Skulptur

Die Ausstellung *Post / Postminimal* im Kunstmuseum St. Gallen konfrontierte 2014 herausragende Werkgruppen der Postminimal Art – Bill Bollinger,

Gary Kuehn, Richard Serra, Keith Sonnier – mit Skulpturen zeitgenössischer Kunstschaffender von Katinka Bock bis Christoph Weber. Sie alle griffen in ihrem Schaffen die skulpturalen Möglichkeiten der späten 1960er- und frühen 1970er-Jahre auf. Im Gegensatz zu damals geht es heute indes weniger um eine kulturelle und gesellschaftliche Revolution, um ein Überwinden eines künstlerischen Kanons, sondern eher um deren inhaltliche und materielle Neubestimmung. Die künstlerischen Ansätze müssen sich nicht mehr als heftige Geste bzw. als radikaler Bruch mit der Tradition bestimmen, sondern bauen vielmehr ganz selbstverständlich auf den formalen Recherchen der Vergangenheit auf, verbinden diese mit den Erfahrungen von heute und schaffen Werke, die von einer eigenen Sensibilität getragen sind und die Möglichkeiten zeitgenössischer Skulptur in unterschiedlichster Richtung souverän ausloten. Das zeigt sich exemplarisch in den vier in der Ausstellung gezeigten Skulpturen von Christoph Weber: **Beton (gehoben)**, **Beton (gerollt)**, **Beton (gewickelt)** und **not yet titled**.

Im Begleittext zur Ausstellung fasst Céline Gaillard wesentliche Momente seines künstlerischen Ansatzes zusammen: „Für ihn [den Künstler] sind sowohl Beschaffenheit wie Symbolkraft des Materials von immanenter Bedeutung. Damit lässt sich im Prozess des Trocknens der Akt der Bearbeitung als performatives Moment sichtbar machen. Einer Versuchsreihe gleich lotet Weber die Möglichkeiten des Werkstoffs aus, indem er den idealen Moment der Härtung sucht. Ob gehoben oder gerollt trotzt er diesem geradezu archetypischen Baumaterial des 20. Jahrhunderts unterschiedliche Zustände ab, die dem üblichen industriellen Gebrauch des Betons grundsätzlich widersprechen. Weber [...] spielt im Grunde mit den Materialeigenschaften genauso wie mit den Gebrauchskonventionen.“[2] Thomas Trummer spricht im Zusammenhang mit diesen Betonskulpturen vom „Stresstest des Dinglichen“[3] und eröffnet metaphorisch jene für die zeitgenössische Kunst so entscheidende Doppelperspektive – auf die materiellen Eigenschaften zum einen und auf die inhaltliche Dimension zum andern. Gerade in deren enger Verschränkung, im Material angelegt und zugleich gedanklich überhöht, scheint mir das eminent Zeitgenössische von Christoph Webers Skulptur zu liegen. Sie zeichnet sich eben nicht allein nur durch ihre Stofflichkeit und die damit zusammenhängenden künstlerischen Prozesse aus, sondern gleichermaßen durch das metaphorische Potenzial, das in den Dingen selbst angelegt ist und durch künstlerische Transformationen im Grunde erst sichtbar wird. In diesem Sinne handelt Christoph Webers Skulptur von ihrem materiellen Grund, ihrer Entstehung, sie ist zugleich Sinnbild für die prekäre „conditio humana“ einer Welt, wie sie Gerhard Polt so kongenial besingt als „Paradies aus Farbig-Beton.“

1 Vgl. dazu Thomas Trummer, „Precariously Balanced Roughness“, in: *RES*, Juni 2013, S. 50–54. Deutsches Manuskript unpubliziert. Der Autor verweist auf die symbolische Macht von Beton, explizit auf die Punk-Bewegung der 1970er Jahre, sowie die Hausbesetzerszene und die Anti-Atomkraft-Bewegung.

2 Céline Gaillard, „Saalblatt“ zur Ausstellung *Post / Postminimal. Die Sammlung Rolf Ricke im Dialog mit zeitgenössischen Kunstschaffenden*, Kunstmuseum St.Gallen, 2014, unpubliziert.

3 Siehe Trummer, S. 50.

Methodologie und Prozess.

Über die Entwicklung Christoph Webers nachvollziehender Handlungen mit Material

Fiona Liewehr

In einem vorbereitenden Gespräch mit Christoph Weber zu diesem Text bezeichnet er seine künstlerische Entwicklung als eine „vom methodologischen Nachvollzug" ausgehende Praxis bei früheren Arbeiten hin zum Handeln mit und gegen ausschließlich ein Material: Beton. Bereits die Titel der Skulpturen **Beton (gehoben)**, **Beton (gefaltet)**, **Beton (gerollt)**, beschreiben prozessuale Vorgänge, die den üblichen Gebrauchskonventionen des Materials geradezu zu widersprechen scheinen, verbindet man den archetypischen Baustoff des 20. Jahrhunderts doch mit Formstabilität, Massivität und Unverrückbarkeit, Härte und Belastbarkeit. Doch wickelt sich der Beton in Bündel elegant um Bewehrungseisen, quillt in **Beton (gerollt)** aus einer an der Wand hängenden Abdeckplane, biegt sich in **Beton (gewickelt)** bzw. **not yet titled** geschmeidig über Holz und Stahlplatten, steht in **bent inversion** filigran, wie ein unsicherer Körper an die Wand gelehnt oder scheint, zu einer Art Wippe oder Bogen geformt, auf dem Boden zu balancieren und seiner eigenen Schwerkraft zu widerstreben. Die Arbeiten wirken roh und weich zugleich, massiv und doch fragil, starr und beweglich, wie geronnene Zeit, die einen Augenblick festzuhalten und eine Handlung zu konservieren scheint, um sie für den Betrachter sichtbar zu machen. Die gründliche Vorbereitung der Gussform und das genaue Wissen um den Aushärtungsvorgang von Beton sind für das finale Ergebnis ausschlaggebend. In dem Moment in dem sich der Aggregatzustand von zähflüssig zu fest transformiert, hebt, kippt oder faltet Weber den Beton und zwingt ihm eine Form auf, für die das Material ursprünglich nicht vorgesehen ist. Zufall ist genauso intendiert wie das Scheitern ein ständiger – wenngleich durchaus konstruktiv verstandener – Begleiter seiner experimentellen Versuchsfolgen ist.

Christoph Weber interessiert die Prozessualität und die kontextuelle Verschiebung durch die substantielle Metamorphose vom Formlosen zum Konkreten,

Beton (gehoben) → p. 90
Beton (gefaltet) → p. 66
Beton (gerollt) → p. 92
Bündel → p. 102
Beton (gewickelt) → p. 58
not yet titled → p. 56
bent inversion → p. 82 / 98
Contradiction → p. 104
Schade, dass Beton nicht brennt → p. 74 / 78
Untitled (Gegenstück) → p. 150
Untitled (Ramponeau) → p. 126
Objets externes → p. 140 / 142
Untitled (Chunks) → p. 144
Trauma → p. 134

innerhalb derer er das Material einer extremen Belastungsprobe aussetzt. Anstatt *a priori* vollkommen festgelegt werden zu können, bestimmt das Material durch seine physikalischen Eigenschaften und seinen Herstellungsprozess die Form der Werke. In seinen jüngeren Betonskulpturen manifestieren sich Webers performative Handlungen und die Prozessualität des Materials in gleichsam „schockgefrorenen"[1] Formen.

Selbst wenn der künstlerische Handlungsakt und die schier unendlich scheinenden Gestaltungsmöglichkeiten von Beton im Mittelpunkt zu stehen scheinen, so ist Christoph Webers Werk jedoch keineswegs aus rein formalen Gesichtspunkten zu betrachten. Er ist stets auch an inhaltlichen Dimensionen interessiert, an dem, was er – wie eingangs erwähnt – den „methodologischen Nachvollzug" nennt. Entscheidend ist für ihn die Suche nach einer bestimmten Technik der Umsetzung von Konzepten, nach den Kriterien, wann und warum eine bestimmte künstlerische Methode und Material zur Anwendung kommen muss. Ausgangspunkt ist demnach die konzeptionelle Analyse, die Idee eines Gegenstandes, der die Wahl des Materials und den Umsetzungsprozess nach sieht zieht, selbst wenn dieser wiederum – trotz aller künstlerischen Beherrschung – immer auch unberechenbar bleibt.

Mehrfach spricht Weber davon, dass Beton für ihn ein Material der Gewalt sei, eines das für Zerstörung, für Okkupation steht. Tatsächlich können seine ersten Betonarbeiten genau diesen Eindruck auf den Betrachter hinterlassen. Da stechen Bewehrungseisen in **Contradiction** gefährlich aus der Wand in den Raum, während sie gleichzeitig in ihrer systematischen Akkuratheit dem sorgfältig freigelegten Betonquadrat als fast melancholischer „Bildrahmen" dienen, da besetzen mittels Flammenwerfer gewaltsam aus ihrer Verschalung befreite Betonquader in **Schade, dass Beton nicht brennt** den Raum, die gleichzeitig von Verletzlichkeit und einer fast sentimentalen malerischen Schönheit zeugen.

Stets ist Christoph Webers Arbeiten eine Dichotomie von Aufbau und Zerstörung, von Gewalt und Sanftheit, von Depression und Hoffnung inhärent, ist ihnen eine „lakonische Traurigkeit"[2] eigen, wie sie der Künstler selbst nennt. Keine anderen Skulpturen vermitteln diese Dichotomie besser als eine Serie von Arbeiten, die alle mit **Untitled (Gegenstück)**, ab 2010 betitelt sind. Immer stehen sich zwei monolithische Betonquader, durch einen Riss getrennt, einander gegenüber und scheinen aus einem massiven Block gebrochen zu sein. Während dem einen der Quader ein riesiges Eckstück fehlt, findet dieses in dem Gegenstück eine exakte Entsprechung. Aufgrund der teilweise glatt verbleibenden Flächen zwischen den beiden Quadern offenbart sich die Absurdität des Bruches und somit der künstliche Herstellungsprozess: ein Quader wurde in Beton gegossen und nach der Aushärtung eine Ecke herausgeschlagen. Die Oberfläche der so entstandenen Bruchstelle wurde in Silikonkautschuk ab- und gegenabgeformt und als Ergänzung der Gussform des zweiten, danach gegossenen Quaders hinzugefügt. Die beiden Objekte verweisen darauf, dass nicht nur die dem Werkstoff eingeschriebene Metaphorik sondern auch die spezifische Beschaffenheit des Materials Christoph Webers künstlerischer Praxis besonders entgegenkommt. Als künstliches Gestein durchläuft Beton verschiedene Aggregatzustände von flüssig zu fest und lässt sich demnach in eine zuvor festgelegte Form gießen, sowie in gehärtetem Zustand bildhauerisch bearbeiten. Beton ermöglicht zugleich „Plastik", die im additiven Verfahren durch Materialzufügung zustande kommende Form als auch „Skulptur", das im subtraktiven Verfahren durch Abarbeiten geschaffene Werk.

Webers Gegenstücke folgen stets der gleichen Vorgangsweise: Einem rationell kalkulierten Aufbau folgt die physische Zerstörung, die wiederum Voraussetzung für einen neuerlichen Aufbau ist. Konstruktion bedingt Dekonstruktion und umgekehrt. Entscheidend bleibt dabei stets die menschliche Beherrschbarkeit. Nie würde Christoph Weber sein prozessorientiertes Handeln zugunsten eines rein maschinellen Verfahrens aufgeben; nie würde er, wie beispielsweise die Minimalisten, maß- oder massengefertigte Industrieprodukte verwenden. Selbst wenn seine Skulpturen durch ihre Formensprache an die der Minimal Art erinnern, leugnen sie nie die Spuren ihrer Produktionsbedingungen, bleibt die Beschaffenheit des Werkstoffes stets sichtbar und transportieren sie nie die rigide Selbstreferenzialität und kühle Strenge der Minimal Art. Auch die teilweise übermannshohen, tonnenschweren Gegenstücke werden von Christoph Weber alleine manuell bearbeitet, nur während der Ausschalung und Versetzung der Betonblöcke greift er auf einen Kran und die Hilfe von Assistenten zurück. In diesem Sinne ist Weber ganz klassischer Bildhauer, der sich an seinen Werkstücken abarbeiten muss.

Nicht immer war Beton vorrangiges künstlerisches Material seiner Skulpturen, immer schon ging es aber um den „methodologischen Nachvollzug", um die Bedeutungsträgerschaft von Materialien, um Fragen von Konstruktion und Dekonstruktion oder, ganz allgemein gesprochen, um die unauflösbare Verschränkung von materiellen, formalen und inhaltlichen Dimensionen. Im Unterschied zu den aktuellen Betonskulpturen tragen Webers ältere Arbeiten ihre Materialität nicht offen zur Schau, sondern die verwendeten Werkstoffe wurden derart bearbeitet und transformiert, dass sie auf die Metaphorik anderer Materialien oder Objekte verwiesen. Während sie früher auf historische oder gesellschaftspolitische Implikationen deuteten, sind diese im Beton selbst bereits eingeschrieben. Die intermediale Transformation von einem Werkstoff zu einem anders aussehenden und anders konnotierten wird nun innerhalb des Materials und dessen Aggregatzuständen verhandelt.

In seiner Installation **Untitled (Ramponeau)** arrangiert Weber beispielsweise Pflastersteine aus Papiermaché, deren Vorlage ein aus der rue Ramponeau heraus gebrochener Stein ist, in der 1871 die letzte Barrikade der Pariser Kommune stand. Indem Christoph Weber für das Papiermaché ausschließlich Bücher verwendet, die vor dem Revolutionsjahr erschienen sind, schreibt er den abstrakten Objekten nicht nur einen konkreten historischen Diskurs ein, sondern stellt auch Fragen nach dem Wechselverhältnis von Fiktion und Realität, von Signifikant und Signifikat. Ähnliche Prozesse durchläuft das Material in den **Objets externes**, für die er Oberflächenstrukturen von Häuserfassaden mit Silikonkautschuk abgenommen, sie mit koloriertem Wachs zu Platten gegossen und zu post-minimalistisch anmutenden Kuben gefaltet hat. Durch die Abformung mit Silikon blieb jedes einzelne Detail und die genaue Oberflächenbeschaffenheit der Fassaden sichtbar und verhandelt Fragestellungen zu Kategorien von Öffentlichem und Privatem, von Außen- und Innenraum. Da die Texturen einiger der Fassaden längst Veränderungen oder Übermalungen unterworfen wurden, können die Objekte als eine Art Time Capsule gelesen werden, in der historische Informationen der Vergangenheit für die Gegenwart und Zukunft einerseits eingeschrieben anderseits durch die spezifische Materialeigenschaft der Veränderung und Vergänglichkeit preisgegeben werden.

Entscheidend für den „Nachvollzug" eines historischen oder persönlich erlebten Ereignisses ist die Erinnerung. Sigmund Freud definierte 1914 das Erinnern, Wiederholen und Durcharbeiten als Methode um ein traumatisches Erlebnis durch die Vergegenwärtigung der Vergangenheit zu verarbeiten.[3] Jacques Lacan hat Freuds Theorie 1953 neu interpretiert und insofern radikalisiert, als er die Wiederholung als symbolischen Akt gegen die Erinnerung als imaginären Akt beschrieben hat.[4] Die Wiederholung wird von der postmodernen Philosophie als positive Möglichkeit von Handlung, als Tat der Differenz gesehen, da ein „Wieder" nie zur selben Zeit stattfindet und diese selbst den Unterschied setzt. Durch den Akt der Wiederholung wird Erinnerung produziert, die Tat soll einen Unterschied zum Wiederholten setzen und Anderes, Neues möglich machen. Die Handlung selbst setzt die Differenz.

In Arbeiten wie **Untitled (Chunks)** oder **Trauma** setzt sich Weber bewusst mit der Thematik von Wiederholung als Mittel der Vergegenwärtigung von verdrängten Ängsten und Erinnerungen auseinander. Beiden geht ein Akt der Zerstörung der Wiederholung voraus. Für **Untitled (Chunks)** vervielfältigte er einen zuvor gewaltsam auseinander gebrochenen Betonblock täuschend echt aus grau gefärbtem, gipsartigem Kunststoff und stellte die Blöcke akkurat hintereinander gereiht in den Raum. Die Installation mag wie eine wehrhafte Barrikade anmuten, dennoch wird der gewaltsame Akt durch die exakte Wiederholung seiner Form und räumlichen Inszenierung ins Absurde verkehrt. Eine Absurdität und Künstlichkeit, die sich hier insofern direkter als in späteren Skulpturen offenbart, als sie nur auf den Werkstoff Beton verweisen als tatsächlich daraus gemacht zu sein. Ebenso spielt **Trauma** mit der Verunsicherung, die sich durch die exakte mehrfache Wiederholung von Zerstörung einstellt. Weber zersplitterte mit einer Axt eine Zimmertüre, formte die Bruchstelle sorgfältig mit Silikonkautschuk ab und übertrug die Abgüsse auf sechs identische Türen. Das Arrangement der Türen in einem geschlossenen Raum, der lediglich durch das Loch der originalen Türe den Blick auf die exakt identisch gebrochenen Kopien zulässt, kann als Verweis auf die zerstörerische Kraft des Menschen und die psychischen Traumata sowohl bei den Tätern, als auch bei den Opfern gelesen werden.

In all seinen Arbeiten setzt sich Christoph Weber mit Realität, deren Wiedergabe und Wahrnehmungsmechanismen auseinander, untersucht Begriffe, Vorstellungsmuster und gesellschaftspolitische Ordnungssysteme. Konstitutiv ist eine inhaltlich-konzeptionelle wie formal-materielle Doppelbödigkeit seiner Werke, die eine Dichotomie von Zerstörung und Aufbau, von Dekonstruktion und Konstruktion in sich tragen. Nie sind sie entweder das Eine oder das Andere, sie sind stets Beides zugleich: verstörend und versöhnlich, massiv und verletzlich, aggressiv und passiv, grob-unbeherrscht und elegant-sinnlich und damit stets menschlich. Christoph Webers künstlerischer Weg führte von der kontextuellen Verschiebung durch Materialtransfer zur derzeitigen ausschließlichen Verwendung von Beton, innerhalb dessen formale wie inhaltliche Implikationen verhandelt werden. Man mag auch eine Veränderung im Materialumgang allgemein konstatieren: während in früheren Arbeiten der Akt und die Wiederholung von Zerstörung teilweise eine bestimmende Rolle spielen und diese noch in den verbrannten Betonskulpturen und in den entzweiten massiven Gegenstücken ablesbar sind, mögen die jüngsten Arbeiten von einem selbstsicheren, fast spielerischen Umgang zeugen. Beton ist für Christoph Weber zur Selbstverständlichkeit geworden. Dem Kampf gegen das Material ist ein Spiel mit und innerhalb des Materials gewichen. Bleibend ist der „methodologische und prozessuale Nachvollzug", ein Akt der in seiner jeweiligen Zeitlichkeit nie affirmative Bestätigung sondern stets einer von Vergegenwärtigung, Differenzierung und Versuch sein kann.

1 Thomas Trummer, „Precariously Balanced Roughness", in: *RES*, Juni 2013, S. 50–54, hier S. 52.

2 Weber spricht in diesem Zusammenhang auch über Literatur, dezidiert über die Werke Thomas Bernhards und über Erich Kästners Großstadtroman *Fabian*, deren „lakonischer Traurigkeit" er sich zutiefst verbunden fühlt. Unveröffentlichtes Interview mit Timothée Chaillou, Jänner 2012.

3 Sigmund Freud prägte 1914 in einem kurzen Artikel den Begriff „Durcharbeiten" als psychoanalytische Technik, die auf der Annahme basiert, dass das Erinnern an einen belastenden Vorfall und das Wiederholen für eine dauerhafte Veränderung nicht ausreichen. Siehe: Sigmund Freud, „Erinnern, Wiederholen und Durcharbeiten (Weitere Ratschläge zur Technik der Psychoanalyse, II)", in: *Internationale Zeitschrift für ärztliche Psychoanalyse*, Bd. 2 (1914), S. 485–491; Gesammelte Werke, Bd. 10, S. 126–136.

4 Siehe dazu insbesondere: Jaques Lacan, *Buch I (1953–1954): Freuds technische Schriften*, Weinheim und Berlin: Quadriga, 1990.

Pflastersteine aus Pappmaché Zur Arbeit **Untitled (Ramponeau)** von Christoph Weber

Jens Kastner

Übrigens kann ich Ihnen kein einziges ungewöhnliches Ereignis aus den Jahren 1870–71 erzählen. Ich teilte meine Zeit zwischen der Landschaft und dem Atelier.

Paul Cézanne
(in einem Brief an Ambroise Vollard)[1]

Dass Paul Cézanne, Wegbereiter der modernen Kunst, aus den Jahren 1870/71 nichts Nennenswertes zu berichten weiß, ist bemerkenswert.[2] Immerhin fiel in diese Zeit ein Ereignis, das dem russischen Sozialrevolutionär und Zeitzeugen Pjotr L. Lawrow zufolge „den Sozialisten aller Schattierungen nicht irgendein besonderes Organisationsprogramm, nicht irgendein isoliertes Dogma, sondern jene Ansätze [brachte], die wesentlich die historischen Bedingungen für den bewussten Kampf des Proletariats [...] gegen seine Unterdrücker geschaffen haben"[3]: Die Pariser Kommune.

Cézanne aber konzentrierte sich auf Landschaft und Atelier.[4] Das ist letztlich die paradigmatische Haltung des Künstlers im frisch autonomisierten Feld der Kunst, in dem sich die Radikalität künstlerischer Formgebung von jener politisch-emanzipatorischer Kämpfe abgekoppelt hat. Seither wird Vermittlung versucht. Nicht, dass es nicht politische Kunst oder Kunst mit Politik die gesamte Geschichte der künstlerischen und gesellschaftlichen Moderne hindurch immer gegeben hätte. Gerade für diese am Politischen orientierte Kunst war das Jahr 1871 ein Ausgangs- und Bezugspunkt. Hier hatten auch damals schon namhafte Kunstgrößen wie Gustave Courbet oder Camille Pissarro mit den Aufständischen sympathisiert und den Anlass für die wechselhafte Geschichte der „Verkettung von Kunst und Revolution"[5] markiert. Und dennoch: die Kunstproduktion, die sich auf politisches Engagement einlässt, die motivisch oder inhaltlich mit Politik hantiert oder in der Produzentinnen und Produzenten einfach eine politische Haltung manifestieren wollen, ist seit der Etablierung jenes gesellschaftlichen Sonderbereiches, der gemeinhin „Kunst" genannt wird, in besonderem Maße legitimationsbedürftig.[6]

Untitled (Ramponeau) → p. 126
Untitled (rue Ramponeau) → p. 124
Untitled → p. 130

Der Zugriff auf oder gar der Eingriff in das Politische bedarf einer Vermittlung mit dem Anspruch auf künstlerische Eigengesetzlichkeit. Solche vermittelnde Ansätze hat es viele gegeben, die Arbeit von Christoph Weber ist eine davon. Allerdings eine besonders konsequente. Dies schon deshalb, weil sie sich mit **Untitled (Ramponeau)** an jenen Ort und jene Zeit zurückbegibt, an und in der die Genese der Abkoppelung spätestens ansetzen muss: wo der „Wegbereiter der Moderne" schon gar nicht mehr mitbekommen will, was im Bereich der sozialen und politischen Kämpfe geschieht und seither Gedenken „in allen Sprachen der zivilisierten Welt"[7] auf und nach sich gezogen hat.[8]

Weber hat dort einen Pflasterstein entnommen, wo im Mai 1871 die letzte Barrikade der Kommune stand, in der Rue Ramponeau. Mit Pappmaché, hergestellt aus Büchern aus dem selben Jahr (oder älter), hat er diesen Stein repliziert und einige davon aufgehäuft. Grau-bräunlich schimmernd geben sie noch den einen oder anderen Wortfetzen preis. Sie verbergen nicht, aus dem falschen Material zu sein.[9]

Sie stapeln und streuen sich somit einerseits ein in die anderen Arbeiten des Künstlers, in denen es um Fragen des Materials geht, welche Gebrauchsweisen es jeweils hergibt und was es zu sagen hat. Weber knickt, faltet oder kippt Beton und das ruft natürlich Irritationen hervor. Das sind, wenn man so will, Akte der Respektlosigkeit gegenüber der Stabilität und Bombastik, die den Beton – neben Glas und Stahl – zum paradigmatischen Zeichen der ökonomischen Modernisierung und damit selbstverständlich auch zum Referenzmaterial in der Kunst haben werden lassen. Das Ungewohnte und Überraschende, das der gefaltete Beton auslöst, tritt den Betrachtenden sicherlich auch in den Steinen aus Papier entgegen. Aber sie leisten noch mehr. Sie tragen nämlich andererseits auch noch zur Reflexion über die künstlerischen Prozesse des Aufgreifens und Adaptierens und der Verwertung und Inwertsetzung bei.

Denn anders als der Beton sind Webers Pflastersteine nicht aus wertlosem Zeug wie Sand hergestellt, sondern aus selbst bereits Wertvollem, aus – mit Pierre Bourdieu gesprochen – „objektiviertem Kulturkapital"[10], nämlich aus alten Büchern. Die Empörung, die deren Zerstörung bei den Gebildeten normalerweise auslösen würde, kann allein durch ihre Kunstwerdung abgefangen werden.[11] Weber und seine wuchtigen Papiersteine führen damit auch verschiedene Legitimationsmodi vor: Welches Material ist in welchem Zustand und in welchem Kontext etwas wert? Und sie zeigen die Fragilität solcher

1 Zit. n. Ulrike Becks-Malorny. *Paul Cézanne (1839–1906). Wegbereiter der Moderne*, Köln, London u.a.: Taschen Verlag, 2007, S. 19.

2 Ich danke Tom Holert für seine kritischen wie hilfreichen Anmerkungen zu diesem Text.

3 Pjotr L. Lawrow, *Die Pariser Kommune. Geschehnisse – Einfluss – Lehren*. [1880], Münster: Unrast Verlag, 2003, S. 182.

4 Dass diese Konzentration nicht Ausnahme, sondern die anerkannte Regel ist, weil sie sich ganz dem widmet, was sich als das Eigentliche der Kunst etabliert hatte – Wahrnehmen und Formgeben – ist vielfach bestätigt worden. „Es gibt keinen Zweifel" schrieb etwa der Kunsthistoriker Herbert Read über Cézanne, „dass das, was wir die Bewegung der Moderne in der Kunst nennen, mit der zielstrebigen Bestimmtheit eines Französischen Malers begann, die Welt objektiv zu sehen." Herbert Read, *A Concise History of Modern Painting*, [1959] London: Thames & Hudson, 2006, S. 13 [Übers. J.K.]

5 Gerald Raunig, *Kunst und Revolution. Künstlerischer Aktivismus im langen 20. Jahrhundert*, Wien: Turia + Kant, 2005, S. 7 und S. 63ff. Auch die 2007 von Charles Esche und Will Bradley organisierte Ausstellung in der Tate London und im Vanabbemuseum Eindhoven und die dazugehörige Textsammlung zum Verhältnis von Kunstproduktion und sozialem Wandel setzt programmatisch mit der Pariser Kommune ein, vgl. Charles Esche und Will Bradley (Hg.), *Art and Social Change. A Critical Reader*, London: Tate/Afterall, 2007.

6 Vgl. u.a. Helmut Draxler: „Der Fluch der guten Tat. Autonomieanspruch und Ideologieverdacht in der politischen Kunst", in: *Texte zur Kunst, Nr. 80*, Dezember 2010, S. 34–41.

7 Pjotr L. Lawrow, *Die Pariser Kommune*, a.a.O., S. 181.

8 Mit solch historischer wie materieller Treffsicherheit hat Weber auch die Arbeit (*Untitled [Kupferstich, 1631]*, 2008) produziert: In ihr sind Kupferstreifen in Form modifizierter Rauchwolken an die Wand montiert. Sie sind den Linien aus einer Karikatur von einem Flugblatt aus dem Jahr 1631 nachempfunden, als während des 30jährigen Krieges Flugblätter gerade erfunden und – wegen der hohen Analphabetenrate – auf visuelle Elemente stark angewiesen waren.

9 Teil der Arbeit ist auch noch ein Foto von der Straße mit dem tatsächlich fehlenden Stein und eine Kiste mit nicht mehr oder noch nicht gebrauchten alten Büchern.

10 Pierre Bourdieu, „Ökonomisches Kapital – Kulturelles Kapital – Soziales Kapital", in: ders., *Die verborgenen Mechanismen der Macht. Schriften zu Politik & Kultur I*, Hamburg: VSA, 2005, S. 49–79, hier S. 59f.

Legitimierungsweisen auf. Was heute für die einen wertvoll ist, kann zugleich und erst recht am nächsten Tag schon für die anderen wertlos sein. Es ist selbstverständlich nicht ganz so arbiträr und kontingent, weil es Normen und Institutionen gibt, die die relative Dauerhaftigkeit von Wert garantieren, aber das Prinzip ist klar: Wert von Bestand muss hergestellt und kann nur geschaffen werden, indem sich bestimmte Bedeutungen in sozialen Kämpfen durchsetzen und etablieren. Damit sind nicht allein Auseinandersetzungen im Format Pflasterstein gegen Polizeiknüppel gemeint, sondern soziale Kämpfe beschreiben vielmehr das Ringen um legitime Sichtweisen, um Geltung und Gültigkeit von Werten, Normen und Bedeutungen, also ein allgemeines Prinzip gesellschaftlicher Dynamiken.

Hier, in diesem Kämpfen um Bedeutung, sind sich Kunstproduktion und Straßenproteste schließlich immer am nächsten, auch wenn sie nach sehr unterschiedlichen Regeln funktionieren.

Die Regeln der Kunst haben eine wichtige Tradition erzeugt, in der die bei Cézanne schon angelegte, objektivierende Grundhaltung – „die Welt *objektiv* zu sehen“ (Read) – stets weiter verschärft wurde, um vor allem persönlichen Ausdruck, aber auch verschlüsselte Narration überhaupt, aus der Kunst auszuschließen. Ein Konzentrationsprozess zieht sich durch die moderne Kunst, in dem das Spiel mit den Materialien entscheidender wird (für „gute Kunst“) als das, was mit ihnen dargestellt werden kann. Dabei hatte dieses Spiel häufig weniger spielerischen als eher analytischen Charakter: ein Durchspielen von Möglichkeiten. Die 137 Schamottsteine, die mit der schmalen Seite nach oben vom Minimal Art-Künstler Carl Andre in eine Reihe auf den Boden gelegt worden waren (*Lever*, 1966), sollten nicht mehr entziffert und dekodiert, sondern vor allem als Material im Raum erfahren werden.[12]

Diese vermeintlich abschließende Reinigung der Kunst von allen ihr als äußerlich postulierten Aspekten allerdings blieb in seinen Effekten immer ambivalent. Die Einbeziehung der Betrachtenden (in dieser Raumerfahrung etwa) mündete schließlich immer auch in der Frage nach den sozialen und kulturellen Ordnungssystemen, denen diese angehören. Zwar sollten bestehende Muster und Raster (des Denkens und der Wahrnehmung) nicht über die Entschlüsselung und Informationsverarbeitung ins Wanken gebracht werden, wohl aber über die Erfahrung mit dem Material im Raum. Es ging um die etablierten und prägenden Räume von Vor- und Darstellungen, auf deren Erschütterung die von noch so metaphysischem Firlefanz entledigte Kunst häufig setzte.[13] Zumindest der von Carl Andre verkörperte Strang der Radikalisierung künstlerischer Verfahren trifft in seinen Effekten so schon wieder auf die andere Tradition, die der gewollten künstlerischen Einmischung ins Politische: „Maler bauen Barrikaden“ (Ludwig Rubiner).[14]

Gleichzeitig brachten auch die verfeinerten Sichtweisen auf die innerhalb der Regeln des Politischen auftretenden Aktionsformen neue Einsichten hervor. Im kollektiven Protest wurde nicht mehr nur die gleichsam strukturlogische Reaktion auf Not und Unrecht erkannt, sondern eine ungeahnte Bandbreite an Motivationen gesichtet. Etwa die Diskrepanzen in den Vorstellungen von der Welt (oder auch nur der eigenen Situation), wie sie vorgefunden wird und wie sie sein könnte oder sollte. Soziale Bewegungen wurden gewissermaßen als Produzentinnen von Bedeutungen entdeckt, die weit über die Artikulation ihrer konkreten Forderungen hinausgehen.[15]
Sie agieren auf dem Terrain von Konnotationen, von Definitionen und Klassifikationen, die den ganzen sozialen Raum betreffen. Mit den Neuen Sozialen Bewegungen seit den 1960er Jahren geriet also die Dimension von Kultur, verstanden als Praktiken und Prozesse der Sinn- und Bedeutungsgebung, ins Zentrum der Bewegungsforschung. Aber auch in den tatsächlichen Auseinandersetzungen, nicht nur in der sozialwissenschaftlichen Rezeption, hatte diese Dimension mehr Gewicht bekommen.

Die Praktiken selbst also schienen diesen Fokus zu rechtfertigen: Im legendären Mai 1968 etwa gab es – um ein hier relevantes Beispiel zu nennen – Barrikaden, aber sie waren weniger militärischer als vielmehr ästhetischer Art. Das Auftürmen der Pflastersteine während der Kommune diente noch vornehmlich militärischen Zwecken, der Abwehr des Gegners. Aber bereits hier wurden moralische Wälle gleich mit aufgebaut und die Barrikaden förderten, wie Carl Douglas aufgezeigt hat, dazu noch die Entstehung eines sichtbaren Kollektivsubjektes „as a communal construction“[16]. In der Revolte von 1968 waren sie dann vollends des militärischen Zweckes entledigt. „Die Barrikaden von Paris in der Nacht vom 10. auf den 11. Mai 68 sind ein historisches Zitat“, schreibt Ingrid Gilcher-Holtey in ihrer Analyse der Bewegung.[17] „Errichtet von Schülern und Studenten in Kenntnis der Bedeutung der Barrikaden in den Tagen der Commune und während der Befreiung der Stadt von der deutschen Besatzung, beschwören sie die Erinnerung an diese historischen Vorbilder, doch erweisen sie sich in Form und Zielsetzung nicht als deren Abbilder."[18] Diese Barrikaden waren also bloß Zitate und dennoch (oder gerade auch in dieser Form) waren sie Einsätze im Kampf: um das historische Gedächtnis ebenso wie um die Vorstellungen von einer anderen Welt, um Utopien.

Die Arbeit **Untitled (Ramponeau)** reagiert schließlich auf beide Entwicklungen – jene in der Kunst und die in den und hinsichtlich der sozialen Bewegungen. Sie betont erstens die Prozesse der Ver- und Umwertung von Material als zentrale für die Kunstproduktion. Sie hat somit weder mit der Materialfixierung im puristischen Setzungsakt der Minimal Art viel zu tun, noch mit dem Übergang in aktivistische Logiken und der damit verbundenen Auflösung von Ambiguitäten, wie sie etwa in den 1968 vom brasilianischen Konzeptualisten Antonio Dias auf einen Galerieboden gelegten handgroßen Steinen zum Ausdruck kommen. An jedem Stein hing ein kleines Schild mit der Aufschrift „To the Police" (*To the Police*, 1968). Weniger als um das Aktivistisch-Werden der Kunst und die Übertretung des „Dispositionsrahmen(s) ‚Gegenwartskunst'"[19] geht es Weber um das Ausschöpfen der Bedingungen und Möglichkeiten dieser Kunst-Dispositionen und ihrer Rahmungen.

Die Arbeit integriert – zweitens – den performativen Recyclingaspekt politischer Kämpfe, in denen das Aufschichten von Mülltonnen, Autos und anderen Alltagsgegenständen zu Barrikaden sich auf *vorherige* Gefechte bezieht und zugleich die *gegenwärtige* Infragestellung bestehender Wertesysteme symbolisiert. (Mit „integriert" ist gemeint, dass die Steine aus Pappmaché einige der neuen Logiken der politischen Aktion bereits in sich aufgenommen haben: das Verfahren des Aufgreifens und Umwertens des Materials weiß – es kennt die Zitatbarrikaden von 68 oder ähnliche Vorgänge – wie wichtig ein austariertes Verhältnis von Geschichtsverhaftetheit und Zukunftsorientierung für die effektive Durchsetzung politischer Vorstellungen ist.)

Was hier als Annäherungstendenz zwischen Aktivismus und Kunstproduktion beschrieben wurde – Wertsetzung und Umwertung von Vorstellungen in materiellen Prozessen –, wird in **Untitled (Ramponeau)** benannt, zur Aufführung gebracht und zugleich reflektiert.

11 Wo es sich um alte Autos handelt, die zu Kunst werden, wie in Nam June Paiks *32 cars for the 20th century: play Mozart's Requiem quietly* (1997) war das nicht ganz so einfach, weil die Kunstwerdung im Milieu der Autoliebhaber nicht ganz so hoch geschätzt ist wie in jenem der Buchliebhaberinnen und Buchliebhaber. Nichtsdestotrotz machen Paik wie Weber auf genau diesen Wechsel zwischen den Sphären der Anerkennungs-, Legitimierungs- und Inwertsetzungsweisen aufmerksam, was einem dafür gefeierten Werk wie dem diamantenbestückten Totenschädel von Damian Hirst (*For the Live of God*, 2007) in Wirklichkeit viel weniger konsequent gelingt, weil er die Materialien unangetastet lässt. Die Diamanten ließen sich auch wieder als Diamanten verhökern, mit den Büchern und den Autos geht das nicht.

12 Denn Kunst, so Andre programmatisch, „ist eine direkte Erfahrung mit etwas in der Welt", zit. n. Tony Godfrey, *Konzeptuelle Kunst*, Berlin: Phaidon, 2005, S. 302.

13 Insofern waren gerade Carl Andre, der die BetrachterInnen dazu einlud, auf seinen Arbeiten herumzulaufen und tatsächlich körperliche Erfahrungen zu machen, die ambivalenten Effekte seiner Kunst durchaus recht. Obwohl an der Entledigung der künstlerischen Produktion von allem Nicht-Künstlerischen arbeitend, konnte er so – wie Julia Bryan-Wilson betont – zugleich „at the forefront of an abstract, politically committed art practice" sein, Julia Bryan-Wilson, *Art Workers. Radical Practice in the Vietnam Era*, Berkeley: University of California Press, 2009, S. 49.

14 Ludwig Rubiner: „Maler bauen Barrikaden", in: ders., *Künstler bauen Barrikaden. Texte und Manifeste 1908–1919*, Wolfgang Haug (Hg.), Darmstadt: Sammlung Luchterhand, 1988, S. 81–86.

15 Vgl. etwa Stuart Hall, „Bedeutung, Repräsentation, Ideologie. Althusser und die poststrukturalistische Debatte", in: ders., *Ideologie – Identität – Repräsentation. Ausgewählte Schriften 4*, Hamburg: Argument, 2004, S. 34–65.

16 Carl Douglas, „Barricades and Boulevards: Material transformations of Paris, 1795–1871", in: *Interstices. Journal of Architecture and Related Arts*, Nr. 8, 2007, S. 31–42, hier S. 39.

17 Ingrid Gilcher-Holtey, ‚Die Phantasie an die Macht'. *Mai 68 in Frankreich*, Frankfurt am Main: Suhrkamp, 1995, S. 240.

18 Ebd.

19 Tom Holert, *Übergriffe. Zustände und Zuständigkeiten der Gegenwartskunst*, Hamburg: Philo Fine Arts, 2014, S. 9 f.

Das Obskure im Konkreten.

Überlegungen zu **not yet titled** (pinhole camera stop-motion setup)

Andreas Duscha &
Christoph Weber

Zwischen zwei Dingen besteht eine Analogie, wenn sie sich durch ein Merkmal ähnlich sind, auch wenn sie sich in anderen Merkmalen unterscheiden.

Was passiert, wenn die Produktionsbedingungen eines Mediums auf ein zweites Medium übertragen werden, welches ganz anderen Gesetzmäßigkeiten unterliegt? Ist die Tatsache, dass es sich sowohl beim Betonguss als auch bei der Fotografie um ein Negativ-Positiv-Verfahren handelt, deren einzige Ähnlichkeit, oder lassen sich weitere „Verwandtschaften" finden? Kann ein Vorgang wie der Betonguss, dessen konstituierender Faktor bei seiner Erstellung die Zeit ist, in seiner Essenz auf ein fotografisches Bild übertragen werden, und wie wirkt sich diese Übertragung auf die Abbildung aus? Das waren Überlegungen, die zu der gemeinsamen Arbeit **not yet titled (pinhole camera stop-motion setup)** führten.

Im Vordergrund stand die Idee, diese Prozesse miteinander zu verschränken: In einer Art Versuchsanordnung zu testen, was passiert, wenn bestimmte Rahmenbedingungen unterschiedlicher Medien analog zueinander angewendet werden? Ein zentraler Faktor für unser Vorhaben war die Zeit. Für den Betonguss spielt die Verweildauer des Betons in seiner Schalung die wichtigste Rolle im Hinblick auf seine Festigkeit. Wie in einer fotografischen Belichtungsreihe wurde bei Christoph Webers **not yet titled** schrittweise die Dauer des Aushärtens in der Form verlängert. Die so entstandenen fünf Objekte erinnern in ihrer sequenziellen Reihung an die frühen Bewegungsstudien von Eadweard Muybridge. Eine Bewegung wird in fünf autonome Bilder aufgespaltet, deren cinematografische Abfolge aber die Darstellung einer zusammenhängenden Bewegung bildet.

not yet titled → p. 40
not yet titled (pinhole camera stop-motion setup) → p. 203–213

Während das Stück mit der kürzesten „Trocknungsphase“ den Gesetzen der Schwerkraft am stärksten nachgibt, in sich zusammenfällt, und seinen geformten Charakter am wenigsten behaupten kann, steigt die „Stabilität“ mit Zunahme der Dauer graduell, bis der letzte Betonguss die vorgegebene Form fast beibehält. Die Zeit und die aus ihr resultierende Festigkeit definieren die Manipulierbarkeit des Materials. Während es anfänglich noch wie „Wachs in den Händen“ ist, widersetzt es sich später jeglichem Eingriff.

Die Zeit (im Verhältnis zur Blende und der Lichtempfindlichkeit des Bildträgers) ermöglicht dem Fotografen, die Realität nicht einfach nur indexikalisch abzubilden, sondern sie zu gestalten, zu manipulieren, die künstlerische Idee in das Bild einzuschreiben, es sich gefügig zu machen. Mit zunehmender Belichtungszeit nimmt die Möglichkeit der Manipulation ab, bis das Bild schwarz wird, sich schließlich selbst auslöscht und somit jeglicher weiteren Bearbeitung entzieht. Ein schwarzes Fotopapier, ein ausgehärteter Klumpen Beton, stellen die jeweiligen Endpunkte eines unumkehrbaren Prozesses dar, wenn eine Reduktion auf das bloße Material vorhanden ist.

Was passiert, wenn man den Faktor Zeit von einem Medium auf das andere überträgt: die unterschiedlichen Zeiten, die Christoph Weber seinen Güssen zum Aushärten gewährte, bevor sie aus der Schalung genommen wurden, als Belichtungszeiten für die fünf Fotografien eben jener Objekte verwendet? Hier werden Dinge zueinander in Beziehung gesetzt, die eigentlich nicht miteinander in Beziehung stehen, vergleichbar mit jenem intellektuellen Spiel, das die Protagonisten in Umberto Ecos Roman *Das Foucaultsche Pendel* erfinden. Sie kombinieren permanent Fakten und Dinge, die in keinerlei Zusammenhang miteinander stehen, und generieren so eine Realität, die sich behaupten kann, weil sie von anderen als solche akzeptiert wird.

Eadweard Muybridge hat für seine Aufnahmen von Bewegungssequenzen mit bis zu 36 nebeneinander positionierten, sukzessive auslösenden Kameras gearbeitet. Da für unser Unterfangen die bei ihm erforderlichen sehr kurzen Belichtungszeiten keine Rolle spielen, weil die Objekte bereits in einem „eingefrorenen“ Zustand verharren, hat sich die Anfertigung mehrerer Lochkameras angeboten. Als Variation der Camera Obscura (dunkle Kammer), und im Gegensatz zu herkömmlichen Fotoapparaten besitzt die Lochkamera keine Linse, sondern lediglich ein sehr kleines Loch. Durch diese Reduktion auf die einfachste Grundform einer Kamera bietet sie den größten Spielraum um an spezifische, persönliche Notwendigkeiten angepasst zu werden. Die Größe der Schalungen wurde 1:1 auf die Größe der Kameras übertragen wodurch die zu belichtenden Flächen kongruent mit der Ausgangsgröße der Skulpturen vor ihrer Verformung waren. Für die Konstruktion der Lochkameras wurde dasselbe Material wie für die Schalungen – nämlich Pressspan – verwendet, Kamera und Schalung so formal angeglichen, unterschieden allein durch ihre Funktion.

Bei einer Lochkamera wird das zu fotografierende Motiv auf der dem Loch gegenüberliegenden Seite der Apparatur spiegelverkehrt und auf dem Kopf stehend abgebildet und auf einer lichtempfindlichen Oberfläche (Fotopapier) als Negativ entwickelt und in unserem Fall ohne Umkehrung in das Positiv verwendet – hier kommt die eingangs erwähnte Analogie zum Betonguss zum Tragen, da die verwendeten Schalungen auch die Negativform der Objekte vor ihrer Manipulation waren. Durch die kleine Blendenöffnung der Lochkamera wird die Tiefenschärfe drastisch erhöht, was der Nahaufnahme entgegenkommt, darüber hinaus lange Belichtungszeiten erfordert und somit ermöglicht, die sukzessive ansteigenden Aushärtungszeiten direkt zu übernehmen.

Die Lochkamera funktioniert in diesem Fall als epistemologischer Apparat, denn sie erzeugt kein bloßes Abbild, sondern stellt auch die „Gemachtheit“ der Fotografie selbst aus. Die scherenhafte Verschränkung von Abgebildetem und Abbildendem manifestiert sich in mehrfacher Hinsicht: Die formale Angleichung von Gussform und Kamera und die daraus folgende lange Belichtungszeit überführte den Prozess der Objektwerdung in ein fotografisches „Destillat“, dem sowohl das fotografische Bild als auch sein individueller Entstehungsprozess inhärent ist. Es wurde nicht nur das Objekt abgebildet, sondern seine jeweilige „Geschichte“ mit eingeschrieben.

List of Works

p. 18–26 / 40–43 / 165
not yet titled, 2015
Concrete
5 parts
140 × 766 × 77 cm
Courtesy
Galerie nächst St. Stephan –
Rosemarie Schwarzwälder,
Vienna
Exhibition views:
Galerie nächst St. Stephan –
Rosemarie Schwarzwälder,
Vienna, 2015

p. 44 / 45
not yet titled, 2015
Concrete, steel
18 × 130 × 60 cm
Courtesy
Galerie Jocelyn Wolff, Paris
Exhibition view:
Passion, Galerie Jocelyn Wolff,
Paris, 2015

p. 46 / 47
not yet titled, 2015
Concrete
120,5 × 44 × 22,5 cm
Courtesy
Galerie Jocelyn Wolff, Paris
Exhibition view:
Passion, Galerie Jocelyn Wolff,
Paris, 2015

p. 48 / 49 / 170
not yet titled, 2015
Concrete, steel
53 × 107 × 141,4 cm
Courtesy
nächst Galerie St. Stephan –
Rosemarie Schwarzwälder,
Vienna
Exhibition views:
ELSEWHERE. Observations
on Islands, Franz Josefs Kai 3,
Vienna, 2015

p. 50 / 51
not yet titled, 2015
Concrete, steel
17 × 111 × 150 cm
Courtesy
Galerie nächst St. Stephan –
Rosemarie Schwarzwälder,
Vienna
Exhibition view:
Galerie nächst St. Stephan –
Rosemarie Schwarzwälder,
Vienna, 2015

p. 52–55 / 216
not yet titled, 2015
Concrete
128 × 103 × 55 cm
Courtesy
Galerie nächst St. Stephan –
Rosemarie Schwarzwälder,
Vienna
Exhibition views:
Galerie nächst St. Stephan –
Rosemarie Schwarzwälder,
Vienna, 2015

p. 56 / 57
not yet titled, 2014
Concrete, steel, wood
18 × 105 × 125 cm
Österreichische Galerie Belvedere
Studio view

p. 39 / 58 / 59
Beton (gewickelt), 2014
Concrete, particleboard
14 × 33 × 130 cm
Alexandra and Rolf Ricke
collection, Berlin
Exhibition views:
Post/Postminimal,
Die Sammlung Rolf Ricke im
Dialog mit zeitgenössischen
Kunstschaffenden,
Kunstmuseum St. Gallen, 2014

p. 30 / 33 / 60–63
not yet titled, 2014
Concrete
58 × 149 × 103 cm
Kunstmuseum St. Gallen
Exhibition views:
Post/Postminimal,
Die Sammlung Rolf Ricke im
Dialog mit zeitgenössischen
Kunstschaffenden,
Kunstmuseum St. Gallen, 2014

p. 64 / 65
not yet titled, 2013
Concrete
37 × 38 × 10 cm
Courtesy
ibid., London
Exhibition view:
uncast, ibid.,
London, 2013

p. 66–69 / 172
Beton (gefaltet), 2013
Concrete, cotton
7,5 × 58 × 62 cm
Courtesy
ibid., London
Exhibition views:
uncast, ibid.,
London, 2013

p. 70–73
not yet titled, 2012
Concrete
29 × 98 × 75 cm
Courtesy
ibid., London
Exhibition views:
uncast, ibid.,
London, 2013

p. 74 / 75
Schade, dass Beton nicht brennt, 2012
Concrete
40 × 60 × 20 cm
Courtesy
Galerie Jocelyn Wolff, Paris
Exhibition view:
In the Shape of Things to Come,
Ve.Sch, Vienna, 2013

p. 76 / 77
Untitled (getauchtes Holz), 2013
Concrete, lumber
17 × 145 × 36 cm
Courtesy
ProjecteSD, Barcelona
Exhibition view:
Map, Record, Picture, Sculpture,
ProjecteSD,
Barcelona, 2013

p. 78–81 / 175
Schade, dass Beton nicht brennt, 2012
Concrete
45 × 30 × 15 cm
Courtesy
ProjecteSD, Barcelona
Exhibition views:
10, 25, 80, ProjecteSD,
Barcelona, 2012

p. 82–85 / 184
bent inversion (lehnend), 2012
Concrete
109 × 37 × 0,7 cm
bent inversion (seitlich stehend), 2012
Concrete
36,6 × 115 × 0,7 cm
Courtesy
ProjecteSD, Barcelona
Exhibition views:
10, 25, 80, PROJECTESD,
Barcelona, 2012

p. 86–88
Untitled (Wachsfaltung), 2012
Concrete, wax
13 × 75,5 × 57 cm
Courtesy
ProjecteSD, Barcelona
Exhibition views:
10, 25, 80, ProjecteSD,
Barcelona, 2012

p. 34 / 90 / 91
Beton (gehoben), 2012
Tarp, concrete, wirerope
359 × 62 × 59 cm
Collection Gabriel Nallet,
Grenoble
Exhibition views:
10, 25, 80, ProjecteSD,
Barcelona, 2012

p. 36 / 92 / 93
Beton (gerollt), 2012
Tarp, concrete, nails
82 × 58 × 11 cm
Private collection, London
Exhibition views:
Galerie Jocelyn Wolff,
Paris, 2012

p. 94–97 / 187 / 188
unfold, 2011
Concrete, plank
2 parts
198 × 19 × 5 cm each
Private collection, Marseille
Exhibition views:
Galerie Jocelyn Wolff,
Paris, 2012

p. 98–101
bent inversion, 2012
Concrete
50 × 208 × 80 cm
Courtesy
Galerie Jocelyn Wolff, Paris
Exhibition views:
Galerie Jocelyn Wolff,
Paris, 2012

p. 100–103 / 166 / 169
Bündel, 2012
Rebar, cement, cloth
11 × 700 × 11 cm
Courtesy
Galerie Jocelyn Wolff, Paris
Exhibition views:
Galerie Jocelyn Wolff,
Paris, 2012

p. 104 / 105
Contradiction, 2011
Peeled concrete wall, rebar
100 x 100 x 40 cm
Courtesy
Galerie Jocelyn Wolff, Paris
Exhibition views:
Archivisions #2 Quand l'œuvre
a lieu – Le Parvis – scène
nationale Tarbes Pyrénées,
Ibos, France

p. 106 / 107
inversions, 2011
Concrete, nails
29,7 × 42 × 3 cm
Collection Charlotte Beauvisage,
Paris
Exhibition view:
Les amis de mes amis sont mes amis,
Hommage à Ján Mančuška,
Galerie Jocelyn Wolff,
Paris, 2011

p. 108–111
not yet titled, 2011
Concrete, paper
6 × 100 × 88 cm
Exhibition views:
Villa Tokyo, Tokyo, 2011

p. 112 / 113
Untitled (Baseline), 2009
Sand, cement, water, lumber
Dimensions variable
Here: 5 × 35 × 350 cm
Private collection, Madrid
Exhibition view:
Villa Tokyo, Tokyo, 2011

p. 114 / 115
not yet titled, 2010
Concrete, clamps
63 × 37 × 60 cm
Private collection, Los Angeles
Exhibition view:
Open Studios, ISCP,
New York City, 2010

p. 116–119
Untitled (bewehrtes Wachs), 2014
Wax, aluminum mesh
65 × 34 × 35 cm
Pedestal 9 × 68 × 68 cm
Courtesy
Galerie Jocelyn Wolff, Paris
Studio view

p. 120–122
Heap, 2008
Variable dimension
Variable amount of aluminum sheets
13 × 49 × 66 cm each
Courtesy
Galerie Jocelyn Wolff, Paris
Exhibition view:
Sleepwalking,
Temporary Gallery Cologne,
Cologne, 2009

p. 122 / 123
Stack, 2008
29 × 66 × 65 cm
19 aluminum sheets
13 × 49 × 66 cm each
Lumber
Courtesy
Galerie Jocelyn Wolff, Paris
Exhibition view:
Sleepwalking,
Temporary Gallery Cologne,
Cologne, 2009

p. 124 / 125 / 194
Untitled (rue Ramponeau), 2008
Lambdaprint
25 × 21 cm
Courtesy
Galerie Jocelyn Wolff, Paris

p. 126–129 / 132 / 133 / 191 / 192 / 201
Untitled (Ramponeau), 2008
Papier-maché cobblestones
made of historic paper
Dimensions variable
12 × 13 × 15 cm each
Collection Josiane Coudray,
Lausanne
FRAC Franche Comté
Exhibition views:
Galerie Jocelyn Wolff,
Paris, 2008

p. 130 / 131 / 196 / 199
Untitled, 2008
Ripped books, cardboard box
38 × 51 × 24 cm
Courtesy
Galerie Jocelyn Wolff, Paris
Exhibition views:
Galerie Jocelyn Wolff,
Paris, 2008

p. 134–139 / 179
Trauma, 2008
Installation consisting of 7 doors
Dimensions variable
Courtesy
Galerie Jocelyn Wolff, Paris
Exhibition views:
Galerie Jocelyn Wolff, Paris, 2008

p. 140 / 141
Objets externes, 2005
Wax, pigment, foil
5 parts
100 × 307 × 35 cm overall
NO Collection, Berlin
Exhibition view:
Galerie Jocelyn Wolff, Paris, 2005

p. 142 / 143 / 183
Objets externes, 2005–2007
Wax, pigment
5 parts
Approx. 130 × 300 × 35 cm overall
Courtesy
Galerie Jocelyn Wolff, Paris
Exhibition views:
On Fait Le Mur, l'Espace de l'Art Concret, Mouans-Sartoux, France, 2007

p. 144–147
Untitled (Chunks), 2004
Sewacryl laminate
85 × 13 × 70 cm each
85 × 172 × 130 cm overall
Edition of 4+1AP
Collection Isabelle and Pierre Bertiaux, Paris;
Leitner collection, Schröcken, Austria; Speyer family collection, New York;
Private collection, Berlin
Private collection, Vienna
Exhibition views:
Kopf oder Zahl,
Kunstraum Niederösterreich, Vienna, 2007

p. 148 / 149
Untitled (Gegenstücke), 2014
Concrete, steel, acrylic glass
127 × 145 × 30 cm
Private collection, New York
Studio view

p. 151–153 / 180
Untitled (Gegenstück), 2012
Concrete
2 parts
130 × 135 × 90 cm overall
r/e collection
Exhibition views:
Galerie Jocelyn Wolff, Paris, 2012

p. 154–163
Untitled, 2010
2 parts
16 contact sheets 8 × 10", framed
111,5 × 91 cm
Plaster cast
13 × 94,5 × 76,5 cm
r/e collection
Exhibition view:
loose concrete,
Galerie nächst St. Stephan — Rosemarie Schwarzwälder, Vienna, 2010

p. 7–15 / 203–213
Collaboration with Andreas Duscha
not yet titled (pinhole camera stop-motion setup)
Concrete, baryta paper, black particleboard, aluminum, Auer-crates, plywood board, LED floodlights
165 × 250 × 125 cm
Moulds
White particleboard, cotton
35 × 43 × 37 cm
Courtesy the artists
Exhibition views:
Das Obskure im Konkreten,
O.T., Vienna, 2015

Christoph Weber
Uncast

Editors:
Georgia Holz, Christoph Weber
Concept:
Anna Lena von Helldorff,
Georgia Holz, Christoph Weber
Authors:
Konrad Bitterli, Andreas Duscha &
Christoph Weber, Jens Kastner,
Fiona Liewehr, Sadie Plant
Text Editing:
Georgia Holz
Translations:
Sadie Plant, Jake Schneider
Copyediting:
Mischa Guttmann, Georgia Holz
Proofreading:
Georgia Holz (German),
Kellie Rife (English)
Graphic Design:
Anna Lena von Helldorff [buero total]

Typeface: FaktPro (Thanks to T. Thiemich)
Paper: DuO-Oktav Dünndruck
Print: DZA Druckerei zu Altenburg GmbH

Published by
Spector Books
Harkortstraße 10, 04107 Leipzig
www.spectorbooks.com

ISBN 978-3-95905-030-2
First Edition, Printed in Germany

Distribution
Germany / Austria:
GVA, Gemeinsame Verlagsauslieferung
Göttingen GmbH&Co. KG
www.gva-verlage.de
Switzerland:
AVA Verlagsauslieferung AG,
www.ava.ch
France / Belgium:
Interart Paris,
www.interart.fr
UK:
Central Books Ltd,
www.centralbooks.com
USA / Canada:
RAM Publications+Distribution Inc.,
www.rampub.com
Australia / New Zealand:
Perimeter Distribution,
www.perimeterdistribution.com
Other Countries:
Motto Distribution,
www.mottodistribution.com

Photography Credits
All images courtesy the artists,
except for the following list,
keyed to page numbers, for which
seperate credits are due:
Markus Wörgötter
p. 40 / 51 / 53–55 / 155
Roberto Ruiz
p. 77 / 79 / 81 / 82 / 84 / 85 / 87 / 88 /
91 / 175 / 184
François Doury
p. 36 / 45 / 47 / 92 / 94 / 95 / 97 / 99 /
100 / 101 / 103 / 106 / 126 / 128 / 129 /
131 / 132 / 133 / 135–137 / 139 / 141 / 151 /
152 / 153 / 166 / 169 / 179 / 180 / 191 / 192 /
196 / 199 / 201
Joe Clark
p. 65 / 66 / 71–73 / 172

Christoph Weber would like to thank:
Konrad Bitterli, Silvia Dauder,
Sandrine Djerouet-Stenstad,
Andreas Duscha, Magnus Edensvard,
Judith Fegerl, Matilda Fegerl,
Mischa Guttmann, Anna Lena von Helldorff,
Georgia Holz, Jens Kastner,
Anne König, Fiona Liewehr, Max Lust,
Heike Maier-Rieper, Samuel Mizrachi,
Raphael Oberhuber, Sadie Plant,
Rosemarie Schwarzwälder, Thomas Trummer,
Alex Weber and Friends, Jan Wenzel,
Nasim Weiler, Marlies Wirth, Jocelyn Wolff

Bibliographic information published by the
Deutsche Nationalbibliothek: The Deutsche
Nationalbibliothek lists this publication
in the Deutsche Nationalbibliografie;
detailed bibliographic data is available on
the Internet at http://dnb.ddb.de.

This publication was supported by:
Bundeskanzleramt Österreich, Kunstsektion
Galerie Jocelyn Wolff
Galerie nächst St. Stephan – Rosemarie Schwarzwälder
ProjecteSD
ibid.

BUNDESKANZLERAMT ÖSTERREICH